D1519307

THE ALIBABA W

THE ALIBABA WAY

Unleashing Grassroots Entrepreneurship to Build the World's Most Innovative Internet Company

YING LOWREY
TRANSLATED BY MARTHA AVERY

Mc
Graw
Hill
Education

New York   Chicago   San Francisco   Athens   London
Madrid   Mexico City   Milan   New Delhi
Singapore   Sydney   Toronto

1 2 3 4 5 6 7 8 9 0   DOC/DOC   1 2 1 0 9 8 7 6 5

ISBN   978-1-259-58540-1
MHID   1-259-58540-9

e-ISBN   978-1-259-58541-8
e-MHID   1-259-58541-7

McGraw-Hill Education books are available at special quantity discounts to use as premiums and sales promotions, or for use in corporate training programs. To contact a representative, please visit the Contact Us page at www.mhprofessional.com.

Library of Congress Cataloging-in-Publication Data

Author: Lowrey, Ying.
Title: The Alibaba way : unleashing grass-roots entrepreneurship to build the
   world's most innovative internet company / Ying Lowrey.
Description: 1 Edition. | New York : McGraw-Hill Education, 2016.
Identifiers: LCCN 2015032907| ISBN 9781259585401 (hardback) | ISBN 1259585409
   (hardback)
Subjects: LCSH: Alibaba (Firm)—History. | New business
   enterprises—China—Management. | Small business—China—Management. |
   Success in business. | BISAC: BUSINESS & ECONOMICS / E-Commerce / Internet
   Marketing.
Classification: LCC HD62.5 .L697 2016 | DDC 381/.14206551—dc23 LC record
available at http://lccn.loc.gov/2015032907

This book is dedicated to two giants in the field: Professor William Baumol for his seminal work on innovation and entrepreneurship, and Professor Edmund Phelps for his contributions to the understanding of the importance of institutions and grassroots dynamism to economic growth and well-being.

I want to thank them for being mentors in my economic research.

CONTENTS

INNOVATION AND GRASSROOTS ENTREPRENEURSHIP: KEY INSTRUMENTS OF ECONOMIC GROWTH

Throughout history, China has been a guide to economic progress, in many eras serving as a model for other nations—though sometimes showing what approaches are best avoided. Now it has returned to its role as a source of guidance and is again achieving domestic progress and offering the promise of future prosperity. The lessons to be learned will surely be useful to China itself because much of its economy has not yet abandoned older and less productive modes of operation and management. This valuable book offers a guide to the activities that will contribute to China's success.

However, such a book will also serve as an instrument that benefits China indirectly by enhancing the purchasing power of other countries that are China's customers. Here we must remember that impoverished customers are not good customers. It follows that China stands to benefit both directly and indirectly by understanding the economic activities that enhance prosperity.

A key to progress in this direction is the opportunity for encouragement of entrepreneurial activity, within small enterprises and large firms. Both have already made substantial contributions and promise to remain a source of these benefits in the future. These observations may appear to be self-evident, but it is important to bear in mind that entrepreneurs can be relied on to seek to promote their own gains, whether or not the actions adopted are beneficial to other enterprises.

Recent developments in China have shown dramatically how such a society can benefit from the contributions of entrepreneurs and their colleagues in carrying out the activities of a firm. However, they also have provided unfortunate examples in which entrepreneurs put their own well-being ahead of society's welfare. Evidently, the general welfare requires the adoption of incentives that encourage those entrepreneurs whose activities are beneficial, while discouraging others, whose actions conflict with the interests of society.

In China, some of these incentives already have been put to use. In other cases, the orientation of the firms themselves has contributed to achievement of such goals. But there is still more to be learned from the beneficial undertakings of enterprises that are laggards on the road to progress. Indeed, in China and other countries that have experienced substantial growth, some enterprises have explicitly designed their activities to achieve private benefits at the expense of their employees and their customers.

This book focuses on the firms whose activities contribute to the general welfare through the use of innovation—both in producing and in bringing goods and services to the public—that also multiplies the benefits to society provided by small entrepreneurs. Based on both observed experience and years of research, Professor Lowrey's discussion brings out the developments of the recent past that have enhanced the general welfare.

More than that of any other nation, China's history entails a story of invention that is unique in its abundance and, thereby, illustrates dramatically how grassroots entrepreneurship can contribute to the general welfare—or, in other circumstances, how it can fail to do so. Such contributions clearly offer extraordinary enhancements to economic growth and, thereby, to the general welfare. The analysis offered in this book indicates directions that will enhance both by using innovation to unleash productive grassroots entrepreneurship.

William J. Baumol
Professor Emeritus of Economics,
New York University, and
Professor Emeritus of Economics,
Princeton University

My book, *Mass Flourishing*, argues that the surge in economic activity and the emergence of widespread growth and prosperity observed during the 1800s and first half of the 1900s cannot be understood solely as a consequence of scientific discoveries or changes in government policies or institutions. An important factor, often disregarded, was a change in attitudes, which finally led to the unleashing of entrepreneurs and, in turn, innovation. New or improved products and methods resulted in the spread of more rewarding work and a sense of flourishing—of personal growth.

Professor Lowrey's book, which describes and analyzes the tremendous dynamism created by Alibaba's ecosystem, exemplifies my basic themes transported to China's modern age. Rather than the steam engine of the nineteenth century, Alibaba uses information technology to enable mass innovation to flourish. Thanks to this technology, "growing by unleashing grassroots entrepreneurship" can be adapted by companies as a new strategy to win markets; it also can become a nation's strategy to improve the lives of its people.

China has changed greatly in the last 35 years: Markets have been created, skyscrapers are everywhere, people are migrating in pursuit of jobs, and urbanization is taking advantage of the country's late development. Perhaps most important, companies such as Alibaba have become leaders of the international trend in e-commerce. Using Internet technology, Alibaba and others are creating environments where grassroots entrepreneurs can easily enter markets with little or low cost. This new ecosystem allows small businesses to avoid middlemen between them and consumers. The ecosystem also includes open, transparent, efficient, and accountable services, such as logistics and finance, for millions of e-commerce retailers.

E-commerce has changed attitudes toward the possibility of individuals using their initiative and creativity to become entrepreneurs. This is extremely important in countries such as China, where, traditionally, business has held low status. Thousands of years of the education and examination system molded the elite to follow orders, serve the emperor, and seek high government positions. A high government position offered high social status and personal wealth.

This book shows that Alibaba is changing the culture: millions of entrepreneurs got online and started their businesses. Jack Ma started as a grassroots businessman and became a modern icon for youth. This dynamism can be contagious. Ordinary individuals can influence regional development by showcasing their success in online businesses; Taobao Villages can help to fast-forward the process of hundreds of years of urbanization. This book demonstrates that in China at present, economic dynamism is alive and well and that grassroots innovation of products, processes, and markets is occurring at an increasing rate. Keep up the dynamism; what will follow is sustainable mass flourishing.

Edmund S. Phelps
Nobel Laureate in Economics 2006
Professor, Columbia University
Director, Center on Capitalism and Society
Dean of the New Huadu Business School

Things like "innovation," "startups," and "small is beautiful" were a focus of attention from the 1990s as I pursued a career in teaching and economic research. The lack of real data at the time kept me from delving into these phenomena, however. The situation only changed in 2000, when I was hired as a senior economist by the Small Business Administration in the United States.

In September 2011, I received an invitation to work at the Social Sciences Institute of Tsinghua University in Beijing, and in November of that year, I began preparations for early retirement. In March 2012, the first thing I did after arriving at Tsinghua was to begin looking up statistics on small business in China. What I found was dismaying. In such a great country, not a single place could provide me with data on small businesses. My only recourse was to approach eminent economist Professor Wu Jinglian for help. He said to me, "You need to go to Alibaba. They have quantities of data on small businesses. Somebody like you who has lived and worked for so many years abroad should become acquainted with one of China's more outstanding enterprises. Go and do some research there."

My cooperation with Alibaba began in July 2012, when I organized the first research forum on big data. The head of the Alibaba Research Center (recently renamed the Alibaba Research Institute) at the time was Liang Chunxiao, and both he and a member of his staff, Dr. Zhang Ting, attended the forum. From that time on, I became a "student" within the center. The thing that initially excited me most about Alibaba was the manuscript of a report that Chunxiao asked me to read and critique. It was entitled, "Small Is Beautiful: Development Report on

E-commerce in 2012." What was this?! E. F. Schumacher had written the book, *Small Is Beautiful*, long before; a friend had recommended it to me in 1982 when I was just starting my studies at Yale University. I had been particularly taken with the confirmation and appreciation of small businesses at the time.

Reading and critiquing this report was a wonderful experience. I was moved by the vision of the company and the way Alibaba's concept of "making it easy to do business anywhere" bestowed confidence on millions of industrious "beautiful small" startups. The great mass of China's grassroots-level impoverished farmers really could set up business on Taobao's platform. By running a business, people could express their individual willingness, capability, and aspiration to innovate. They could enjoy the great thrill of unleashing their own entrepreneurship. The whole idea was aligned with preserving respect for the individual in business, with looking for new-age production methods, gathering together the positive energies of the economy and society, creating mechanisms for generating sustainable growth, and embracing a future in which all prosper together.

After being moved by this new reading of *Small Is Beautiful*, I immersed myself in understanding Alibaba itself. I came to appreciate the "Six Swords" of its code of values and the way it makes innovation a routine part of corporate culture. I came to have tremendous respect for the Alibaba people whom I now know. From the angle of a renegade who goes against mainstream economics, in which there is no role for entrepreneurs in the economy, I understood in a very brief period of time at least one small part of the mighty iceberg of Alibaba. I recognized the validity of a whole new kind of business ecosystem in which "One is for all, and all are for one" and the validity of a new economic growth model—"growing by unleashing grassroots entrepreneurship."

Starting in the spring of 2013, I began writing about the economic significance of platform economies using Alibaba as an example. My intent was to show how they could play a critical role in realizing China's dream of being a strong nation and a prosperous people. At the end of June 2013, I delivered a paper in Rome on Alibaba's innovations. There I again met up with Mr. and Mrs. Edmund Phelps and learned that Professor Phelps' newest book was about to be published, titled

Mass Flourishing. In September of the same year, I purchased the English e-version of this book via the Internet while at the same time buying a whole box of the book in Chinese, for friends, students, and colleagues, including those at Alibaba.

In the fall of 2013, I created a new course at Tsinghua called "The Economics of Innovation and Entrepreneurship in the Age of Big Data." I asked students to get out of the classroom and go find innovative enterprises such as Alibaba and entrepreneurs such as Jack Ma. I asked them to share their insights about innovation and their research on entrepreneurship. By the end of the semester, my intentions had been realized as students recognized the dynamism or energy fields within China. Given the force of this dynamism and these fields of energy, once our young people begin releasing their own entrepreneurship, China's creative capacities will be sparked in a way that makes its growth prospects encouraging indeed.

Traditional economic analysis has lost much of its luster given the financial crisis that so damaged the vigor of advanced Western economies and given the way new technologies are propelling different kinds of corporate growth. The traditional model, based as it is on economy of scale and a desire to maximize profits over the short term, is now being replaced by new models. These instead are based on platform effect and sustainability and seek to achieve prosperity for all groups on the platform. Alibaba has taken a path that is quite distinct from the traditional model as well as from typical modern corporations of the twentieth century. It has grown by unleashing the entrepreneurship of the grassroots. The grassroots innovations that Alibaba supports come, on the one hand, from society at large but, on the other, from within Alibaba's own staff.

In order to provide fertile soil for grassroots innovations and small businesses to grow, Alibaba has done many new things: Founded the Taobao University, cleared the way for a new kind of industrial supply chain, opened up the whole realm of e-commerce and the spillover effect, and continued the exploration of microfinancial services that are based on integrity capital. It is using Internet grassroots forces to consolidate positive energy to eliminate negative approaches in business practices. It is itself creating the rules of the game in platform economies, creating the ecosystems of a new age. Alibaba's own process of maturing has a very grassroots aura to it as well. Grassroots innovation and entrepreneurship are what spurred its own growth, while Alibaba people are constantly unleashing their own entrepreneurship as they grow.

In the second half of 2013, a film entitled, *Crocodile in the Yangtze*, was popular on WeBlog (China's blog site). Directed by Porter Erisman, a former Alibaba vice president, it narrates the story of the first decade in the turbulent life of Alibaba. The film opens with a scene from the tenth anniversary of the company, at the Huanglong ("Yellow Dragon") Stadium. Jack Ma, already legendary, continues to be what he was before. Wearing rather unusual clothes, he describes in vivid and emotional terms the process by which Alibaba came about. People think back to when 18 people squeezed into a small room and put their efforts into creating the Chinese Yellow Pages. Not a princeling, no rich uncle, yet in short order here he is, head of an "information economic ecosystem," an "Internet empire." His voice takes people back to his life-and-death battle with eBay and how, in 2000, after getting investment from Goldman Sachs and SoftBank, he decided to move the headquarters to Silicon Valley in the United States to create a truly international Internet company. He quickly ran into problems and moved back again in a few months, having been forced to fire his American staff. That particular experiment in going abroad was a failure.

Fast-forward to May 6, 2014, as Alibaba hands over its F-1 qualifications to the Securities and Exchange Commission of the United States in order to be listed on the U.S. market. This is a formal declaration by the "Crocodile of the Yangtze" that he is now moving his troops back into international waters. On September 19, 2014, Alibaba was listed on the New York Stock Exchange. The listing price for each share was US$68, which rose to US$93.89 by the close of the market that day. The total market value of Alibaba came to US$23.14 billion,[1] exceeding the entire gross domestic product (GDP) of one of China's midranking provinces. The crocodile had become a shark whose stage had moved from the Yangtze River to the wide oceans of the world. It dared to challenge others but also to break through its own confines and change itself.

---

[1] In the end, the value came to US$25 billion because the SEC allowed an additional distribution of shares. Among other sources, see Reuters.com article of September 22, 2014, written by Elzio Barreto.

Innovation—"routinized" innovation—remains the necessary precondition for Alibaba's existence and sustained growth.

Questions remain. How can Alibaba set up rules of the game for Taobao and Tmall and provide outstanding service so that the company ensures indispensable platform services in increasingly fierce competition? How can it spur the formation of microfinance markets that finance grassroots economic activity and create microfinancing services that are open, transparent, efficient, and accountable? How can it open a new Silk Road in the Internet era and thereby overturn the traditional ways that international trade blocks small enterprises? How can Alibaba deal with the conventional inefficiencies of the twentieth century when companies grew into gigantic corporations in order to provide shareholders with real value for a realistic share price today, as well as satisfy expectations for excellent long-term returns? These questions are something that Alibaba, now listed on the market, must consider every moment of the day.

Meanwhile, I would like to find out how this company, called Alibaba Online back then, has gone from being an 18-person team to being the megapower that it is today. In this book, my team and I have focused our attention on the profound impact that Alibaba's approach can have on China's economic development and social progress. That approach essentially relates to the "routinization" of innovation in unleashing grassroots entrepreneurship and in galvanizing and supporting China's small businesses.

This book has sought to uncover the secrets of Alibaba's unprecedented growth in China. Innovation is the uncovered secret of how Alibaba emerged and strode out into the world! If Alibaba can prosper by unleashing entrepreneurship, so can the nation. I hope that our research and conclusions will contribute to Alibaba's continued success, but more important, I hope that it will be helpful to the evolution of a healthy ecosystem for small businesses and to the sustainable economic development of China.

I began writing this book in the spring of 2013, and it was finally published in Chinese in November 2014. I am now amazed and greatly pleased that the book is being published in English as well as a number of other languages. As I note in the text, however, writing a book is a slow process compared to the fast-moving innovations of Alibaba. It took me a year to interview people; to visit Taobao vendors, Taobao villages, and Taobao counties; and to collect information and settle on the outline of the book. During that time, many changes took place. In this brief Preface, I would like to update readers on what Alibaba has been doing since publication of the Chinese version of *Alibaba*.

Once Alibaba was listed on the New York Stock Exchange, on September 19, 2014, it set up three key strategies for long-term growth. These include globalization, use of big data, and rural e-commerce.

Alibaba's global ambitions were apparent even during the company's startup period, as discussed in this book, but its global strategy has matured over time. As Jack Ma has emphasized, the strategy now relates not so much to Alibaba alone as to e-commerce as a whole. The new slogan for the company is "Buying from the world, selling to the world," which is one expression of the Alibaba mission of "Making it easy to do business anywhere." This declared mission helps consumers and producers not only inside China but also throughout the world. Alibaba's new vision is to foster a collaborative e-ecosystem of a multiplicity of international partners that will serve the world's 2 billion consumers. The aim is to have global logistical services that enable 72-hour delivery within the next decade. So far, this ecosystem includes four platforms, Aliexpress.com, Alibaba.com, Alipay ePass, and Tmall.hk. The first two are to enable China's exporting to the rest of the world, with Aliexpress.com for retail and Alibaba.com for wholesale. The second two are to make it easier for foreign exporters to do business in China.

Alipay ePass is for enabling cross-boarder payment, and Tmall.hk is for enabling the import into China of products produced in the rest of the world. One good example of this is the success of Costco in selling 300 tons of dried fruit and nuts to China during the one-day 2014 11.11 Shopping Festival. Given this impressive sales volume, Costco then quickly decided to open two stores in China, after 15 years of prolonged due diligence and equivocation.

Alibaba believes that an entity's competitiveness will increasingly be defined by its level of computing, whether that entity is a country, a business, a school, or even an individual. Alibaba hopes to change its own business in this regard via a robust AliCloud, and it hopes to help China transform from information technology (IT) to data technology (DT). AliCloud is already a powerful engine: it has the capacity to support 17 million people accessing the Alibaba website in any given minute. On November 11, 2014, it enabled a record turnover of US$9.3 billion (57.1 billion RMB, calculated at the exchange rate of August 3, 2015) in the course of the 11.11 Shopping Festival. Alibaba's volume of e-commerce has surpassed the combined volume of Amazon and eBay in the United States. The company accounts for 80 percent of China's e-commerce. As promised by the president of AliCloud, "AliCloud is dedicated to acting as a public grid that serves millions of innovative small- and medium-sized enterprises." In addition to individual startups, it is now speeding up its outreach to large enterprises.

In October 2014, Alibaba announced an initiative for promoting rural e-commerce business on the Taobao platform, with an anticipated investment of US$1.6 billion (10 billion RMB) over three to five years. The plan is to set up 1,000 e-commerce operation centers at the county level and 10,000 e-commerce service stations at the village level. Each of these involves five different kinds of infrastructure: a village center, a dedicated network cable, a set of computers, a superlarge screen, and a group of trained technicians. The goal is to bring a modernized form of buying and selling to backward rural areas that currently lack adequate retail services. It is to serve the daily shopping needs of China's rural population.

I have visited many Taobao villages and Taobao counties and seen this in action. Most recently, I visited two Taobao villages in LinAn County in Zhejiang Province, where I witnessed the impact that this initiative is having. Maxiao Village ("horse roaring village") is located in a mountainous area of Zhejiang. Very little of the terrain is cultivatable owing to a topography that has only 5 percent level ground. In the past, young people mostly left to become migrant workers in cities, leaving the elderly at home to care for younger children. This entire village now has access to 4G high-speed wi-fi. Women wear high heels; children play with the latest toys. I visited one family that is engaged in e-commerce operations in which all family members participate in the business. As the father told me with apparent pride, "E-commerce has made our family one of the happiest in the world. My two sons can stay here—they do not have to work in far-off places. My wife and I live with our sons, daughter-in-laws, and two grandsons. We make good money, and we all live under one roof."

Bainiu Village ("white cow village") is better known than Maxiao Village because two well-known persons visited it in early 2015, Wang Yang, vice premier of China's State Council, and Jack Ma, of Alibaba. This village epitomizes the way that e-commerce is driving the future—college graduates have been returning here to set up businesses and are making enormous contributions in disseminating new technologies and new kinds of culture. The village has only 1,500 people, yet over 50 e-commerce retail businesses have been established that are operated by local people. In addition, the county has developed online purchasing services for local residents. In 2014, online sales of local businesses exceeded US$30 million (200 million RMB). The net income of local people was nearly 23 times the national average (226,000 RMB instead of 9,892 RMB).

In 2014, Alibaba held a summit at its headquarters to present awards to the best Taobao counties in the country. It sold tickets, and the organizers were amazed that not only was the event sold out, but people were sitting on the floor and even outside the conference hall. In 2015, Alibaba had a bidding campaign for hosting a similar summit event, and 66 counties presented their proposals. I was a member of the reviewing committee for the proposals. I witnessed the tremendous excitement of local government officials about the possibilities that e-commerce can bring to their regions and their people.

On July 8, 2015, I attended a two-day conference in Tonglu County, Zhejiang Province, entitled, "Small County, Giant Ecosystem." Tonglu County had won the bidding campaign mentioned earlier. More than 1,500 people from around the country attended, including government officials, Internet experts and scholars, and representatives of the "Best 100 Counties in E-Commerce Practices." This was an unprecedented event in terms of its collaboration between government and the private sector on e-commerce. Tonglu County includes around 408,300 residents and was selected as the site for hosting this second summit because of how it developed a replicable new way to do e-commerce in rural areas, a way that is being described as the "Tonglu model." It consists of having one operational center in the main city of Tonglu, providing e-commerce, warehousing, and logistical services, and then a service station in each of the 183 villages in the county.

Most people who attended the summit did not intend to copy the Tonglu model but instead presented their own ideas on how to handle their own affairs. This concept of county governments handling their local public administration has historic roots in China that can be said to go back to the Qin Dynasty, that is, back to 221 BCE. The early historian of China, Sima Qian (145–86 BCE) wrote about the practice in *Records of the Grand Historian*: "People are settled in counties, counties are gathered in a nation; if each county is well governed, the nation is well governed." China's current administration[2] recently reconfirmed this doctrine by inviting the heads of 102 "model counties" to the Great Hall of the People on June 30, 2015. This was one day prior to the 94th Anniversary of the Communist Party of China. It is fortuitous that Alibaba's post-IPO rural initiative has coincided with the Chinese administration's needs in terms of governing the nation.

Three models for developing county-based e-commerce emerged in the course of the e-commerce summit. The first relies on a strong manufacturing base. The most successful counties in e-commerce also have successful manufacturing sectors that tend to be focused on specific products. Tonglu County produces pens and pencils for the world market and

---

[2]Xi Jinping (General Secretary of the Communist Party and President) and Li Keqiang (Premier).

is also famous for producing textile products. Qinghe County of Hebei Province is known for producing cashmere products. The economy of Haining City of Zhejiang Province took off on the basis of leather production and brand-named leather goods. The second model is based on a strong culture and established traditions. For example, e-commerce has turned China's food culture and craftsmanship into a formidable marketing tool. Suichang County's sellers have formed an e-commerce association and sell green products nationwide, in addition to having B&B businesses that provide local lodging and specialty foods. Bo'xing County of Shandong Province has developed its legacy of crafts that use locally grown water rushes[3] as well as traditional cotton fabrics that are woven manually on old looms. These traditional products can be designed to customers' specifications and ordered online. The third model emphasizes a grassroots startup model that has been widely adopted in China's most impoverished regions. Shaji Town in Suining County, Jiangsu Province, is an example of how a poverty-stricken place with few resources can use e-commerce and begin to thrive by building a manufacturing cluster from scratch.

As of the end of June 2015, based on this county approach to developing e-commerce, China's 17 provinces have seen the establishment of 63 e-commerce operational centers in county seats and 1,803 e-commerce service stations in county villages.

In writing this new Preface to the English edition of *Alibaba*, I would particularly like to share with readers my sense of excitement about what a giant platform company can do for an economy. As I have said in this book, Alibaba has been doing what a government would normally do for its citizens. Its contributions have been enormous, and they also have huge ramifications. Taobao.com has enabled more than 10 million grassroots people to do business online at low cost. It has fostered online consumption in rural areas, opened up access to financial support for common people and small businesses, and created a bridge between small businesses and international markets. Alibaba is now working with local governments and many parts of the private sector to encourage entrepreneurship in China's rural areas and to accelerate their modernization.

---

[3] *Typha angustifolia* in Latin.

There are, of course, many unanswered questions. How do such giant corporations as Google and Alibaba strike the right balance between maximizing business profits and maximizing the social welfare aspects of their platforms? How does a government serve its citizens by expanding the positive network externalities that are embedded in platform companies while still ensuring free competition in the economy?

In addition to these considerations, I wonder about the role that e-commerce can play in advancing technological progress in China. China's manufacturing sector is sorely lacking in the necessary support of engineering and technical services. As a result, the country is unable to commercialize many good scientific results and patents. Small manufacturing businesses, mostly privately owned, are finding it hard to survive as they churn out low-end goods, both those being assembled into other products and in final products themselves. China is in urgent need of a way to link its research sector with its manufacturing sector via a kind of Internet of engineering/technological services. Without upgraded and attractive consumer goods, and without a strong manufacturing sector that makes use of modern industrial equipment, it will be very hard to have a sustainable e-retail sector in China. As the country's economy develops, people's tastes are changing. The Chinese people's zest for shopping is well known, from purchasing Louis Vuitton handbags in Paris to electronic toilets in Japan. I therefore hope that Alibaba will focus its attention on the real sector and help to create a market for engineering and technological services that can contribute to transforming China's backward small-manufacturing sector.

As Alibaba institutes a "routinized" form of innovation,[4] it is hard to predict how far and in which direction the company will go. What is certain is that Alibaba is creating an astounding twenty-first-century platform by pulling together productive and innovative energies. As I continue to research the company, I intend to focus on Alibaba's microfinance in particular—how this particular mechanism uses not only the "invisible hand" but also the "invisible moral standard" to guide economic behavior, including that of governments, businesses, social organizations, and

---

[4]This is described in the text of the book; in addition, please see Chapter 3 in William Baumol (2002), The Free-Market Innovation Machine: Analyzing the Growth Miracle of Capitalism, Princeton, N.J.: Princeton Press, for his idea of "routinized" innovation.

individuals. It is my belief that once the new IT-DT-Internet-based technologies replace old technologies, small business and microfinance will dominate the economic ecosystem of the twenty-first century. Principles of openness, transparency, efficiency, and accountability will contribute to making the world a better place in which to live.

Finally, I would like to take this opportunity to thank all who have contributed to this English edition of the book. My special appreciation goes to Martha Avery for her superb English translation; to Zhang Qiaoyun, Ding Chuan, and Li Yinghong of CITIC Publishing House; and to the team at McGraw-Hill. Most of all, I am indebted to friends at the Alibaba Research Institute who provided me with tremendous access to Alibaba for my research into the company's ongoing innovation. I treasure the opportunity to watch how this company is growing by unleashing grassroots entrepreneurship both in China and abroad.

CHAPTER 1

THE ALIBABA WAY

New York University's William Baumol, nominee for the Nobel prize in economics, has pointed out that in some economic systems innovation can happen by chance or by choice but that in capitalist systems it is mandatory. The attribute of innovation in a nation depends on the political system and the incentive structure shaped by the society. To the enterprise in a market-oriented system, innovation is a matter of life or death. The diffusion of new technologies often requires decades or even a century in other systems—under capitalist systems, it can happen in a day. The motivation for this kind of superfast innovation is very simple because time is money.

If innovation is so necessary in capitalist economies, it must be even more important to China today. China has firmly aligned itself with the "international track" of development. The moment you step onto an international track, you have someone opening the way before you but also someone following right behind. China is squeezed in the middle and has no time now for regrets. In terms of the majority of its population, however, China is still agrarian. In terms of technological levels, China has not yet fully completed the first industrial revolution. Luckily, China has a large population, and optimism runs high. If state-run business is not working out, we have people-run businesses.[1] If the Central Committee is not coming through, we have local[2] governments. If our technology is

---

[1]Translator's note: One term for *private enterprise* that is used in contrast to state-owned and -operated businesses.

[2]Translator's note: The term as used in Chinese includes provincial governments.

backwards, we enjoy the advantage of later-to-develop countries, and we can leapfrog over whole periods as we develop! In this fashion, we have been able to foster a group of companies that represent international levels of advanced technology and quality services on behalf of China, companies such as Xiaomi, Huawei, and Tencent.

More important, however, we now have Alibaba, a platform that has unleashed the grassroots entrepreneurship of millions of people. Alibaba is the product of a world that has entered a digital age. It is a modern enterprise that represents a classic example of Internet technology and big-data analysis based on information and communications technology (ICT). Nevertheless, it is not in fact an enterprise so much as it is what Professor Baumol has called an "innovation machine."[3] Privately operated entities in China have by now created numerous commercial successes despite the fact that they operate under the shadow of the planned economy, do not enjoy equal access to resources, do not work in an environment of consistent and reliable policies, and do not have any precedent they can look to as a model. They have made outstanding contributions to the growth of China's economy and to China's social progress.

Alibaba is one of these privately operated entities. As a new kind of *diaoyutai*,[4] Alibaba has taught people how to fish rather than just giving people fish. Alibaba's innovation machine has enabled those who are unwilling to remain poor to step up onto that fishing platform, take action, and fulfill their wildest dreams. Some have learned to fish, others have learned to make fishing boats, and some have even learned how to trawl the distant oceans.

The Astonishing Way in Which Alibaba Grew

The Alibaba Group began with the stated intention of being in business long enough to straddle three centuries. It started as a grassroots enterprise

---

[3]William Baumol, *The Free-Market Innovation Machine* (Princeton University Press, 2003).
[4]Translator's note: The term *diaoyutai* literally means "a platform for fishing." It takes off on the name of the central location of China's Communist Party and government officials in Beijing. The "platform" of Alibaba is in fact a new form of governance.

with 18 people and 500,000 RMB in capital, scrounged from wherever people could find the money. In the short space of some 12 years, it has "grown up" to become a world-class e-commerce empire. Today Alibaba has 35,000 employees and a constantly growing number of subsidiaries.

Alibaba's business-to-business (B2B) enterprise was established in 1999. Taobao was created in 2003 and Alipay in 2004. In October 2005, Alibaba began to cooperate with Yahoo in setting up China Yahoo. AliSoftware was established in January 2007 in Hangzhou and Shanghai. These five separate spheres of business have long since become outstanding subsidiaries of the Alibaba Group. They represent five main aspects of the group's structure, its integrity systems, and market, search, software, and payment components. Each subsidiary is in itself a subsidiary platform. Each of the platforms links together an unimaginable number of grassroots factories, retail businesses, and services. Alibaba's rapid growth as an e-commerce business entity has by now become an indispensable part of China's economy.

In addition to these five subsidiaries is the Alibaba Group's Research Institute. This Research Institute was established in April 2007 with the mission of forging a new form of business civilization that will change how business operates throughout the world. It concentrates on creating the strategic vision for such a civilization. It has an extremely active and highly professional research team. No innovative company can be without a research and development (R&D) team, but most such R&D teams are focused on technology. Alibaba's innovative concepts drive the Research Institute to take a global stance and to focus on both the theory of the information age and its existing practicalities, developments, and trends. Its purpose is to gain insight into how e-commerce is overthrowing traditional commerce, and it is to build an "ecosystem" and a "civilized order" for new-age commerce.

For years, the Alibaba Group's Research Institute has cooperated closely with institutes and universities, government departments, and public institutions. It has published large quantities of research results with topics ranging from the social sciences, economics, finance, and computer sciences to information sciences. In addition to contributing to specific areas of study, research has contributed to the creation of various economic indicators by constant use of the database embodied in the Taobao platform. This supplies data that can be put to effective use in the formulation of policy. Given the support of the data platform, the Research Institute has made contributions in many areas of government policy in China. Among other things, it has contributed to understanding how micro-sized Internet merchants affect issues of consumption, labor, employment, production, regional economies, and the "three agricultures."[5] In its conceptual approach and its applied research, the Research Institute has far surpassed the level of China's other specialized research centers. Previously called a "Research Center," the name was changed to reflect the greater reach of its activities, so the entity is now called the Alibaba Research Institute.

From "Small Is Beautiful" to "Small Is the New Big"

In the 1960s, when industrialization was enjoying unprecedented growth, Western economists such as John Kenneth Galbraith declared categorically that America had entered an age of big industry and that the traditional small-business structure would no longer exist. Given the strength of the American government and the low-cost goods produced by big industry, Americans could now enjoy a beautiful life in their "affluent society."[6] Galbraith's thinking and policy recommendations, as well as the way he spoke on behalf of large corporations, faced opposition from a number of scholars. In addition to criticism from Nobel laureates such as Milton Friedman and Paul Krugman,[7] many scholars who believe in the market, grassroots innovation, and entrepreneurship began to show that Galbraith's ideas were factually incorrect.

Joseph Phillips, in *Little Business in the American Economy* (University of Illinois Press, 1958), emphasized two important values of small

[5]The "three agricultures" refers to the agricultural industry, the rural economy in general, and people with a rural household registration status.
[6]John Kenneth Galbraith, *American Capitalism Trilogy: The Affluent Society* (Houghton Mifflin, 1958), *The New Industrial State* (Houghton Mifflin, 1967), and *Economics and the Public Purpose* (Houghton Mifflin, 1973).
[7]For example, Paul Krugman, *Peddling Prosperity: Economic Sense and Nonsense in an Age of Diminished Expectations* (W. W. Norton, 1994), pp. 10–15.

businesses: (1) small business is "the backbone of the American system of free enterprise"; it "serves as a providing ground for new technologies and new, vigorous entrepreneurial talent"; and (2) the preservation of small business "is essential to the maintenance of the middle class."[8]

John H. Bunzel, in *The American Small Businessman* (Knopf, 1962), pointed out that small business is an American heritage: the small businessman "appears to have few enemies and is, in fact, something of a national hero."[9] He further noticed that "living in a country that places heavy emphasis on material success and pecuniary rewards, the small businessman had managed to be a symbol of success even in times when he has not … been financially successful."[10]

In his world-awakening book in the midst of the oil crisis, *Small Is Beautiful: Economics as if People Mattered*, Ernst Friedrich "Fritz" Schumacher (Harper & Row, 1973) indicated a firm belief in "small" as the basis for freedom, efficiency, creativity, joy, and sustainability in business. He called for a "restructuring [of] large-scale industrial ownership without revolution, expropriation, centralization, or the substitution of bureaucratic ponderousness for private flexibility." In his view, "All the indications are that the present structure of large-scale industrial enterprise, in spite of heavy taxation and an endless proliferation of legislation, is not conducive to the public welfare."[11]

Steven Solomon, in *Small Business USA: The Role of Small Companies in Sparking America's Economic Transformation* (Crown Publishers, 1986), claimed that "by injecting aggressive, free-market forces into a modern economy, small businesses permit the 'invisible hand' to play an important part in selecting those innovations upon which America will compete in the new global marketplace."[12]

Mansel G. Blackford, in *A History of Small Business in America* (University of North Carolina Press, 1991), claimed that "[f]rom the time of Thomas Jefferson to the present, many Americans have seen the owners

---

[8]Phillips, pp. 113–114.
[9]Bunzel, p. 13.
[10]*Ibid.*, pp. 85–86.
[11]Schumacher, p. 275.
[12]Solomon, p. 140.

of small businesses as epitomizing all that is best about the American way of life." He noted, "Small businesses have often received special treatment in state and national legislation."[13]

John Case, in *From the Ground Up: The Resurgence of American Entrepreneurship* (Simon & Schuster, 1992), clearly saw that "[t]he economic stability that Americans once took for granted was gone. We could no longer count on big companies for what they used to provide." He envisioned that we "will need a highly dynamic business world, once characterized by high levels of innovation, technical progress, and entrepreneurship."[14]

Small businesses play a very real role in stimulating economic growth—they are not merely an academic topic for books such as those noted earlier. After the financial crisis of 2008, people in both the United States and Europe drew lessons from the painful experience and urgently began to reconsider the contributions that small businesses can make to economies. China shares this sense of urgency, given the country's recent economic history. After 1949, China swiftly assembled its limited resources—drawing on the available forces of the nation, it used the scale effect of large industry to rebuild a home on a tragically ravaged land. Heavy industry, large-scale industry, and state-owned enterprises made an undeniable contribution to "new" China's development. The drawback of a state-owned sector operating according to a government plan, however, was that it was inefficient and lacked the dynamism of a market. By the end of the 1970s, this brought China's economy to the brink of collapse. Once market mechanisms were allowed to release the entrepreneurship of long-suppressed forces, tens of millions of enterprises and entrepreneurs were able to bring forth an economy in China that could be called the opposite of what had come before, namely, the ultimate in vitality. The tremendous increase in the number of enterprises in China is an indication of this. In 1978, there were a total of 348,000 enterprises in the country. By 1990, the figure had increased to 7,957,800, and by 2013, it was 60,623,800.

---

[13]Blackford, p. 4.
[14]Case, p. 224.

Small Is the New Big

In his book, *Small Is the New Big* (Penguin, 2006), marketing guru Seth Godin points out that big-box companies such as Walmart and The Home Depot, which had been forcing small businesses out of the market, are now themselves facing intense competition from niche markets and high-efficiency e-commerce. Today, he notes, success will no longer belong to large enterprises that are closely allied to Wall Street or to those that enjoy a completely globalized supply chain. Instead, latter-day arrivals that make use of platforms and that run two-sided markets, such as Google, Amazon, eBay, and Alibaba, are the new model for success. He notes that there are two secrets to using a platform successfully. The first involves amassing a sufficient number of creative entrepreneurs who are operating at the most basic levels and doing it at the lowest cost. The second involves providing the highest-quality service on the platform so that businesses on the platform can create their own commercial space for themselves.

In today's information age, specific production characteristics determine the viability of small enterprises. The marvelous thing about platform businesses is that whoever "owns" the most creative grassroots participants is the one that can occupy the entire space, who can "take the field." Faced with a competitive environment that changes constantly, small enterprises that are nimble and creative have the ability to prosper in a moment of time, but they also can disappear in a second. The creative intent and the capabilities of a small enterprise may be successful, but they also may fail. Nevertheless, through *dynamism* and *innovation*, the mass of entrepreneurs proliferates and creates a spillover effect, thus creating the positive energy field for building a prosperous and strong society.

One reason "small is beautiful" is that people matter. The U.S. Small Business Act puts it simply and clearly: "Only through full and free competition can free markets, free entry into business, and opportunities for the expression and growth of personal initiative and individual judgment be assured. The preservation and expansion of such competition is basic not only to the economic well-being but to the security of this Nation. Such security and well-being cannot be realized unless the actual and potential capacity of small business is encouraged and developed."[15]

Godin writes further in *Small Is the New Big*

> *Small is the new big because small gives you the flexibility to change your business model when your competition changes theirs. … Small means you can tell the truth on your blog. … Small means that you will outsource the boring, low-impact stuff like manufacturing and shipping and billing and packing to others while you keep all the power because you invent something that's remarkable and tell your story to people who want to hear it. …A small law firm or accounting firm or ad agency is succeeding because they're good, not because they're big. So smart, small companies are happy to hire them. … A small restaurant has an owner who greets you by name. … A small venture fund doesn't have to fund big, bad ideas in order to put their capital to work. They can make small investments in tiny companies with good ideas. … Small is the new big only when the person running the small thinks big.[16]*

Alibaba is precisely this kind of company. It has been able to create an infinite number of "small is the new big" types of companies.

A New Growth Model: Growing by Unleashing Grassroots Entrepreneurship

Classical Model of Economic Growth

Economic growth refers to growth in the market value of goods and services of a given economy over a specific period of time. The traditional way of measuring this was to calculate the percentage increase of real gross domestic product (GDP). The classical (Ricardian) growth model

---

[15]From Small Business Act as amended (1/13/13); available at: http://www.sba.gov/sites/default/files/Small%20Business%20Act_0.pdf.

[16]Godin, pp. 217–218.

was described in terms of production and increases in production in an agricultural economy. As the theory went, if any one production factor increased, it would cause overall production to increase, but at a progressively lower rate. (This assumed that other factors did not change, including technology. It defined *production factors* as being labor, capital, and land.) Ultimately, given diminishing returns, the rate of overall increase would decline until it approached zero.

The neoclassical growth model was a product of the industrial revolution. In this model, labor time, capital, production volume, and investment remain important, and the law of diminishing returns still applies, but changes in technology become more important than the accumulation of capital. In this model, an economy's long-term growth rate is determined by the savings rate (*Harrod-Domar model*)[17] or by changes in technology (*Solow-Swan model*).[18] However, the rate of capital accumulation (savings) and advances in technology remain unexplained by the model.

The *internally generated* or *endogenous growth model* attempts to overcome the dogma of progressively declining returns as well as the presumption of a steady state. It does this by injecting *human capital* into the equation. That is, it increases productivity by increasing the skills and knowledge of workers. This model provides an explanation for the long-term sustained economic growth of many Western countries. The model posits that the return on human capital increases progressively, while the return on financial capital does not change. Because of this, economic growth does not slow down with the accumulation of capital and therefore can never reach a steady state. The focus of research in this area is on increasing the factors that are decisive in increasing either human capital (such as education and training) or technological change (such as innovation).

---

[17]Translator's note: The *Harrod-Domar model* is an early post-Keynesian model of economic growth.

[18]Translator's note: The *Solow-Swan model* is an exogenous growth model, an economic model of long-run economic growth set within the framework of neoclassical economics.

New Economic Growth Model

Edmund Phelps, Nobel laureate in economics in 2006, has declared his belief that only sustained grassroots innovation can ensure the prosperity of a country.[19] He does not believe in the explanatory powers of classical models of growth based on resources, nor does he believe that the neoclassical model is sufficiently persuasive, with its focus on human resource capital and technological change. He feels that the wellsprings of sustained economic growth are to be found in economic dynamism, that is, in people's desire, ability, and intent to be innovative. Phelps cites the results of a McKinsey study: among every 10,000 ideas for new businesses, 1,000 companies are actually founded, 100 receive venture funding, 20 go through an initial public offering (IPO) and raise funds from the stock market, and 2 become market leaders. Given these odds, having broadly based grassroots participation in innovation is the key to fostering more market leaders that can make a contribution to economic growth.

Phelps' ideas with respect to how dynamism stimulates economic growth have been systematically tested and verified. He divides the time that an entrepreneur puts into his or her work into two different categories. The first is time put into producing enough to ensure the ongoing necessary aspects of life. The second is time put to *innovative production*, the kind that provides individuals with the pleasure of success. *Entrepreneurship* has three constituent parts. First, it involves the entrepreneurs themselves, who are working not only to sustain their livelihoods but also to grow. The second involves the social institutions that bestow on the entrepreneur the ability to carry on unencumbered business operations. The third involves a government that has organized its systemic framework so as to protect the innovative abilities of individuals and their ability to create startup companies.

Ying Lowrey has gone a step further in developing her own theory about entrepreneurs, with a focus on innovative labor. This challenges the dogma of the neoclassical school that maximizes the effect of humans as rational agents. Moreover, she borrows from the classical theory of

---

[19]Edmund Phelps, *Mass Flourishing: How Grassroots Innovation Created Jobs, Challenge, and Change* (Princeton University Press, 2013).

the entrepreneur in the tradition of Max Weber and Joseph Schumpeter. From this classical tradition and from empirical data, she feels that creative labor and vitality are what most characterize entrepreneurs. She hypothesizes two categories of labor, one that is engaged in producing subsistent goods and one that is engaged in creative production, and she assumes that an entrepreneur would prefer to engage in creative labor as a rational agent and not just "work" to support himself or herself. The necessary conditions for *maximizing personal satisfaction* therefore require that the marginal value of necessary-goods production must be greater than or equal to the marginal value of creative production. Lowrey has designed a dynamic model that incorporates the two types of labor, two periods, and two products. She injects *initial capital* into the equation of maximizing the happiness of this rational entrepreneur. The model predicts that an additional unit of initial capital generates a substitution effect in the first period but then a complementary effect that is positively associated with initial capital.

Lowrey (2005) asserts that people's economic well-being relies on the strength of the economy and that behind a robust and balanced economy must be a vibrant market system in which private business ownership is pervasive, small, and local. Using business and macroeconomic data from all states in the United States, she introduces the concept of *business density*. A spatial economic model and statistical testing demonstrate a significant correlation between business density and economic well-being at the state level. Results also indicate that a higher business density is associated with lower poverty and lower disparity between rich and poor.

Lowrey (2011) differentiates between two different types of employment in the process of starting up a company. One type uses a contract to confirm the employment that the employer provides to employees. It is therefore defined as *contractual employment*. The other is the *startup employment* that the entrepreneur provides for himself or herself. Only a small percentage of the startup employment is included in (any country's) official employment statistics. The U.S. Census Bureau distinguishes business into two categories: employer firms that hire employees versus nonemployer firms that do not hire employees. Using data from three databases regarding the situation in the United States, namely, the Panel Study of Entrepreneurial Dynamics, the Kauffman Firm Survey, and the 2002 Survey of Business Owners the research shows the following results. On average, each new startup employer firm can generate 5.8 job positions, including 4.4 contractually employed jobs and 1.4 startup jobs. Each startup non-employer firm can generate an average of 1.2 startup jobs. On average, each company founder puts 33.1 hours per week into entrepreneurial or startup labor. According to estimates derived from these three databases, between 1997 and 2008, in addition to creating over 1 million contractually employed job positions, another 2.5 million people were at the same time creating their own startup job opportunities in the United States. This is significant in terms of China's own government policy: policies clearly should promote entrepreneurial activity that results in startup companies. Entrepreneurs not only generate contractual employment for others but also—and even more important—they create jobs for themselves.

In this regard, it may well be that Alibaba's greatest contribution has been to provide millions of ordinary people with the chance to start their own companies.

Alibaba's Success Stems from Unleashing the Forces of Grassroots Entrepreneurship

Alibaba's great innovation was to base its own growth and development on the unleashed entrepreneurship of grassroots enterprises. Previously in China, an individual's creativity, capabilities, and ambitions were inhibited by social institutions that did not guarantee the rights of free enterprise and by a government that did not protect individuals' creative ability to start companies. When we now champion grassroots entrepreneurship, we include not only individuals among the public at large but also primary-level communities and primary-level government organizations.

By adhering to the concept of *customer first* and the motto, "Make it easy to do business anywhere," Alibaba has used the dynamism that has been gestating within the public at large to create one astonishing feat after another. The company set its sights on being in business for 102 years and being "China's greatest and most unusual major company to span three centuries." To achieve this, it had to institute a sustained and routinized form of innovation.[20] The value concept of customer first is not built on the basis of altruism. Instead, it is determined by the ecosystem needs of the platform economy of e-commerce in the digital age.

This value concept and its positioning require unusual comprehension and long-term vision. The concept of customer first enabled Alibaba to build a platform based on the digital age. Highly effective hardware and software enabled it to develop a massive customer base, both of which then enabled Alibaba to employ the scale effect of technological innovations. All this counted toward what the company did itself and so was only one side of the story. On the other side, Alibaba bestowed enormous capabilities on grassroots entrepreneurs, which allowed them to unleash their own entrepreneurship. In this process, Alibaba and millions of small companies formed a digital-age mutual interdependency that allowed the "stars and the moon" to reflect light off one another.

There are 7 million extremely active merchants on Alibaba. Not only have they created their own business turf, from which a large number of outstanding enterprises have emerged, but in the process they have catapulted the growth of Alibaba.

Jack Ma is the chairman of the board of the Alibaba Group. In 2009, on the tenth anniversary of the company's founding, he described the secret of the company's success: "We have been willing to do what others were not willing to do but also what they could not do. Over this past decade, we have written our script solely for micro and small enterprises, that is, for the 'forsaken daughters' that no-one else wanted."

Orders and cash flow are the lifelines of companies. Through Alibaba's e-commerce platform, by participating in the formation of a sturdy supply chain, micro and small enterprises have discovered a way to exist and to grow in a manner that represents a completely new path. By now, the Alibaba Group has entered the ranks of global Internet giants. The real power behind it, however, lies in the tens of millions of astonishingly dynamic small Chinese companies.

Alibaba's mission is to create a situation that "makes it easy to do business anywhere." Before making any decision, Alibaba first takes into consideration how any action may contribute to increasing benefits to

---

[20]See Baumol, Chapter 3, for the idea of routinized innovation.

its customers, by allowing them to make more money, save on costs, or manage employees better. As Jack Ma says,

> After we came up with this phrase about creating a world that makes it easy to do business anywhere, it became the sole criterion by which we judge the launch of any service or product. When our engineers and designers design new products, I always try them out first. If I can't use them myself, 80 percent of the world's people won't be able to use them either and I immediately toss them out. As a result, we make products extremely simple. We make it easy for the customer and put all the trouble of doing so on ourselves. Our aim is to enable micro and small enterprises to truly make money.

Zeng Ming, Alibaba Group's deputy CEO, who is also chief strategic officer, echoes this approach:

> For the past ten years we have focused exclusively on micro and small enterprises, and exclusively on e-commerce. Our mission is to create a world that makes it easy to do business anywhere. Our own existence and growth lies [sic] in how well we are able to support the existence and growth of small companies.

Given the number of occasions on which Jack Ma has reiterated that the company puts the "customer first, employees second, and shareholders third," he has encountered some resistance on this front from shareholders. Unperturbed, he continues to hold that customers must always be the very lifeline of Alibaba. The best customer service is the key to Alibaba's long-term growth. "The situation that micro and small enterprises within China have to cope with is intimately related to Alibaba's own future." He also confirms that Alibaba will continue to "write its script" for micro and small enterprises in the decade to come.

Despite the shock of the financial crisis, Alibaba was able to build a substantial customer base of small Chinese companies, and Jack Ma believes that this is something that cannot be duplicated in any short time.

"Our micro and small enterprises have formed a relatively complete production chain. This is the advantage of a 'later-to-develop' manufacturing country and is something that would be hard to duplicate."

On a number of occasions when traveling abroad, Jack Ma has heard people express views to the effect that the Chinese government actually controls the market economy. He feels that this is a biased opinion and has refuted it many times by saying that people are "looking at but not actually seeing the mainstream in China. ... To this day," he continues, "Alibaba has never asked for one penny in bank loans. Even more to the point, it does not have any kind of so-called 'complicated background.'"

In Jack Ma's eyes, some people in Western countries seem predisposed to misjudge the reason some privately owned high-tech businesses are flourishing in China. These people feel that the "life histories" of such businesses are complex. He says, "Not Alibaba. Alibaba can announce with all integrity that we are in complete alignment with international standards, and we are not, as some Western people have said, 'a product of policy.'"[21] He adds that the emergence of Alibaba proves to the world that "China's market economy has developed to the extent that its 'soil' can support the growth of world-class companies."

Many young people idolize Jack Ma for his entrepreneurship but assume that he was given a helping hand, boosted by things they don't have access to. He responds to this by saying that many young people make excuses for not starting a company, for instance, by saying, "My father doesn't have any money" or "Our family doesn't have any *guan xi*."[22] He says, "We at Alibaba want to provide a role model for China's youth. You can start a company even if you don't have parents with money or family connections." As noted earlier, the data show that there are several tens of millions of merchants on the different Alibaba platforms, people starting up companies, trading, and providing both real and digital products and services—and this is the best confirmation of his statement.

Alibaba has done a great number of things that the Chinese government should have been doing but has not done in terms of unleashing

---

[21]Translator's note: That is, policy support from different levels of the Chinese government.
[22]Translator's note: Relationships, so they can pull strings.

creativity, encouraging people to start companies, and supporting the innovative efforts of small entities. Meanwhile, Alibaba's "star-moon relationship" with countless grassroots enterprises is something that the United States has put enormous effort into for 60 years and not been able to accomplish.

In 1953, America passed the Small Business Act,[23] which explicitly stated that 23 percent of the enormous quantity of the federal government procurement must be done by small businesses—that is, large corporations must find small entities with whom to partner to do the business. Congress hoped that this would ensure fair competition and would stimulate large companies to foster cooperative relationships with small companies. While still enabling economies of scale in large enterprises, it would encourage the sound growth of small enterprises.

What happened, however, is that this kind of "quota" approach to business instead spawned all kinds of rent seeking and fraudulent behavior. A minority of large enterprises still monopolizes the great majority of the trillions of dollars of purchasing done by the American government every year. Other than a very few years, the 23 percent quota has never actually been achieved. Despite this, however, given its protections for fair and equal competition, the Small Business Act does in fact stimulate greater initiative on the part of small businesses.

Alibaba's Job Creation

Existing enterprises generally do not contribute to new employment—in fact, their contribution is often negative. Because of this, the United States depends on newly established enterprises to generate jobs. Statistics from the U.S. Department of Labor show that between 1997 and 2009, new employment generated by newly founded enterprises dropped precipitously from an average of 6 (fourth quarter of 1997) to an average of 3.5 (after the first quarter of 2009). New jobs created by newly established companies went from a total of 2 million in the late 1990s to 1.2 million in the most recent figures. At the same time, the number of enterprises with no hired employees at all went from 5.44 million

---

[23]From Small Business Act as amended (1/13/13); available at: http://www.sba.gov/sites/default/files/Small%20Business%20Act_0.pdf.

in 1997 to 22.5 million in 2011. This represents an annual increase of 500,000 enterprises. Every year in the United States, roughly 300,000 employing entrepreneurs create more than 1 million new job positions, but in addition, there are another 2 million entrepreneurs who do not hire employees who are starting up all kinds of commercial activities and providing goods and services to the market (Figure 1.1).

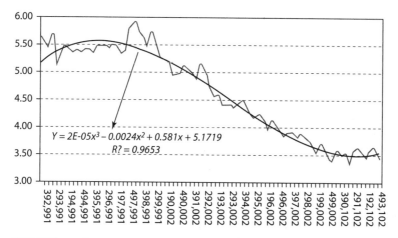

FIGURE 1.1 *Number of people employed in startup companies in the United States between the third quarter of 1992 and the fourth quarter of 2012*

According to a conservative estimate derived from a recent study of the big data behind Alibaba's platform, Alibaba has directly created 9.72 million jobs (including hired employment and startup employment), and it has indirectly created 2.04 million jobs. Not only has it become necessary for the millions of merchants on Alibaba's platforms to "found and also operate their own companies," but it also has become the prevailing mode of operation.

In 2011, Alibaba's Research Institute published a study entitled, "Lighthouse: Lighting up the Path of Business on the Internet." This is a collection of 100 case studies drawn from global Internet businesses in 2011. It records the way in which 100 of the most successful enterprises got started and grew. Alibaba helped to resolve the job difficulties and basic survival of these people, but it also amassed a very powerful force of entrepreneurship and positive energy in the process. Quite a few university students are returning to their rural roots after graduating these days and using their knowledge as well as their awareness of the outside world to start up Internet shops in their hometowns. They are developing the material economy by setting up "Taobao villages" (Table 1.1). They are carving out a new course of urbanization in China, one that is in line with China's unique circumstances. This new form of urbanization is quite different. It is more natural and harmonious in terms of social structure, and it allows China to leapfrog over one age and into the next.

TABLE 1.1 *Core data on people engaged in retail sales on the Alibaba platform*

TYPE OF E-COMMERCE EMPLOYMENT	CATEGORIES OF EMPLOYMENT	NUMBER OF EMPLOYED (MILLION)	TOTAL (MILLION)
Direct employment involving retail sales	Employment on the Taobao platform	9.27	9.72
	Employment on the Tmall platform	0.45	
Indirect employment involving services	Employment relating to transaction services (Alibaba network retail platform)	0.01	2.04
	Payment services (logistics, express delivery, payment, finance)	0.94	
	Derivative services	1.09	
TOTAL (million)			11.76

Source: Alibaba Research Institute,
Report on Employment by Alibaba Retail Platform, November 2013.

Spillover Effect of Alibaba

On July 3, 2014, the first summit ever held to discuss the subject of China's county-level economies and e-commerce was held on Alibaba's Xi Xi campus in Hangzhou.[24] Close to 180 leaders from county-level municipalities attended. This was yet another expression of how Alibaba

---

[24]Translator's note: *Xi xi* means "Western stream." *Xi* is pronounced "she."

has unleashed the forces of grassroots entrepreneurship over the years. In 2004, the company had started a contest to choose "the ten best e-commerce merchants in the world." This annual contest became a "Star-Light Pathway"[25] encouraging millions of startup entrepreneurs for personal achievement. While chasing their individual dreams, these outstanding entrepreneurs could have role models to follow. Meanwhile, the 2014 summit displayed how Alibaba exercised its spillover effect by exercising positive energy in the form of community development.

In the eighteenth and nineteenth centuries, Jeffersonian ideals in the United States created the foundations for small businesses, entrepreneurial startups, and community development. In the twenty-first century in China, the 2014 summit indicates that the dynamism of entrepreneurial startups is now irreversible. The summit first presented a report on China's county-level e-commerce developments. Areas with a relatively high density of e-commerce are also areas that are already fairly well developed. At the same time, the report revealed two important discoveries. First, in the decade 2003–2013, China's e-commerce passed through three successive stages. The beginning stage occurred between 2003 and 2005, with only a small number of county-level online vendors and slow growth. Between 2006 and 2009, a stage of modest incremental growth began, with county-level online vendors being added every year at an increasingly fast pace. (The term *online vendors* includes both individuals who sell online and online stores.) From 2010 onward, operations began to scale up rapidly, with a notable expansion of county-level online vendors every year. In terms of numbers during these three stages, county-level online vendors went from tens of thousands to hundreds of thousands to millions.

Second, prior to 2010, counties with e-commerce were concentrated primarily in the key growth area of China's southeast, as represented by the Jiangsu-Zhejiang Region. Since 2010, however, a new stage of multiple-level growth has developed in other parts of China, including northern, southern, and central China. Starting in 2010, although e-commerce maintained fast growth in Jiangsu and Zhejiang, for the first time, the combined figures in these provinces represented less than 50 percent of

---

[25] "Star-Light Pathway" is a very popular TV program that is similar to the "Star Search" TV program in the United Kingdom and United States. Many talented singers become very popular because of their performances on the program.

the total. At the same time, growth in the northern, southern, and central parts of China has been especially notable, with combined totals for these three approaching 30 percent of the total for 2013. The chief sources of growth have been Hebei, Guangdong, and Henan.

As Internet startups penetrate into other parts of the country, and as the density of online vendors increases, regional economies begin to be supported by the Internet advantages of decentralization displaying their own unique regional qualities and characters. Zeng Ming, chief strategic officer of the Alibaba Group, summarized the speeches that had been given during the summit, and in the course of his talk, he noted that "[w]e have discovered that China's counties may become the important core of China's future e-commerce." China is divided into more than 2,800 county-level units, that is, separate government administrations at a county level. Many of these counties contain over 1 million people. Grassroots entrepreneurship starts with individuals opening up Taobao shops, which then converge into Taobao villages and coalesce into Taobao counties. This kind of dynamism is currently in the process of creating the mass flourishing in the twenty-first-century China.

An Entrepreneurial Economy and Its Social Attributes

Entrepreneurs are the *allocators* of scarce resources, but they also represent a resource that is itself being allocated.[26] As a term derived from the French, *entrepreneur* refers generally to a businessperson who both founds and then operates a company. Joseph Schumpeter is regarded as one of the main scholars who studied entrepreneurship in the early twentieth century.[27] He defined *entrepreneurs* as those who use creative approaches or new methods to do things that are already being done in other ways. More important, entrepreneurs "can get things done."

William Baumol pointed out that while entrepreneurs have a twofold role in innovation (both the allocators of scarce resources and a resource

---

[26]William Baumol, *Entrepreneurship, Management, and the Structure of Payoffs* (MIT Press, 1993).

[27]Joseph Schumpeter, "The Creative Response in Economic History," in *Essays on Entrepreneurs, Innovations, Business Cycles, and the Evolution of Capitalism* (Transaction Publishers, 1947; 3rd edition, 1997), pp. 223–224.

that is itself being allocated), mainstream economics as based on neoclassical theories not only does not focus on this twofold role but also has no consistent and standardized definition of entrepreneurs at all. The twofold role of entrepreneurs may well not have been very pronounced in the age of major industrialization, but this is not true in the digital age. Cheaper transaction costs are dividing up large industrial production into smaller components, whereas the constant increase in labor costs is making enterprises that employ others try their best to outsource production processes or to substitute machines for human labor.

For example, Apple has outsourced a portion of its products to the e-commerce manufacturer Fushikang. Once labor costs became a problem for Fushikang, that company then purchased 1 million robots to replace most of its labor force. By now, robots are responsible for such daily tasks as spray painting, welding, and basic assembly. Substituting robots for human labor is merely another indication of how history moves forward. Unfortunately, though, the recent financial crisis has made this particular stage in the process far more tragic. People do not have much choice: either they are a resource that is to be "allocated" and they wait to be replaced by machines, or they begin to exercise their own ability to allocate themselves as a limited resource. They stand on their own two feet and found a company—create new endeavors in the new age.

As the development history of Western countries shows, when the use of machinery in manufacturing led to a severe surplus of labor, entrepreneurs began to develop such service industries as finance, logistics, education, and health care. Such service industries became the engine driving economic growth after World War II. Service industries grew the fastest in the United States, which entered the ranks of the world's economic powers as a result. As America enters the digital age, whether or not it can yet again transition smoothly to a human-machine substitution—and emerge from the problems of high unemployment created by the financial crisis—will depend on whether or not a new engine for growth is sufficient to bring into being a large number of new entrepreneurial startups.

Since 2013, the Defense Advanced Research Projects Agency (DARPA) in the United States has been focusing its R&D efforts on the development of robots (DARPA is part of the U.S. Department of Defense Department that functions as a platform to encourage scientific R&D). It is providing college students, professors, and professionals in virtually all fields as well as entrepreneurs with business opportunities. It is enabling them to allocate limited science and technology resources in ways that they themselves are free to determine. In China, the question now is how the country can use Alibaba's platform to similarly stimulate science and technology, to serve the unleashing of entrepreneurship, and to encourage innovation not only in the fields of B2B, retail, logistics, and microfinance but also in other spheres of science, technology, and services.

For example, opening up the Alibaba platform to community hospitals and clinics of all kinds could enable people to use (their own) medical big data as a valuable resource. Similarly, Alibaba could share the big-data resource with medical personnel to develop the best preventative and treatment methods for large-scale infectious diseases as well as the most difficult and complicated cases of illness. Or another example: if the Alibaba platform were opened up to universities, small high-tech companies, and venture investors, funding could flow directly to science and technology. People with human resources and those with financial resources not only could use the platform to allocate resources but even more significantly could be the scarce resources themselves that were being allocated.

Attributes of Social Entrepreneurship: Productive, Unproductive, and Destructive

William Baumol has pointed out that the entrepreneurship of a society can be productive but also unproductive and potentially also destructive.[28,29] The attributes of a society's entrepreneurship are determined by the society's social institutions and incentive mechanisms. Alibaba has done a great deal of experimentation in coming up with ways to build productive types of incentive mechanisms and platform "institutions." It has made *credibility* the corporate culture of the platform. At the same time, it has turned this into an important resource in the digital age by making it a

---

[28]William J. Baumol, "Entrepreneurship: Productive, Unproductive, and Destructive." *Journal of Political Economy* 98(5): 893–921, 1990.

[29]Translator's note: In Baumol's words, it is "disharmony creating."

quantifiable "integrity capital." Based on the record of credit of 7 million active online vendors, Alibaba Micro Financial Service Group has extended credit to 4 million online vendors. These people can make loans from Alibaba without a large amount of deposit in banks, collaterals, or third-party guarantees. This single fact alone is somewhat phenomenal in the history of finance in the West.

Small businesses face tremendous difficulties in getting loans given their lack of any kind of collateral or credit record and without anyone to guarantee repayment. This has been a problem in China but also around the world in the financial sphere, and many individuals as well as international organizations have tried to deal with it in creative ways.

Mohammad Yunus is one such individual.[30] He is a financial scholar from Bangladesh who has created a microloan service within the traditional realm of finance that offers loans to impoverished entrepreneurs who otherwise would not be able to receive traditional bank loans. In 2006, Yunus and the Grameen Bank[31] were honored with the Nobel prize for their work in promoting economic and social progress by working at the lowest levels of society. This demonstrates a global recognition of how microloans are an important factor in helping to alleviate poverty by funding startups. Through efforts similar to those of Yunus, Alibaba's microlending has taken an even more creative approach. The reason is that Grameen microloans are built on the foundation of a banking system that is post–industrial revolution, whereas Alibaba's microloans are built on the basis of the Internet after the digital revolution. They are built on the foundation of a *big-data-based financing service*.

Compared with the methods employed by the Grameen Bank, Alibaba has lower financing service costs, less risk, and much greater coverage, plus it is open, transparent, effective, and accountable. As a financial innovation, it is historically significant and highly constructive. The concepts behind it and its application will in the future overturn the traditional way in which impoverished people at the grassroots level have been denied entry into the "great gate of finance which faces only toward the riches." Microfinancing services will be a gate that is open to

---

[30]http://www.nobelprize.org/nobel_prizes/peace/laureates/2006.
[31]Translator's note: In Chinese, this is the "Bangladesh Rural Bank."

all. It will provide the liquidity, the bloodstream as it were, for all kinds of startups as well as ongoing operations.

In moving into a whole new age of commerce, unproductive, and destructive behavior is bound to occur among online vendors. In recent years, e-commerce platforms in China have all been embroiled in issues relating to fraudulent practices, including such companies as Jingdong, Taobao, Dangdang, and Suning. Malicious ordering, unqualified merchants, and lawsuits regarding orders and other unlawful activity have been a frequent occurrence.

The design of an Internet-based credit-rating system must involve an evaluation system that protects the rights and interests of buyers, vendors, and third-party online vendors. It may be that when this evaluation system was set up, however, it focused on the "hoped for" results too exclusively and did not analyze the unexpected consequences that also might occur. As a result, destructive innovations have severely damaged the reputations of blameless vendors and done tremendous damage to their businesses. Although e-commerce platforms themselves can adopt measures to guard against and counterattack all kinds of fraudulent and criminal activity, the force of government action is extremely important. An e-commerce platform is not after all an enforcement agency. Such platforms can devise incentive mechanisms in scientific ways, but the key to guiding all social innovation in a productive direction lies with government. Not only must the government set up better legal institutions, but it also must increase the severity of enforcement.

Alibaba has taken major innovative steps on the human resources side of this whole issue to ensure the productive entrepreneurship of staff as it sets up internal management systems and incentive mechanisms. It has taken a number of actions to pull together positive energy. These include setting the principles of recruiting staffs, encouraging competition for innovation, and even extending to bulletin boards in restrooms for collecting good ideas and information about the employees' moods. At the same time, Alibaba has been firm in attacking any behavior that is detrimental to the culture of Alibaba as a corporation.

In 2009 and 2010, Alibaba investigated thousands of cases in which "China Suppliers" were suspected of being involved in fraudulent activity. Evidence indicated that some Alibaba staff in direct-sales teams of the B2B company intentionally allowed certain companies to come onto the Alibaba platforms purely for the sake of improving their own performance ratings and thereby gaining more income. Nearly 100 sales staff were directly involved. These people were then dealt with according to the company's internal governance systems, including being fired. At the same time, Alibaba took steps to punish higher officials. The CEO of the Alibaba B2B company, Wei Zhe, and the Chief Operating Officer, Li Xu hui, were both fired. In order to prevent such unproductive rent-seeking behavior, Alibaba set up disciplinary systems that are similar to those required of public servants in the United States—for example, staff may not receive any gifts or any other form of compensation from outside parties. As Alibaba personnel conduct their research, they may well be offered various inducements, such as wining and dining and gifts from local governments and merchants, but they are not allowed to accept these.

Microfinance Based on "Integrity Capital"

Adam Smith's *The Wealth of Nations* provided the solid theoretical system behind today's mainstream economics, whereas the "invisible hand" of the market may well guide market economies. Moral integrity is still the foundation for human societies, however, as described in Smith's *Theory of Moral Integrity*. The invisible hand has become the core of economics, yet, whereas moral integrity and an invisible moral standard are scarcely seen in mainstream economics at all.

Today's economies employ extremely complex banking, virtual, and monetary transactions to accomplish the highly fragmented production of goods and provision of services. Because of this, personal reputations and mutual trust are of ultimate importance in maintaining normal business operations. An effective financial market should be able to stimulate positive commercial activity and business creation. In an age of *financial capitalism*, however, if the microloan market is imperfect or not functioning properly, reputation and trust are also not functioning properly.

Three hundred years ago, the author of *The Fable of the Bees* extolled the virtues of being "rapaciously avaricious" and was severely criticized for this by Adam Smith. Nevertheless, some professors and some people on Wall Street still take delight in this kind of distasteful story. To this day, the parable is taught in some MBA and executive MBA classes. A great deal of research indicates, however, that avaricious behavior on the part of individuals can lead to large-scale financial crises, indeed to global economic crises. On April 5, 2012, Reuters reported in a story that the head of the U.S. Treasury Department, Tim Geithner, made the comment, "Most financial crises are caused by a mix of stupidity and greed, and recklessness and risk-taking and hope."[32]

In 2014, a British scholar[33] discovered while researching the annual reports and financial reports of five banks during the period 2004–2009 that the initial customer-driven culture of these banks had turned into a culture that was driven by sales and that during these five years, these five banks were dominated by a kind of rapaciously avaricious culture that disregarded consequences. The financial crisis of 2008 swept aside the reputation of financial capitalism in Western countries. As a 2011 Gallup poll in the United States indicated, more than 75 percent of those interviewed no longer trusted banks.

The global crisis in the reputation of the financial world did not influence the reputation-based foundations of the Alibaba platform. As a third party between buyers and vendors, Alipay only remits payment to vendors once buyers have received their goods. This payment innovation resolved a fundamental issue in e-commerce and spurred the establishment of a trust relationship on both sides of the platform. At the same time, it gave individuals the chance to accumulate what is now being called *integrity capital*. Ali-Loan (aliloan.com, now renamed as Ant Microloan) is an Internet microloan service that is based on integrity capital. A separate service called Yu'ebao provides the economic decision makers themselves with the opportunity to make choices regarding their consumption and their savings in the most transparent of all markets. Alibaba Group's financial branch now is renamed as Ant Financial Service Group. It provides microfinancial services including Alipay, Yu' eBao, Sesame Credit, and Ant

---

[32]A financial insider, former U.S. Treasury Secretary Timothy Geithner acknowledged this fact, as reported by Reuters on April 5, 2012.

[33]Alison Lui, "Greed, Recklessness and/or Dishonesty? An Investigation into the Culture of Five UK Banks between 2004 and 2009." *Journal of Banking Regulation* 16(2): 106–129, 2014.

Financial Cloud.[34] The appearance of these financial services and tools has filled a gap in global microfinance markets. They have fundamentally changed a situation in which small businesses were unable to get financing, and they have made a historic contribution to unleashing grassroots entrepreneurship.

One of the Nobel prizes in economics in 2013 went to Yale University's Robert Shiller,[35] who emphasized two key concepts in his book, *Finance and the Good Society*. First, the essence of finance is to provide funding for economic activity. It is not done to maximize profit for itself. Second, financial systems should be democratized. These two concepts may be regarded as a provocative challenge in the age of big industry, but openness, transparency, high efficiency, and an orientation toward grassroots are not only possible in the digital age but also imperative. Since the 1980s, the financial industry in Western countries has been controlled by a small number of oligarchs. Politicians are manipulated by them, and policies provide them with open sailing. People in finance have devised all kinds of ways to maximize profits—to the extent that countless people have lost their life savings and many have lost their homes.

Only when information technologies develop to a sufficient degree can they eradicate the problem of asymmetrical information. Only then can they turn around the monopoly situation in the financial sector, and only then does it become possible to set up this kind of microfinance market.

As for China, the severely negative spillover effects of the financial crisis in America and the West are currently spreading within the country as its own economic growth rate slows. China's unemployment rate has been rising, and its exports have dropped precipitously. China's highly centralized financial sector is simply unable to resolve the recession now hitting enterprises. It certainly cannot address the lower levels of economic dynamism in the country. As a result, microfinance has emerged to meet the need. Its existence and sound development depend on ongoing updates of information technologies and powerful and effective regulatory systems. Even more important, microfinance, as based on information technologies

---

[34]http://www.antgroup.com/zh/antFamily.htm.
[35]Robert Shiller, *Finance and the Good Society* (Princeton University Press, 2012).

and regulatory systems, in the future will force people who are engaged in economic activity to comply with a form of invisible moral standard, namely, *reputation*. Microfinance services in the new age should come from the grassroots, and they should serve the grassroots.

During a lunch that Edmund Phelps had with the deputy editor of the *Financial Times*, Martin Wolf, Wolf asked Phelps what he thought about the bank rescue that had such a "bad odor" to it in the 2008–2009 period. Phelps admitted that American banks were a problem. If banks were going to be "too big to fail," there should be a firm bottom line. Nevertheless, every bank tries to get as big as possible as it takes advantage of a flourishing real estate market, and there is less and less of a bottom line as a result. Phelps said, "Part of my vision is that the big banks should be broken up. I would like to see the American economy go back to small banks rooted in communities where the bankers know something about the local startups."[36]

Through open, transparent, efficient, and accountable microfinance services that are based on Internet technologies, not only should we be able to realize Phelps' vision—and realize Jeffersonian ideals that are centered on community development—but we also should be able to lower the costs of innovative startup activity and thereby increase returns to investors.

Alibaba's Next Decade

Chris Anderson, author of *Makers: The New Industrial Revolution*,[37] has said that "[o]ver the last ten years, through jointly using the Internet, we invented new paths via our exploratory innovations. Over this next ten years, we will be taking these paths out into a new real world." The new age has brought new challenges as well as opportunities to business-people. Not only do "makers" have the professional ethics of craftsmen, but they also have the high-tech tools of the new age, tools that enable creativity and low costs and that therefore can keep production small scale while allowing it to coexist in a globalized world.

---

[36]http://www.ft.com/cms/s/2/c88b2610-f095-11e3-b112-00144feabdc0.html.

[37]Chris Anderson, *Makers: The New Industrial Revolution* (Crown Publishing, 2012), p. 17.

"Killer" applications and 3D printing are a good example of things that begin in small places and grow to affect large areas. Who can say that the Taobao network, Alipay, Ali-Loan small loans, and Yu'ebao will not be the killer app of e-commerce and online payment? Tens of millions of "makers" are linked to one another on the Taobao platform. They use Alipay to carry out online transactions. Those with good credit are getting loans through Ali-Loan, those with extra cash are handling their personal finances via Yu'ebao. Alibaba is definitely not going to rest on its laurels and remain at this level, however.

The United States is the leading force in e-commerce in the world, the bellwether of the industry. By 2011, U.S. e-commerce held 49.3 percent of all sales volume in manufacturing industries, 24.3 percent of all wholesale business, 4.7 percent of all retail sales, and yet only 3.0 percent of all services business. At present, China's e-commerce enjoys the great advantage of being later to develop in the areas of retail and service industries.[38] When the previous chief operating officer of Alibaba's B2B business, Wei Zhe, was recently interviewed by a CNN reporter, he pointed out, "Unlike in America, many retailers and consumer products have not yet penetrated China's smaller cities. This provides an opportunity for the growth of e-commerce in these cities. Indeed, e-commerce will become the mainstream method of retailing." In the process of realizing the "new four-izations,"[39] we can anticipate that the force of China's e-commerce growth in other industries also will be unstoppable.

China's financial markets have not developed to a point of creating unproductive and indeed damaging types of financial vehicles, as the industry in the United States has done. I refer to certain kinds of derivatives and hedging that are far removed from the real economy. In similar fashion, China's retail industry has not been taken over by countless numbers of middlemen. On the contrary, China's retail e-commerce is well grounded in the real economy; that is, it is backed up by the processing

---

[38]David Wei, "E-Commerce Bigger in China than United States," CNN, September 19, 2013; available at: http://edition.cnn.com/2013/09/19/business/on-china-alibaba-e-commerce/index.html?iid=article_sidebar.

[39]Translator's note: These are "marketization," "platform-ization," "ecological-ization" (which refers to a greater diversity of species), and "data-ization." Use of the "four-izations" is a spin on the "four modernizations," as promoted during 1980s.

industry. The success of e-commerce platforms depends on winning over grassroots online vendors so that they position themselves on your platform. As Wei Zhe observed, "Behind the millions of merchants [selling on Internet platforms], you can find tens of millions of Chinese factories. In America, in contrast, it is very hard to find any real factory." Similarly, right now, many Chinese have idle cash in hand that they do not immediately need. Through e-commerce, an open, transparent, highly efficient process, they do not need to go through middlemen, and certainly, they do not need to go through underground banks or credit unions. Their funds can flow directly to short-term forms of liquid capital (e.g., money markets) or to longer-term investments.

Micro entrepreneurs who came into being on the Alibaba grassroots platform, and whose thinking has never been subject to the usual constraints, will without any doubt whatsoever create new and unprecedented forms of supply and demand in the world for new products and services. As we work to develop e-commerce service industries, we should think quite dispassionately about how to avoid so-called innovations that do not provide any socially redeeming value. I refer, for example, to the kinds of financial innovations that are in fact opportunistic and damaging.

Alibaba still has a long road ahead of it. Microsoft has entered middle age, and the ills of larger companies have begun to afflict this company that was once so full of dynamism. A company that generated such revolutionary innovations in its youth has begun to get a little paunchy around the middle. In contrast, Alibaba is only 14 years old. Not long ago, however, an incident occurred that came to be called the "security brother incident." In order to reduce costs and strengthen controls, Alibaba decided to outsource its security. As soon as the news got out, it stirred up an enormous furor on the internal network. Alibaba was then caught in a dilemma, namely, the conflict between fairness and efficiency. Which should it choose?

Meanwhile, starting in 2013, the company has decided not to continue the practice of holding the annual event that elected and celebrated outstanding online vendors. This event had played an important role in unleashing entrepreneurship and pulling together energies. Did the great commander-in-chief really have the interests of only grassroots startups at heart? Many other platform companies had begun to copy Alibaba's business model and were now taking away some of the vendors previously on Taobao and Tmall. Faced with competition, Alibaba was being confronted with the problem of how to balance the traffic flow between large and small vendors. The question for the company increasingly became one of defining its winning model.

In the past, China's retail industry was marginalized in the overall economy, and it remained underdeveloped. Alibaba took smooth advantage of this to unleash grassroots entrepreneurship as a growth model for the retail arena. It turned itself into a giant in the realm of e-commerce in the process. How Alibaba will grow its microfinance service platform in the future remains to be seen. Two powerful forces are influencing Alibaba's financial platform strategy. One is the way the government strongly controls the financial industry in China. The other is the financial capitalism of the West. The government of China, as a party with de facto interests at stake in the traditional financial system, is unwilling to see the growth of a powerful privately operated enterprise in this area. Meanwhile, Western financial capitalism has enormous seductive power. Alibaba could make use of its powerful platform to grow into a Goldman Sachs in a very short period of time. But, does the world need another "Goldman Sachs" that serves the "big guys"? If Alibaba is to succeed in the financial area, it therefore must go up against pressures from interests in the existing Chinese financial industry. It must continue to establish a strong market in the microfinance area, something that had been lacking for a long time, and it must continue to provide services that unleash grassroots entrepreneurship.

In the United States, 4 of every 100 enterprises are providing financial services. In China, the ratio is 4 of every 10,000. Alibaba should withstand the temptation to be a financial capitalist. It should continue to explore platform models that enable both sides of a microfinance market to flourish. That is, the platform can meet the huge demand for microfinancial services such as microloans and personal financial management. On the supply side, it can enable more grassroots entrepreneurs to enter into the financial services industry as small businesses that can provide all kinds of microfinancial services.

CHAPTER 2

ALIBABA'S EFFICIENCY AND THE ALIBABA ECOSYSTEM

CHEN LIANG, SENIOR RESEARCHER
AT THE ALIBABA RESEARCH INSTITUTE

The "Holy Land" of China's e-commerce is located on the western side of Hangzhou. Near a small village, tall office buildings appear to have grown out of the earth—this is Alibaba's Taobao Town. The "Town" encompasses 300,150 square meters and is covered by 250,000 square meters of new buildings. The cost of designing and constructing these came to 1.36 billion RMB.[1] This new campus formally began to welcome its owners to their new home in the second half of 2013. Companies and employees under the banner of the Alibaba Group began moving in—people from the various business groups of Taobao, Tmall, eTao, Alibaba Cloud Computing, and others. Taobao Town now holds the core of Ali's businesses. It is where the Alibaba "miracles" are created and where the business of the entire ecosystem of Alibaba is managed.

An Overview of Alibaba

Alibaba's Big Move to New Quarters (2013)
The design of Taobao Town is highly original. Not the traditional bricks and mortar, it has grassy slopes, wetlands, fields, and even a small village. The environment is open and quiet, full of poetic and painterly aesthetics. Six buildings have been completed. Their glass-sheathed sides come down to the ground, making them seem transparent as they reflect the nearby

[1]Translator's note: Roughly US$217.6 million in 2015.

trees. Perhaps this peaceful scene is intended to soften the impact of the kinds of winner-take-all battles that go on in the e-commerce world, a fierce competition that determines life or death.

This is not the first time Alibaba has moved. Four years earlier, the Alibaba business-to-business (B2B) company made a sensation as it conducted what was called "*A-niu* crosses the river." As a group, Alibaba moved into the new campus situated on the Bin River. At the time, the 6,000 people who were part of this earlier move turned Hangzhou's traffic into complete gridlock. This time, the Alibaba Group set up a temporary command center within the traffic section part of Hangzhou's police department. This approach enabled 10,000 people to move smoothly into the new campus. At the same time, Alibaba made sure that the move was done in groups and conducted mostly on weekends. Each group was composed of around 2,000 people. Alibaba staff had to undergo training in how to move, instructions in how to package and label all their belongings, and so on.

Founded only 14 years before this move, in 1999, Alibaba had already left a deep impression on the ancient city of Hangzhou. As a small example, rents went up steeply after the earlier move to the Bin River as well as this move to Taobao Town. All of Hangzhou's streets and alleyways were buzzing with news of Alibaba and Jack Ma. Those who were unacquainted with the full story would never have been able to connect this mighty army of the Internet industry with a dozen hotheaded youth who gathered in an apartment in 1999 and scraped together enough money to start a company.

In fact, the strong pulse of this enterprise was being felt not only in Hangzhou but also in all of Zhejiang Province, all of China, and even much of the rest of the world. What follows, therefore, does not just tell the story of a successful startup. It also narrates the story of innovation and determination, how innovators fight to realize their ideas and are unyielding in their efforts to find a way forward.

The Great Attraction of Taobao Is that It Enables Others to Be Creative
Unlike China's other Internet entities, illustrious companies such as Tencent, Baidu, and Sina, among others, the Alibaba Group's greatest and most unique appeal lies in its incomparably huge e-commerce ecosystem. Within this ecosystem, millions upon millions of people have found their

own individual value and created their own work. To give one example of Taobao's pull effect on job creation: by the end of 2012, the Taobao platform had been directly responsible for creating 8.6622 million new jobs, whereas the total number of people engaged in Internet startups in China is 9.625 million. Being a "Taobao vendor" has become a whole new occupation that the public is gradually recognizing and embracing. Many of the guests on a highly popular television show describe their occupation as Taobao vendor, for example.

Over this past decade, in line with the swift growth of e-commerce, the Taobao platform has generated countless new occupations. In addition to Taobao vendors, other occupations that nobody has ever heard about are springing up like mushrooms after a spring rain. These Internet-based stores offer products ranging from fashion modeling to advice on how to negotiate prices when purchasing and from consulting services on how to market on Taobao to consulting services for finding the best delivery people. Among occupations, the fastest growing new occupation is providing online services. As the number of Taobao online stores increases, many shop owners, working on their own, are unable to deal with handling all the daily transactions. A new business that deals in customer service for online stores therefore has sprung up. Statistics show that 2.84 million people are already engaged in providing customer service for online stores.

Another occupation that catches people's interest is that of being an Internet model. These models are called "Tao ladies," also known as *Ma Dou*. This refers to people who model products that are being sold by online stores. According to statistics released by the Taobao platform, there are also 37,638 people working on the Tao lady platform, with 86.24 percent of those working part time. Their average age is 23. It is not uncommon for Tao ladies to make a monthly income that is in the thousands of RMB. By now, the highest incomes are in the neighborhood of 50,000 RMB, which is roughly half the annual salary of a white-collar worker in a large metropolis.

From the perspective of someone who works within Alibaba, I can say that Taobao is also a highly creative platform. In 2004, Alipay,[2] previously

---

[2]Translator's note: "Alipay, an online payment escrow service, accounts for roughly half of all online payment transactions within China." *Economist*, March 2013.

an operating unit within Taobao, was spun off and made into an independent company. It has since gone on to become the leading company in the third-party payment industry in China.

In 2008, Taobao Shopping Mall was spun off and made independent from Taobao. Its name was later changed to Tian-mao.[3] Today, this company is known in English and online as Tmall. It has become the largest platform in China's business-to-consumer (B2C) market, having left Jingdong, Dangdang, and Amazon far behind. The eTao, Juhuasuan, and other lines of business also have been spun off from Taobao. It is the base area for spinning off companies on the retail side of the Alibaba Group's Internet business.

Holidays in China have always been considered festivities at which one is allowed to consume a lot, so consumption peaks at such times. There had always been a dearth of opportunities for stimulating mass consumption in the period between the end of Golden Week (Chinese one-week holiday to celebrate the National Day on the First of October) and the Christmas season, however. Taobao therefore proposed what it called the 11.11 Shopping Festival, which filled this need precisely.[4] In an entirely new way, it galvanized tremendous growth in domestic demand. Taobao linked this event with the use of online credit-card payment. This made China's consumers, who had been burying their savings in bank accounts, turn toward unprecedented consumption. The combination opened up a whole new round of economic growth.

Leading the Consumer Trends of the Future

Not only has the Taobao platform been a well-received retail sales platform, but it also has become the concentrated focal point of a community of Chinese consumers who interact with innovative global products. To a great extent, the Taobao platform has thereby changed traditional methods of production as well as the ways in which people consume. Characteristics of the emerging "Tao generation," as it is being called, include comparison shopping among at least three shops, very close figuring when it comes

---

[3]Translator's note: In Chinese, this literally means "heavenly cat," but in English, the word *Tmall* is used, so this translation uses that official name.

[4]Translator's note: In English, on Wikipedia, for example, this is also known as the "November 11 Shopping Festival" and as the world's largest online shopping event.

to what they are willing to pay, a desire for being fashionable, a desire to express individuality, and a highly enthusiastic and open attitude on top of rational decision making. The diversity of consumer experiences on the Taobao platform offers this Tao generation whatever it wants: group design, custom-made anything, keeping up with fashion, and enjoying tradition.

Over the past decade, Taobao has used a unique kind of temperament to influence and change the behavior of Taobao consumers as well as merchants. The trend is toward becoming more popular and fashionable. Purchasing behavior has gone from plucking out what is cheapest and most convenient to choosing more individualistic items. The temperament, or quality, of the trend influences the behavior of the trend, and the platform that enables the trend exposes the direction of the trend. This Tao trend has already arrived and is being led by Taobao.

Alibaba's E-commerce Services Business

A Newly Emergent Business that Has Broken Through 100 Billion RMB
A key indicator of the emergence of an e-commerce ecosystem is the rise of e-commerce services businesses. These businesses have accompanied the growth of e-commerce itself. Based on information technologies, they are able to integrate a variety of industries that serve e-commerce activities.

By operating at different levels of activity and coordination, e-commerce services have been able to generate highly promising prospects for the new types of industry groups that are now vigorously emerging. Vendors want to meet the individualized needs of an ocean of buyers. The multitude of vendors therefore concentrates on e-commerce services platforms. They have effectively hastened the birth of a professionalized division of labor, creating a *network effect* that comes with the interactions between the industries that support e-commerce and the industries derived from e-commerce.

The numbers are impressive. According to calculations by the Alibaba Research Institute, operating revenues generated by China's e-commerce services industries came to US$40.3 billion in 2012 (246.3 billion RMB).[5]

---

[5]Translator's note: At an exchange rate of 6.11 RMB = US$1. The following figures also use this exchange rate.

This was a 72 percent increase over this figure in 2011. Within this figure, income from e-commerce transaction services industries came to US$11.26 billion, an increase of 56 percent over the previous year. Income from e-commerce supporting services industries came to US$19.21 billion, an increase of 113 percent over the previous year. Income from derivative e-commerce services industries came to US$9.84 billion, up 150 percent over the previous year. The total volume of e-commerce transactions in 2012 exceeded US$818 billion—which includes transactions that went through e-commerce trading platforms supported by e-commerce services. Within this amount, the total volume of retail transactions exceeded US$164 billion.

The Alibaba Research Institute predicts that e-commerce services will enter a period of expansion in the next three to five years. E-commerce services[6] are expected to maintain a steady growth rate of 60 to 70 percent per year and therefore are expected to show growth that is even faster than the applications or use of e-commerce itself. According to a survey conducted by Alibaba Research Institute, it predicted that by 2015, operating revenues from e-commerce services are expected to break through 1 trillion RMB. These services will support e-commerce transactions that are on the scale of 13 trillion RMB. The research is not updated, but e-commerce retail services have been growing rapidly. As the foundation for the information economy, e-commerce services are becoming a global leader in strategic emerging industries. China, meanwhile, has the world's largest e-commerce services industry in the world and is therefore leading the way. The strong growth in this industry will propel greater adoption of e-commerce, especially among traditional industries as they shift to e-commerce to take advantage of the growth prospects.

A New Kind of Ecosystem Is Being Formed
by the Rich Diversity of Product Type
E-commerce trading platforms form e-commerce services ecosystems by combining with a diversity of service companies that provide logistics,

---

[6]"E-commerce services" meant to say "services to support e-commerce retail sector."

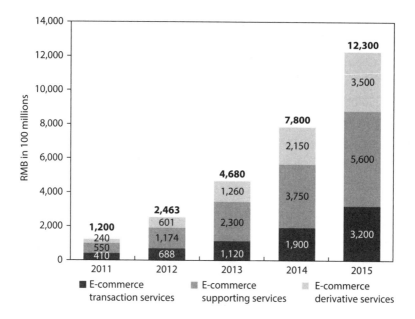

Source: Alibaba Research Institute, March 2013.

FIGURE 2.1 *Turnover of e-commerce retail businesses and the resulting services and derivative industries in China between 2011 and 2015*

payment, software, and agenting services. Together they provide online stores with a rich combination of information, knowledge, and customers themselves. These ecosystems, in turn, provide a strong stimulus for upgrading the level of services of the entire system and expanding the scope of services. The process is calling forth a diversification of product offerings in the system while creating ever-deeper integration among the ecosystem's products and services.

In the retail sphere of the Internet, transaction services platforms universally practice a strategy of *open data*. This greatly enhances the coordinated expansion of service-type groups. When a multitude of professional services vendors enters the services ecosystem, each one constantly creates value for the entire network of vendors. Take the Taobao services market as an example: in 2012, there were 490,000 individual third-party service providers, servicing more than 9 million free-of-charge customers and 1 million paying customers. Operating revenues based on the derivative services of Taobao's platform came to roughly 15.2 billion RMB.

By now, more than 1.56 million sellers are paying to purchase services within the Taobao business circle. Of Taobao Town's online stores, 75.6 percent have chosen 23,000 models from among the network, and the modeling market does business on the order of 396 billion RMB per year.[7] Of providers of traditionally branded goods, 52 percent are considering the use of an agenting service to market their brands online. At present, 0.5 percent of online stores already use an agenting method to operate. These contribute 5 percent of Alibaba's total sales volume.

Innovations in the Dynamic E-commerce Services Sector
The fact that innovation is highly valued in the Internet world is amplified many times over in the specific sphere of e-commerce services. E-commerce services providers generally try to differentiate themselves, and they embed their services in the vehicle of differentiated products. Providers have short research and development (R&D) turnaround times and diverse pricing strategies. Their responses have to be quicker than those of the competition to meet a constantly changing competitive environment. Speed and flexibility determine success.

The coordinated innovations of the e-commerce services ecosystem are mainly divided into three levels: (1) coordinated innovations based on the user entities of e-commerce, that is, coordination among different enterprises that are using the same service but as it relates to different parts of the business chain, (2) coordination that is based on innovation of the e-commerce services ecosystem itself, which requires achieving cross-industry and cross-regional connections that relate to the same project, and (3) coordinated innovations that are based on the interaction between the services ecosystem and its environment. This allows for an outwardly expanding ripple effect, raising the value of the business ecosystem. It influences and changes the external natural, economic, and social environments.

The Application Programming Interface (API) of Taobao's open platform to a certain degree reflects the liveliness of e-commerce innovations that are based on an open foundation. In 2012, 1.2 million vendors

---

[7]Translator's note: These figures are given without currency exchange in order to show direct comparison.

entered the Taobao open platform, which was 2.6 times the number of the previous year. By November 2012, Taobao's open platform recorded a total of 1,025 API data interfaces; the frequency of average daily data transfer is around 2.4 billion times.

Alibaba's E-commerce Ecosystem

An Inventory of Alibaba's Stock in Trade:
Going from an Ecogroup to an Ecosystem
In the field of biology, an *ecosystem* is formed when different species come together to form an organic system that is organized in a certain way. Maintaining the proper functioning of such a system depends on how energy is cycled through its various components in a beneficial way. Making use of this concept, theoreticians as well as people actually doing business have come up with the idea of what is being called a *commercial ecosystem*. This so-called commercial ecosystem happens when related *interest entities* mutually construct a *value platform*. On top of this platform, the capabilities of all participants bring into being and add to existing *value*, which serves the interests of the entire body. The platform is similar to an organic system, whereas the various interests on the platform are similar to species. The joint partaking of value, as well as the dividing up of value, is similar to the transmission of energy. The platform system of commerce is therefore similar to an ecosystem in biology, which is why it is called a *commercial ecosystem*.

By improving strategic choices and upgrading organizational capacity and value creation, Alibaba has gradually formed an ecocommunity made up of e-commerce entities that are engaged in e-commerce. Within this Ali ecocommunity, certain things such as Alipay, Alibaba's search engine, post boxes, and pay for performance (P4P) are like a liquid system. They are resources used by all in the Ali ecocommunity. Alibaba's B2B company Taobao, Yahoo-China, AliSoftware, Ali Mama, and koubei.com are like fields of green grass. Small and microenterprises, individual entrepreneurs, and consumers are the three "tribes" of the Ali ecocommunity. What Alibaba does is to provide a constant stream of services to improve the ecosystem environment so as to expand its own domain and enable the existence, growth, and prosperity of the three tribes of the ecosystem.

Right now, Alibaba is putting all its efforts into making the already existing ecosystem into an open environment so as to allow more partners to enter into cooperative relationships and serve the three Alibaba tribes. Openness endows the Alibaba ecosystem with greater dynamism and more powerful energy and allows greater room for imagining a future that is more worth thinking about.

The Alibaba Group's ecocommunity is basically divided into two parts. One is formed by the mutual intereliance that is generated among all the companies, an ecosystem that is mutually supportive. The other is an ecogroup that allows for common "glory" with third-party participants. Prior to establishment of the new "Seven Swords System," these two groups were not coordinating and sharing mechanisms in the most ideal way. As the Alibaba Group accelerated its efforts to move this ecocommunity toward an ecosystem, in July of 2012, it restructured its subsidiary system into a system of various business groups. After this reorganization, Alibaba included or contained "seven swords," which were Taobao, eTao, Tmall, Juhuasuan, Ali International, Ali Small Business, and Ali Cloud Computing.[8]

The Seven Swords community intends to create the kind of e-commerce ecosystem that enables Alibaba to become the basic infrastructure platform for e-commerce, including all its services, its "water, electricity, and heating." Through unified data, security, risk-prevention, and ground-floor technology, the aim is to construct the Alibaba Group CBBS community of consolidated markets (CBBS stands for *c*onsumers, *b*usiness channels, *b*usiness manufacturers, and e-commerce *s*ervices providers). This will open up one channel that links the whole process—from providers of raw materials to producers to consumers.

The CBBS community of markets is composed of the "C" stores on the Taobao platform, the "B" stores of retailers and channels, the large "B" stores of large producers and manufacturers, and the "S" stores of services providers. In the entire production chain, the ultimate provider should be small businesses on the B2B platform that are linked to one another via "S" services producers. The consumption demand of consumers therefore drives the products and quantities of sales, while the

---

[8]Translator's note: Currently known as Aliyun.

purchasing demand of platform vendors also drives the production types and quantities of small businesses that are involved in production.

Given that small businesses are the fountainhead of the Ali ecosystem, Alibaba has divided its original B2B business into Ali International and Ali Small Business depending on the attributes of each business group. After this division, the new business communities were able to grasp the best of China's production enterprises—the best of its raw materials, purchasing, industrial production, spare parts manufacturers, and services providers—and to integrate each of these with other business groups to open up a platform that accesses all platforms on the Taobao system. Because of this, the Alibaba ecosystem has become a more truly cooperative e-commerce platform based on the Internet. The new Seven Swords business communities will be spurring greater cooperative innovation in the CBBS community.

Alibaba's Innovative Efficiency

The United States has consistently dominated innovation in the Internet domain and is way out ahead of everyone else. Since the 1950s, the United States has instigated and led several revolutions in the information technologies industry and has been able to consolidate its own global economic hegemony each time. From the PC revolution and the Internet revolution to the cloud computing revolution, the United States has played a key role in driving the information economy on a global basis. The reason the country has been able to maintain its long-term position of leadership is mainly the result of the way it has sustained ongoing innovation through conscious development of systems and capacities. It has thereby kept its hold on the central hub of the Internet and kept a clear-minded and forceful national strategy.

However, in the sphere of e-commerce, the strength of China as represented by Alibaba is not in the slightest inferior to companies on the other side of the Pacific when it comes to innovative capacity. Over the past 30 years of reform and opening up and the past decade of the Internet revolution, China has created an astonishing sort of miracle that can be attributed to its enormous enthusiasm, determination, and investment. It has applied itself to constant research, change, and development. Unlike the great majority of other countries, the leaders in almost all spheres of the Internet in China are native-born companies. A number of Internet companies in the country are beginning to be among the global front ranks and to be internationally competitive. The way in which China's e-commerce enterprises have developed so rapidly and have caught up with and in some cases even surpassed those in other countries can be attributed mainly to three things: the country's massive base of "netizens" and huge consumer market, the high-speed growth of its economy, and its advantage of backwardness.[9]

China's Advantage When It Comes to Innovation

China's massive base of "netizens" and its large consumer market provide a firm foundation for the innovations of the country's e-commerce enterprises. The number of people connected to the Internet in China has been growing faster than in any other country. By the end of December 2014, the number of people connected to the Internet in China had reached 649 million. In 2014 alone, another 31.17 million had come online. The penetration rate of Internet use was 47.9 percent, which was 2.1 percent over what it had been in 2013. Moreover, by the end of 2014, the number of people connected to the Internet via cell phones was 557 million, which was 56.72 million more than it had been the previous year. The percentage of those using cell phones to access the Internet went from 81.0 percent of all Internet access in 2013 to 85.8 percent of all Internet access in 2014.

China's consumer market potential is extremely large. The country therefore has what is known as a *large-country effect*. Given its size, enterprises can enjoy economies of scale through cost as well as competitive advantages. From basic necessities to high-end consumer items, China is the globe's largest market. On November 11, 2014, in just one day of the Alibaba Group's 11.11 Shopping Festival, Internet sales came to 57.1 billion RMB (US$9.3 billion).[10] In contrast, the comparable event in the United States, held on a Monday in November 2014, racked up sales

---

[9]Translator's note: Sometimes called *later-to-develop advantage*.
[10]Translator's note: At an exchange rate of 6.11.

of US$2.04 billion. In 2014, China's Internet retail sales volume overall came to a total of 2.8 trillion RMB, which was 10.6 percent of all retail sales of consumer goods in the country. In 2008, the percentage had been just 1 percent, with 100 billion RMB in retail sales via the Internet.

Fast economic growth could be called the wings on which China's e-commerce has taken flight. Growth has moved at high speed ever since 1978. Between 1979 and 2007, the country's gross domestic product (GDP) grew at an actual average annual rate of 9.8 percent. Not only was this notably higher than the country's 6.1 percent average growth rate between 1953 and 1978, but it also was much higher than the 3 percent average growth rate of the global economy. When Japan's economy was in takeoff stage, its GDP was growing at an average annual rate of 9.2 percent, about the same as Korea's average of 8.5 percent. In 2010, China overtook Japan to become the second largest economy in the world, after the United States. The World Bank predicts that China will become a high-income country at some point in the 2030s, when the size of its economy will surpass that of the United States. This is true even though the speed of China's economic growth will be one-third lower in the future than it was over the past 30 years; that is, the economy will grow at an average rate of 6.6 percent per year.

The strength of China's overall economy and the speed at which its per capita GDP is increasing will bring unprecedented prosperity to all industries in the country, including the Internet industry. The Boston Consulting Group forecasts that the scale of China's Internet sector will be on a par with that of the United States by 2016.

At the same time, we should recognize that China also has a very clear advantage in being a "backward" country because it took up e-commerce later than the United States. In contrast to developed countries, the basic infrastructure for China's Internet is not yet well developed, and there are major imbalances between urban and rural areas and the eastern and western parts of the country. Meanwhile, the traditional industries and logistical systems in China are underdeveloped. It is precisely the underdeveloped nature of these things that provides such new commercial value to China's Internet and tremendous opportunities for growth. The development of new forms of industrialization, "informatization," urbanization, and agricultural modernization will be done in tandem with growth of the Internet. This will provide enormous imaginative space for a leapfrogging kind of growth of China's productive forces. In contrast, America's modern retail sales industry is highly developed. Before entering the Internet age, the United States had already realized a fairly high level of "informatization." In creating new value on top of this existing foundation, the U.S. Internet industry faces greater obstacles and has less room to grow.

Alibaba's Innovative Pathway

To someone in the Internet industry in the United States, the success of Alibaba is rather peculiar. Although one can vaguely see some traces of American Internet companies in what Alibaba has accomplished, the overall shape of its innovation has been totally different. Alibaba's success has taken a different path.

1. A B2B Business with Chinese Characteristics

As the global Internet sector heated up in the late twentieth century, e-commerce began to seep into China from the United States. In the course of this "heat wave," Jack Ma accepted an invitation to attend an e-commerce conference in Asia, at which he discovered something that surprised him. In every industry in the United States, which is a mature market economy, the top three companies actually dominate that industry's market and resources. Basically, all (business) e-commerce in the United States is servicing these large companies. By way of contrast, 99 percent of all enterprises in China are small and medium-sized entities, and the market-economy environment is totally different. This was a determining factor in how e-commerce had to develop in China—it had to service small business. It could not resemble the kind of B2B e-commerce in the United States, which was "business to business" or "enterprise to enterprise." Instead, it had to be "businessperson to businessperson."

In the end, this conceptual difference created a Chinese model for B2B that was totally different from that in the United States. B2B was the basis on which Alibaba was founded. Alibaba's original B2B business therefore was divided into a domestic form and an international form—two different market segmentations.

Alibaba's market for international transactions was created to allow small and medium-sized enterprises around the globe to expand into foreign markets on the basis of an English-language cross-border trading platform. By December 31, 2012, Alibaba's market for international transactions had 36.7 million registered users and 2.8 million foreign companies' online storefronts. Its services covered more than 240 countries and regions.

Alibaba's market for domestic transactions was based on the already existing ways in which enterprises exchange information within China—issuing purchasing orders and carrying out large wholesale business. The company decided to provide improved e-commerce services to small and medium-sized companies that were carrying on domestic trade. By the end of 2014, Alibaba's China-based online market, called 1688.com, had become the world's foremost business platform, with over 120 million registered users, more than 12 million visitors every day, and generating more than 150 million online every day. The platform has 10 million business storefronts that sell items that range from clothing to furniture to industrial products.[11]

In both these market segments, Alibaba charged membership fees in order to earn income. Small and medium-sized enterprises could have their own self-operated space on Alibaba's platform by paying a certain fee. Within that space, they could conduct their own business. Sales were mostly generated via the Internet, but the actual transactions were executed offline, in the old manner. Between 1999 and 2007, Alibaba gradually took this B2B model to a higher level of excellence. In 2007, Alibaba's B2B company was listed on the Hong Kong Stock Exchange and raised US$1.7 billion in funding. At the time, this was a record for an Internet company.

2. The Omnipotent Taobao

Taobao's tremendous capacity for innovation was apparent from the time the company came into being. When Taobao was set up in 2003, it was

---

[11]Items being sold include 49 first-level industries and 1,709 second-level industries.

dedicated solely to being a consumer-to-consumer (C2C) website, and eBay/Eachnet stood in front of it like a massively imposing mountain. At the time, eBay's former CEO, Meg Whitman, said that Taobao would last 18 months at the most. Eighteen months later, Eachnet's chief operating officer said, "It's going to be a protracted war—we'll be fighting for some time." At present, Taobao is pretty much calling the shots, while eBay/Eachnet has basically been forgotten.

How did Taobao conquer eBay/Eachnet? The question has been asked by many people with considerable surprise. A simplified analysis shows that Taobao's main innovations included the following:

1. The way in which AliPay serves as a guarantor of transactions eliminated the doubts and distrust that Chinese customers had felt about online payment.

2. eBay/Eachnet did everything it could to prevent buyers and sellers from linking up with one another and conducting business directly in order to ensure that it could keep its own transaction fee revenue. Taobao instead encouraged buyers and sellers to negotiate prices directly. This allowed Taobao to be a free market.

3. While believing that the time was perfect for grabbing the e-commerce market, Taobao put considerable investment into expanding its market, that is, into market promotion. By the time eBay/Eachnet "woke up," China's e-commerce market was already occupied by others, with little left for eBay/Eachnet.

4. Taobao's flexibility in dealing with regional and local markets completely beat the strategy of treating global markets as one entity. Eachnet's platform was linked up to eBay's global platform, and the customer account system of both was one unified system worldwide. This came up against opposition from essentially all Eachnet vendors. In contrast, Taobao could develop functions that were unique to its local native markets.

After beating out eBay/Eachnet, Taobao went on to grow in a way that was basically unobstructed. Guided by correct strategies, the company moved step by step to become the bellwether of China's Internet retail business.

One of Taobao's major innovations was called the *greater Taobao strategy*. In September 2008, the Alibaba Group announced and formally launched the first step of this strategy. Under the banner of a merged Taobao and Alibaba development effort, they created the largest e-commerce ecosystem in the world. This greater Taobao strategy would enable Taobao to surpass itself on the basis of its own foundation and, by means of an unconventional way of developing, would create a unique form of worldwide commerce. The goal was to surpass the global sales figures of Walmart within 10 years. In January 2010, the Alibaba Group announced that it was investing 5 billion RMB into the Taobao platform over the next five years as part of its focus on developing the greater Taobao strategy.

The virtue of this greater Taobao strategy lay in expanding the value that Taobao itself provided to each individual company. Instead of providing simply the Taobao value, each company now was leveraged up to becoming part of an ecosystem and a whole industry. The reason Taobao was able to form e-commerce services valued at 100 billion RMB was closely related to this greater Taobao strategy.

Another of Taobao's major innovations was that it constantly segmented and spun off new businesses. As a highly creative businessman, Jack Ma's tactic with respect to Taobao was to grow the company at exponential speed and then, at the appropriate time, split it up into business segments. Alipay, Juhuasuan.com, and Taobao Commercial City (later renamed Tmall.com) were all the result of this. The most thorough occasion on which Jack Ma played out this strategy, however, was in January of 2013, when he split the entire Alibaba Group into 25 separate business units, a move that astonished everyone on the outside.

Constantly differentiating businesses was, in fact, a manifestation of Alibaba's proactive strategy of constantly changing and improving itself. "Embrace change" is one of Alibaba's Six Sacred Swords. It is an extremely important part of the company's code of values. An even higher-level principle, however, is "Create change"—repair the roof before the rain, make arrangements well in advance. The benefit of this is that even though business units multiply, the core stays the same—all revolve around the backbone of e-commerce. Moreover, each change consolidates and strengthens that backbone. At the same time, the subsidiary businesses that have been differentiated take on a new horizon for growth, a new market space. Each becomes the leader in its own differentiated domain. For example, once Juhuasuan was spun off and made independent, it became the largest online group-purchasing marketplace platform in China. Once Alipay was made independent, it became the leader in the third-party payment sphere in China.

3. Alipay: An Accidental Offspring of Alibaba

When it was spun off from Taobao and made an independent company, Alipay did not anticipate that it would be what it has become today. From being Taobao's earliest "tool" for guaranteeing online transactions, Alipay has now become the leader in third-party escrow services for online payments in China. In fiscal year 2014 (by March 31, 2014), total transactions through Alipay had reached US$623 billion (approximately 3.9 trillion RMB). By the end of 2013, Alipay had close to 300 million named customers, and 12.5 billion transactions had been executed via Alipay's services. What's more, in the course of this, more than 100 million customers had shifted their primary payment site toward the Alipay Wallet, Alipay's mobile service. These customers had completed in excess of 2.78 billion transactions valued at more than 900 billion RMB, making Alipay the largest mobile phone payment service in the world.

From the time it was established in 2004 until the present, Alipay and Alipay Wallet have become the primary method of both online and offline payments for many businesses. They provide basic cash-flow services for millions of customers and commercial entities. During the 2014 11.11 Shopping Festival, orders reached 278 million, and turnover was valued at 57.1 billion RMB. The peak number of transactions handled in one minute was 2.85 million, which was more than three times the figure in the preceding year. The highest monetary value of mobile phone transactions in one single day was 11.3 billion RMB. More than 460,000 businesses routinely use Alipay services to handle payments. Such payments incorporate a wide range of business areas, including Internet retail sales, virtual games, digital communications, commercial services, tickets, and public-service endeavors.

Alipay is no longer a simple payment tool. It has become a "helper in the daily affairs of life" for people in the Internet age. It is putting its efforts into constructing a "life circle" on the Internet, providing ways to make all of life more convenient, faster, and easier in terms of such daily affairs as eating, dressing, housing, and so on. For example, Alipay already has tens of millions of customers using its services to pay utility bills, make credit-card payments, accomplish online remittances, and so on.

The Spring Festival of 2014 can serve as an example. Most banking locations were closed in the course of this seven-day holiday. As a result, 2.2 million person-times used Alipay Wallet services to make payments from 38 different kinds of bank-issued credit cards. In this one instance, payments made by mobile phones came to 7.1 billion RMB. This was 10 times the amount transacted in this manner in the Spring Festival of 2013. The number of credit-card transactions that used Alipay payment services during the Spring Festival of 2014 came to over 100 million separate transactions. Credit-card transactions came to 52 percent of all Alipay-serviced transactions. In these seven days, without ever leaving their homes, Alipay's more than 50 million customers could use their mobile phones to purchase goods, pay for daily needs, pay off credit cards, use the YuEbao service to organize personal finances, and so on.

From this it can be seen that the starting point from which Alibaba unleashes grassroots entrepreneurship is Taobao.com. The Taobao platform is also the foundation and the platform for unleashing grassroots innovation. Numerous beautiful and small e-commerce businesses converge here. In Chapter 3, by looking at the innovative process of the Taobao platform, we will analyze the important role the network plays in "teaching people how to fish."

THE TAOBAO PLATFORM: TEACHING PEOPLE HOW TO FISH

FANG RUONAI[1]

Taobao created yet another miracle on the day known as the 11.11 Shopping Festival in China on November 11, 2013. On that one day, Taobao and Tmall transacted close to 35 trillion RMB in business. This was nearly two times the volume of transactions conducted on the same day one year earlier, when the total came to 19.1 trillion RMB. The 2013 figure represented a new milestone in the history of China's Internet-based retail sales.

If the 2012 figure could be regarded as the start of the dismantling of traditional retail business, the 2013 figure of 35 trillion RMB could be seen as a key moment in the process of transforming traditional sales into e-commerce. Based on the unique characteristics of the Internet, the new economic model of e-commerce was beginning the actual overthrow of traditional commerce.

As an industry that arose like the rising sun, this was not the first time e-commerce had been regarded as a new force for absorbing large numbers of employees. More and more merchants were setting up business on Taobao, which, on the surface of it, seemed a very desirable thing. However, like the bursting of the information technology (IT) bubble a few years earlier and like today's financial crisis, if an industry cannot find a path to sustainability, if it lacks the constant renewal of innovation and vitality, the vision of prosperity remains a far-off dream. Right

---

[1]Kang Lili also contributed to this chapter.

now, for example, the merchants on Taobao are complaining more and more about how hard it is to do business. Even though these grassroots entrepreneurs often came up with astonishing ideas and sales strategies, competition is intense in this market. Many fresh ways of thinking might well get buried by such competition and disappear before you know it. Inside Alibaba, one of the long-term topics of discussion is how to unleash the entrepreneurship of these merchants and also how to make use of this initiative. Taobao University, the Tmall Vendors Training Department, and a number of departments within Alibaba, including the department for developing vendors (bringing them to maturity), spent considerable time and effort on this.

Taobao University

As yet another 11.11 Shopping Festival swept over China like a heat wave, Taobao and Tmall grew another year older. From the day they were established, these two dynamic websites showed a great affinity for attracting business. A number of grassroots brands had made use of the Taobao platform to grow into large businesses and open up their own territory. A number of traditional crafts, such as dying and embroidery, also found loyal customers on Taobao and created a unique kind of adornment. Given increasingly segmented lines of business in China, the innovators of all kinds of unusual and intriguing endeavors found a place to ply their wares on the Taobao website. The creativity of shop owners was allowed full range of expression. Not only did Alibaba constantly stay in the forefront of innovation, but it also mobilized tens of millions of grassroots entrepreneurs to do the same. It built a free and easy "cradle of creativity" for innovators to do their thing.

One might well ask how it was that tiny grassroots peddlers could manage to find business opportunities in the context of fierce online competition. How could they then build themselves up to real strength? What secrets lie behind the legendary stories of so many Internet companies— what are the tricks to being successful, the paths to innovation? How can other potential vendors, lacking experience and yet full of the desire to try, find a way to survive in the stormy turbulence of e-commerce?

In this chapter we get closer to an Alibaba that is not well known to outsiders. We look at the kinds of efforts that Taobao's online customer services providers put into helping grassroots entrepreneurs. We look at what kinds of experiments these entrepreneurs try, what kinds of successes they have, what challenges they face, and what setbacks they have endured.

Taobao University: Serving As Incubator for Training New Vendors

"Unleashing the entrepreneurship of store owners" is easy to say but not so easy to do. A myriad of products is now flooding markets. Products that declare that they are innovative by just sticking on a new label are simply gushing forth. Consumers see such marketing ploys as "Our shop has one of a kind ..." or "Custom made for you ..." or "Made to order," and what started out as interested curiosity turns into a kind of numbness. Meanwhile, the real breakthroughs, the success stories, such as frozen food sold via the Internet and ethnic clothes made to order also have faced all kinds of bottlenecks and problems. They have had to deal with raw materials, logistics (handling and shipping), marketing, and everything else. Alibaba is highly aware that innovation is not just a matter of having a good idea and not just a matter of carving out an innovative path. It is more a matter of turning these new things into successes. Taobao University, which is described next, teaches vendors how to turn innovative ideas into reality.

Taobao University is a training department within the Alibaba Group that provides services specifically to vendors on the Taobao platform. It is positioned as an educational platform. It provides professional training for vendors who are currently operating websites on Taobao as well as vendors who want to start a business but do not have experience. From starting out with the most basic operating training on e-commerce, it has gone on to conduct offline training tours around the country, visiting 50 cities with a team that includes the most successful sellers on the net. It also has gone from being a completely free public good, providing primary training, to positioning itself as an increasing high-level professional service that receives compensation. After nearly 10 years of growth and development, Tao-U, as it is called, also has gone from training supply-chain logistics and transaction credit procedures to preparing people for a more strategic approach to growth. Throughout this process, Taobao University has consistently held to its core mission: helping the world make money rather than making money off the world. Its reflexivity is extremely powerful. It develops itself by constantly thinking about the needs of vendors. It is like a patch of very fertile soil that nurtures the growth of tens of millions of e-commerce entrepreneurs and that then witnesses their miraculous successes, one after another.

The Source of Taobao University

A famous line in Tang Dynasty poetry describes the effects of a gentle spring breeze that passes over the land, putting all the pear trees in bloom in the course of one evening. This elicits comparison with the many e-commerce businesses that sprang up in China at the turn of the twenty-first century. A profusion of "shops" appeared on the Internet selling everything from women's fashion to low-cost household electronics to high-cost luxury items. They emerged and then hoped for business like sunflowers facing the sun. The soil that nurtured these things, however, kept a very low-key and humble attitude. The name of this patch of fertile soil is Taobao.

Many people view Taobao as being akin to Wangfujing in Beijing in that it relies on its premier location. It has the advantage of occupying a unique space all by itself. In fact, just as Wangfujing needs the plans of designers and the cleaning services of a host of sweepers, Taobao also needs designers to help it with the platform that supports the online operations of merchants. It needs their acutely sensitive creativity to constantly adjust its functionality. Wangfujing, located in the center of China's capital city, may have a constant flow of people, but it also still has the underlying precision of excellent management and standardized rules. Every day, Taobao's network carries traffic that amounts to tens of millions of visits. Without a highly refined set of standardized systems, all those large and small, new and old storefronts would be pouring the blood of their efforts to increase traffic out into the sand.

Meanwhile, as everyone knows, when e-commerce was just beginning, traditional branded enterprises kept firmly to their offline mode of operations. As a result, they were not fast enough to catch the wave of Internet sales. The large numbers of online storefronts came from the most simple and unadorned ideas of people at grassroots levels. To use the words of highly qualified Taobao staff, going from 10,000 to 1 million may not have been such a hard thing to do for these grassroots shops, especially given the overall prosperity of e-commerce in that period. Going from 1 million to 100 million, however, began to make store owners feel that perhaps they lacked sufficient experience and professional knowledge. They began to feel that their heart was in the right place, but they did not have everything else that success requires. The question for Taobao then became whether or not to accept the cold logic of the market. Should Taobao allow microentities to go belly up, especially if they had no way to realize their own potential by themselves? Or should Taobao "borrow a ray of light" and serve as a lighthouse for them, guiding their passage, showing them how to break through bottlenecks and bravely keep moving forward? The Taobao platform chose the latter course of action. In June 2007, a department called the Vendors Training Department emerged to meet the needs of the time. This was the precursor of Taobao University.

Maturing of the University

Seedling Stage: 2003–2007

The early period of Alibaba and the Taobao platform did not actually have many elements to it that were original inventions. In 1995, when founder Jack Ma set up China's "Yellow Pages," he imported the e-commerce model of the United States. Later, Alibaba's highly successful business-to-business (B2B) business, which was listed on the Hong Kong Stock Exchange, was still, to a large degree, simply localizing a model copied from elsewhere. The birth of the Vendors Training Department was something Taobao did to reduce the distance that still separated China from America's level of e-commerce.

In 2003, at a time when 100 or more titles on e-commerce could be found in bookstores in America, books on the subject in China were

extremely narrow in focus and mostly were limited to textbooks or educational material. In 2003, when eBay's homepage was alive with the ads
of major international brands, inside China, frontline brands still shrank
from the idea of appearing on Taobao. They did not want to set a foot
in these waters. In that same year, all kinds of Internet sites were up and
contending with one another. Finally, in order not to let the opportune
time pass by, still in 2003, the precursor of Taobao University, the Vendors
Training Department, finally declared its existence.

"If you want to be innovative, first copy others." This realization
was something Alibaba had practiced for many years as an innovative
company. Between 2003 and 2007, the Vendors Training Department
remained at a fairly preliminary stage of development. A team composed
of only four people was responsible for everything it did. To start out,
the team selected store owners who had particular prowess of one kind
or another and asked them to describe their experience for everyone's
benefit. The team was able to find vendors with whom to exchange
information on all aspects of the business, including sourcing goods,
photographing products, marketing operations, logistical management,
customer service, and transaction security. For the first few years, the
Vendors Training Department trained eight lecturers. They came from
the cutting edge of the market and had developed their own set of ways
of doing things that covered all links in the production ecosystem. For
example: How could one predict sales volume over the near term so as
to have adequate stock on hand? From small things, such as servicing
details, to larger things, such as operating rules and regulations, everyone talked about their own successes, and everyone had a good time.
Meanwhile, Taobao staff who were designing the actual platform saw
how these "children" (Taobao vendors) helped one another and found
it hard to express their delight.

Growing Stage 2007
Taobao realized an annual turnover volume of 43 billion RMB in 2007,
and mainstream products began to be sold on the site that same year.
The Taobao platform seemed to have taken some of the wind out of
the sails of Target and Walmart. Also in 2007, the Vendors Training
Department executed an extremely courageous maneuver. It had always

remained behind the scenes, but now it emerged and took a team of Taobao's most proficient vendors on an offline training tour, stopping at 50 cities around China. The members of the team put up notices on bulletin board services (BBS) describing the locations of the training sessions and the qualifications of their lecturers. Once vendors learned about this, they crowded into the sessions. Each of the 50 sessions was totally full. In some cities, where the room was fairly small, attendees spent the entire time standing, drinking in the lessons with rapt attention. The passing along of knowledge, the enlightened understanding, the sharing of experiences, the infectious nature of the enthusiasm all put a kind of magic wand into the hands of these grassroots store owners. Once the evenings came on and they returned home to wave their wands ever so lightly over their own work, the products on their online shops began to glow.

Still in 2007, when the sale of actual goods was enjoying a high tide, traditional forms of training also began to be affected by the spring breezes of e-commerce. At the time, many cities were holding training sessions on the Windows operating system, five-stroke typing training, and computer-aided design (CAD) drafting. These offline training sessions lacked a systematic approach and could not be scaled up, but the market demand for them was enormous. Clear-sighted people recognized a business opportunity. They decided to incorporate skills-based training into the training systems of e-commerce. This idea galvanized the development of a large amount of skills-based training. The mutually stimulating effect among industries also proved infectious.

E-commerce is a very young industry, and it relies on the Internet, with new technologies as the core content. Supply and demand follow the market, while all cutting-edge, fashionable, popular things can see their reflection in the realm of e-commerce. Meanwhile, those engaged in e-commerce are mainly young people who are themselves up with the times. In early 2007, some students from colleges and institutes in Jiangsu, Zhejiang, and Shanghai began to explore the idea of starting their own Internet shops. Without any place to store the goods, they stuffed them into their own bedrooms and along the halls of their buildings. Despite the tough conditions, they found a way to survive. This exploratory kind of self-directed operation was not the way to grow to any kind of scale. Nevertheless, this group of college students was able to build some outstanding stores. At the time, most e-commerce stores simply were lucky to meet with the needs of the times. They did not put too much thinking into their own sales strategies and operating methods, but somehow or other they made money. Wang Jiaying, who sold wrapping paper, said that he did not need to worry about sourcing goods because a relative of his sold paper cartons. He simply registered his shop online and began to do business. However, as more and more people began to participate in e-commerce, this became less feasible as a business plan. Solitary efforts generally meant that the abilities of these sole proprietors did not match their ambitions. Sourcing goods from relatives could not become a widespread business practice, and it definitely was not a long-term strategy. Because of this, Taobao's role in assisting these vendors became all that much more important.

In schools that teach professional skills, such as commercial and industrial institutes, students are taught a certain basic curriculum in such things as marketing and business operations, but this is seldom put to use in any practical application. Given this, Taobao again initiated a quite marvelous practice. It decided to link up with institutes of higher education and provide students with practical training, what the company called "the last kilometer." Starting in 2007, Taobao cooperated with various schools and institutions of higher education in Jiangsu and Zhejiang Provinces. The company appointed a vendor training professor with top-line experience to teach the professors in the school and help them to enrich their courses with case examples. This helped to blend theory with enlightened practice. In addition, the company provided an actual battleground for students. In actual drills, the company sharpened their capabilities and the quality of their work. The original training, which had been adapted to the Internet, was now localized and based on the teaching in schools.

The year 2007 was a milestone for Taobao University's own growth. The training team, like the proverbial Lushan Mountain wreathed in clouds, had not been too willing to show its own face. It now came down to the grassroots level in person and began to meet with vendors face to face. What had originally been a fairly wild and undisciplined form of training used the e-commerce platform to become a more standard track. The original mode of operating by feeling for the stones as you cross the river, using college graduates as representatives of grassroots entrepreneurs, now became professionalized training. In this year, the fertile soil of Taobao University spurred the emergence of one after another and group upon group of superlative e-commerce enterprises.

Opportunities and Challenges Coexist: 2008

In 2008, however, e-commerce began to face unprecedented challenges. First, in the early part of the year, a rare snowstorm blocked all the roads, so shipping was harder than ever before. It was impossible for customers to get the goods they ordered, and public confidence in e-commerce dropped sharply as a result. In May, Wenchuan suffered a massive earthquake, affecting transport in the Sichuan region. Although quantities of material resources were ordered as an emergency measure to be shipped to the affected region, the economic losses were dramatic. In August, the Beijing Olympics opened with great fanfare, creating a period in which businesses hauled in money. People failed to realize that a frozen winter would follow the sunny days, and this, too, was to affect some of the e-commerce enterprises. To enhance security during the Olympics, the government prohibited the air transport of any liquids. This led to a swift drop in online sales volume. How was e-commerce to deal with what appeared to be a real recession in its line of business? The Taobao University team put its head down and kept on moving forward, relying on the strength of innovation to come up with solutions.

On the one hand, the team dealt with an unending stream of natural disasters. On the other, it witnessed an unstoppable wave of "informatization." In 2008, transaction volume on the Taobao platform almost doubled compared with the preceding year, reaching more than 90 billion RMB. In the same year, in order to meet the rapidly expanding demand for its services, Taobao University brought its offline training to an end and formally launched an online training system that centered on an Internet-based curriculum. To this day, members of the Taobao University team are proud of this innovation.

Why choose to set up a highly refined online training system? The answer relates to the primary characteristics of e-commerce. Taobao vendors sit at a computer all day, handling orders and transactions, and it is sometimes hard for them to grab a block of time to go attend a training seminar. Second, vendors have varying levels of education and professional expertise, so a standardized offline training program is a somewhat low-efficiency approach. Finally, it is not cheap to hold offline training in terms of renting space and finding time, and the number of people who can be trained at each session is limited. Faced with these challenges, the Taobao University team came up with its own way to deal with the situation.

First, the team published books and materials relating to e-commerce. In the past, educational materials in the market relating to e-commerce focused on the theoretical side and even then were limited in quantity and variety. They simply did not meet the needs of readers. After 2008, Taobao University published 50 or 60 titles on e-commerce to make up for the lack of case studies and practical experience described in existing materials. Second, the team set up an online educational system. They videotaped a variety of curriculums that were divided up by both subject and degree of expertise and made these available for free to the outside world. At the time, 40,000 people-times received training every day. Third, they set up a training program aimed at each job description in e-commerce. For example, they provided information on what a shop owner might need to know and what each member of the staff might need to know given that the caliber and capabilities of different people would necessarily be different. In designing its curriculum, Taobao University was highly attentive to different administrative levels. Starting in 2008, Taobao University therefore began to move in the direction of providing systematic training, making a smooth and easy pathway for the increasing numbers of vendors on e-commerce.

2009: Collaboration with the Higher Educational Sector

The year 2009 was a year of invention. The training curriculum for enterprise-level e-commerce began to scale up, supplementing the original basic-level curriculum. At the same time, Taobao University began to cooperate with 20 institutions of higher education in the Jiangsu-Zhejiang-Shanghai area. Together they set up base areas for internship. Simulating an actual work environment, they trained students in all the various aspects of the business, including photographing products, warehousing, logistics, and online transactions. The institutions working with Taobao University authorized credit for the courses. For example, students of the Zhejiang Yiwu Institute of Commerce and Industry took courses over the holidays and then got credit for them. These base areas were well received by both teachers and students alike.

In the past, e-commerce training had been rather mysterious and unreal because students were not able to participate directly in e-commerce activities. As people with any experience in the business know, the main thing to avoid is having overly high ambitions and not enough practical experience. One of the clearest examples involves packaging and logistics.

At the end of the day, there are three main determinations you have to make when it comes to packaging and shipping. First, how much material you use for the packaging. The more you save on materials, the lower your packaging costs. Second, the toughness or durability of your parcels. Since goods gets knocked around in the process of shipping, you want to avoid loss due to damage as much as possible. Third, the speed at which things gets shipped. Labor costs are a production cost that must not be overlooked nowadays. Because of this, the more efficient your shipping processes, and the lower the labor costs per time unit, the lower your production costs. If our classmates grasp these three things and work accordingly, they will recognize where they need to improve their performance. They can target their problems more specifically and improve results.

Lessons such as this in packaging and logistics were given the name "the last kilometer." They were intended to enable the classmates to move out of the campus and into the world—to go from theory to actual practice and transition from studying to working. In 2009, Taobao University trained some 150,000 students.

The Year of Reform: 2010
Taobao University began an e-commerce MBA program in 2010. As we all know, in terms of academic disciplines, the field of e-commerce is

regarded as being an emerging industry, and in the early period of this new profession, there was no such thing as a masters or a PhD degree in the subject. Most people entering the profession came from such fields as computer sciences, software engineering, electrical engineering, and so on. They were not at all versed in e-commerce itself and were not adequately specialized in this one topic. The MBA program was set up to provide e-commerce entrepreneurs with systematic training in such things as enterprise management, human resources, operations, marketing, and planning. This was aimed primarily at Taobao vendors whose businesses were already fairly well established.

Taobao's business was becoming more impressive by the day, but the team inside Alibaba faced a dilemma. When the Taobao platform was just being started, a tremendous diversity of what were now regarded as the "old vendors" joined up, and these old-timers were now feeling a certain amount of pressure from the newcomers. Back at the beginning, these old-timers cast their seeds into the fertile soil of Taobao, and it was a result of their efforts as well that this fertile soil became prosperous. In a sense, they had contributed to the founding of the new nation with their loyal service. However, even as Taobao prospered, whether it was as a result of their own limited capabilities or for other reasons, these old-timers were no longer the most shining examples within their particular industries. On the contrary, they were facing considerable attack from the new e-commerce generation. As designers of the platform, the Alibaba team now had to decide whether or not to have some kind of internal protection that opened a back door for these earlier operators. The alternative was to remain impartial as a third-party provider. Alibaba decided to focus on setting up standardized operating procedures that could thereby preserve the long-term health of the ecosystem. In this choice between feelings and rationality, Alibaba did not allow itself to be swayed by emotion. The team coolly and decisively opted for the latter choice—setting up more objective, complete, scientific operating procedures on the platform by which all shop owners, large and small, would be treated with the same respect as long as they abided by the rules. Those who most understood how to do business would be the ones who obtained the greatest rate of flow.

Taobao University undertook another major reform in 2010, which was to bring an end to the era of free training. It began to charge for a portion of its curriculum. Meanwhile, the platform began to transition from being a cost center to becoming a profit center. The team has its reasons for coming to this decision. First, the willingness of students to pay for training was the most direct way to judge the quality of the training. If the training was inadequate, no matter how inexpensive it might be, it would not result in growing demand in the market. On the contrary, if the training was truly useful to e-commerce operators, they would be quite willing to pay for it because it improved their own results. In taking in fees, the pressures on and motivations of Taobao University itself would change, and the drive to succeed would become stronger. Second, the importance of the training link in the ecosystem of e-commerce operations affected not only the caliber of shop owners and their degree of professionalism but also the sound operations of the entire ecosystem. If everything were free, the entire ecosystem would fail to draw in more participants. From a long-term perspective, this would be detrimental to the growth of the industry overall.

The Organization of Taobao University

How were the teachers themselves produced?
Once the precursor to Taobao University was set up in 2003, the training team continuously amassed experience and materials in the course of offline and online training. Eventually, these materials were organized into a full curriculum with sets of lectures, classroom materials, videos, and so on. The first lecturers were sourced from among normal vendors on Taobao. Each lecturer was outstanding in his or her own operating category and had garnered considerable experience in the business. Taobao University provided the training curriculum to these primary-level lecturers and asked them to become familiar with standardized training content so that they could become qualified. Naturally, these people were not selected at random. They had to be excellent communicators, had to have a strong desire to share knowledge, and had to have a clean record

in terms of not violating any business rules and regulations. Only then were they qualified to serve as Taobao lecturers.

In addition, Taobao University also provided opportunities for vendors who were confident of their own operating systems. Any such vendors who wanted to be lecturers could bring their own internally generated materials and training systems to Alibaba. They had their own case studies and course materials and often could be the source of new microinnovations. These lecturers were called *enterprise-level guides*, and they were mainly responsible for Internet-based courses aimed at enterprises.

How Were the Capabilities of Lecturers Evaluated?
Giving a person a fish is not as good as teaching him or her how to fish. Giving a person a fish is easier, however, than teaching a person how to fish. How does one judge whether or not a lecturer has what it takes? Taobao University adopted a democratic method of evaluation. In their initial classes, potential lecturers would be graded by more experienced lecturers and older students. If their marks were not up to a certain level, they would stop being qualified to do further teaching. Listen to the voices of the students and let the students decide on the teachers constituted the core philosophy of Taobao University.

How Were the Main Topics Selected?
After training courses were fully online, it was possible to see which courses were best received and then to select the ones that had received the highest number of hits. This allowed the university to discover which subjects were of most concern to shop owners.

Periodically, Taobao University would send questionnaires to students, asking for their opinions on courses. The students would suggest topics that might be needed and thereby elicit responses from lecturers willing to share their experience.

How to Incentivize Having Vendors Come Share Their Experience?
Reading this, you might wonder why Taobao's store owners would be willing to share their experiences. Weren't they worried that they would

starve as teachers if they taught everything they knew to their students? On this subject, the members of the training team felt that openness and sharing were the bedrock of the Alibaba platform. These tenets had been part of Alibaba's core values from the beginning. Any entity that entered into the ecosystem of e-commerce could only make its own business prosper by a full personal understanding of these principles. In addition, unlike offline competition, the size of a shop or the location of a shop was not a limiting factor in online competition. Each brand had equal opportunity when it came to conditions under which it was to compete. The desire to communicate on the part of each Taobao store was extremely strong. Especially when e-commerce was just beginning, each Taobao store had a strong sense of being "out there alone." If stores in the same line of business did not communicate with one another, they could easily begin to feel that they were alone out there in the fight. As time went on, they would lose the urge to be competitive and innovative. As a result, these stores welcomed the Taobao University method of sharing and communicating. People dealing in the same types of products in particular would form their own communication circle. Not only did this help to grow their own business, but it also enriched their lives—as they say, it killed two birds with one stone. What's more, online business often did not entail any direct conflict of interest. People did not try to hold back when they were sharing information. Over time, this created an extremely beneficial learning environment. In point of fact, the team in the Vendors Selling Department had absolutely no experience themselves, but team members were highly acute in analyzing the characteristics of online business as well as the psychological needs of vendors. They were able to create a comfortable and engaging environment for vendors. Naturally, Tao-U itself had its own set of methods by which to motivate vendors.[2]

Such methods included the following:

1. The team allowed anyone to study for free if they themselves were willing to share their experience. This was a principle to be followed.

---

[2]Translator's note: *Tao* means something akin to "scooping up" in water, with the object of the verb being "treasure." The implication is akin to dredging for gold.

Any lecturers who made particularly large contributions were given a course that was fee based. This was a bonus for voluntarily sharing their experience with others. As the English author Subona has said, "When two people give each other an apple, each one is left with just one apple in his hands. But when two people exchange ideas, each has the ideas of two people in his mind." The more people share ideas, generally speaking, the greater is the harvest. Based on this incentive system, Taobao University attracted hundreds, if not thousands, of vendors into the system to serve as lecturers.

2. Offline training courses continued to be popular with vendors, and the reason was that, like CEO training in the MBA programs in China's more famous schools such as Beijing University, Tsinghua College, Fudan College, and Jiao, people came there to study, but even more important, they used this platform to broaden their connections with the community of other CEOs. They traded experiences, learned things, and made friends. Taobao University organized a similar kind of platform and provided the opportunity for vendors to get to know one another, all in the interest of spurring the growth of e-commerce.

3. Other than certain specialized courses for which a fee was charged, Taobao University did not charge vendors any miscellaneous fees at all, such as membership fees. To this day, the fee-based courses make up only 20 percent of the total. The concept of having a very low barrier to entry is quite intentional. It provides an opportunity for those who truly intend to improve their operations. When the Vendors Training Department was set up, the various management costs in its budget were covered directly by the Alibaba Group. After the higher-level courses began charging fees, any profits that were earned by this were put into operating costs. From start to finish, Taobao University has been regarded as a transmitter of education. Its primary purpose has never been to make a profit. If enterprises are to grow, the heads of those enterprises must first grow themselves. Maintaining this philosophy is what enabled Taobao University to motivate more and more vendors to participate enthusiastically in "circles" for common prosperity and growth.

The Primary Core Reason for the Success of Taobao University

As the saying goes, when you do not have a gourd at hand to copy and you want to draw a gourd, all you can do is go one line at a time. Without the slightest kind of blueprint to serve as a reference, the members of the Taobao University training team made the "soil" of the Taobao platform ever more fertile with each passing day. From sowing seeds to watering to pruning to harvesting, Taobao University supported anything that would help the "seedlings" grow. The thing team members look back on most proudly today is that they were unafraid to create new things. The team did not define any rules or regulations but instead allowed vendors to grow freely so that each member of the Taobao University team was willing to experiment and to make breakthroughs. In this department, the key performance index (KPI) could not really be quantified. The efforts of the team led to an enrichment of the entire Taobao platform and its millions of vendors. The team itself felt that Tao-U was a department created for the benefit of all, so the source of their happiness and sense of accomplishment came from the sound growth of each and every vendor. From offline concentrated training to online direct transmission of courses, from selecting lecturers to establishing methods of evaluation and motivation mechanisms, in the early years, every step that Tao-U took was challenging to itself as well as an astonishing and courageous invention.

Naturally, just as Alibaba ran into turbulence and setbacks as it grew, Taobao University did not always have smooth sailing with the proverbial wind at its back. Because the critical emphasis of each business period and each year was different, and because the energy of the team was, after all, limited, it was unavoidable that some projects had to be abandoned along the way or passed on to other enterprises. For example, basic training is now performed by a specialized training company, whereas Taobao University focuses exclusively on enterprise training. Frequently, it is disappointing to have to give up something. But the willingness of "Ali-people" to do this, to be selective over many years, to break out of constraints, and to constantly innovate, is precisely what has allowed them to stay at the forefront of the times. Their status as frontrunners has never changed. They excel at inner reflection. After every kind of training, they undertake quantified analysis of specific indicators that help to decide how to improve training in the future, such as the amount of pretransaction and posttransaction training, changes in consumer evaluations, and so on. It is hard to hide the excitement in the eyes of an Ali-person when he or she discovers that the training methods are undeniably producing results.

The Theory Behind E-commerce Training

The growth of e-commerce faces a potential bottleneck. This occurs when consumer demand grows too fast for vendors' ability to keep up with it or to keep up with the changing sensitivities of the market itself. The fundamental task of Taobao University is to ensure that vendors do keep up with the pace via all kinds of training. What is the most rational and effective way to do this? In theory, the team responsible for training should first clarify the purpose of and subject matter of training in advance, before creating materials. E-commerce training should combine the realities of all levels of experience as it proceeds. It should apply different types and models of training for different levels of training and for the specific interests of different vendors. From the preceding descriptions, it can be seen that such specialized training relies more on having first-line successful vendors share their experiences, their market analyses, and their self-evaluations through the use of internal exchange and a gradual accumulation mode of training. These successful vendors, that is, training teachers, are the core strength of the entire process. They are responsible for guiding students, recommending this or that advanced concept, analyzing this or that problem in e-commerce operations, and recommending solutions. The form that training takes at Taobao University elicits a tremendous interest among students and generates results based on direct perception. In the training process, the teachers can monitor the responses of students and make adjustments in the training "climate."

In the course of accelerating technical development and the great enthusiasm for e-commerce, training can effectively improve the technical levels of vendors as well as labor productivity. Training offsets a portion of the depreciation of labor capital because it helps students to use new technologies and equipment. The theory of human capital provides the theoretical framework for the role of training in enhancing labor productivity. The theory of human capital was launched in

1962 with the publication of an article by Nobel economics laureate Gary Becker entitled, "Investment in Human Beings," in the *Journal of Political Economy*. The models of early investment in human capital measured the relationship between investment (i.e., anticipated costs) and anticipated benefits. Anticipated costs include two different things: direct costs of training (e.g., fees for training and materials and compensation for teachers) and indirect costs of training (i.e., opportunity costs: the income that a worker might have received by going to work if he or she had not participated in training). The balance of these costs and benefits includes not only a monetary component (i.e., wages and welfare benefits) but also noneconomic elements (e.g., improving the dynamism of the workers' outlook and improving the degree of loyalty within a company that provides training). This very basic cost-benefit analysis shows that a worker will choose training after seeing that anticipated benefits are greater than anticipated costs.

Stevens[3] divides training into three categories, namely, general training, transferrable training, and training that applies to a specific enterprise. In this context, *general training* means training that improves the overall caliber of workers, the results of which can be manifested in the improved ability of such workers to take on any kind of work. Examples include language training and training in computer applications. *Transferrable training* means training or skills that can only be used in similar enterprises or lines of business, such as vocational training and specialized training. *Training that applies to the needs of a specific enterprise* means skills in the machinery and equipment of that specific enterprise. The kinds of training that Taobao University provides include transferrable training as well as specialized enterprise training, and both of these can be used not only on Alibaba's platform but also on the platforms of other e-commerce companies.

Training not only can improve the income of workers and the degree to which they participate in work, but it also can improve the efficiency of the labor services of the enterprise. Efficiency is generally measured in terms of value added or sales volume. By looking at European statistics,

---

[3]Stevens, M. (1994). A theoretical model of on-the-job training with imperfect competition. Oxford Economic Papers, 46, 537–562.

Brunello[4] discovered that training can improve workers' income by 12 percent. By conducting a survey of young people in the United States, Blachflower[5] and Lynch came to nearly the same conclusion. Dearden[6] and colleagues showed that the positive effect of training on Internet efficiency was roughly equivalent to doubling the amount of a worker's salary.

Economic theory in the sphere of human capital has revealed the importance of training. Taobao University recognized this and promptly took action, and the results have been exemplary.

The Future of Taobao University

From the day of its inaugural ceremony, Taobao University has always positioned itself as being a platform. However, Tao-U personnel say themselves that the platform as it exists today is a little like functioning under the planned economy. That is, Tao-U itself analyzes what it thinks the market needs. How does it know? Generally speaking, it does so by the following several channels:

1. It knows what the market lacks (needs) via new training demand, as generated by advances in science and technology. For example, every time a new e-commerce operating tool is launched, there is a corresponding need to know how to manage this tool.

2. It knows what the market needs via changes in the demand for training in line with changes in production relationships. For example, a normal online store may have one fairly singular goal when it first starts out, namely, to make money. Because of this, training must focus mainly on operations, advertising, and sales as the core subjects. Once that store reaches a certain size, however, the owner may decide to do a retail business, set up a retail store, and enter into the next

[4]Brunello, G. (2004). Labour market institutions and the complementarity between education and training in Europe. In D. Checchi & C. Lucifora (Eds.), Education, Training and Labour Market Outcomes in Europe (pp. 188–209). Palgrave Macmillan: Houtmills.

[5]Blanchflower, D. G., & Lynch, L. M. (1994). Training at work: A comparison of U.S. and British youths. In L. M. Lynch (Ed.), Training and the Private Sector:International Comparisons (pp. 233–260). Comparative Labor Market Series, Chicago and London: University of Chicago Press.

[6]Dearden, L., Reed, H., & Van Reenen, J. (2006). The impact of training on productivity and wages: Evidence from British Panel Data. Oxford Bulletin of Economics and Statistics, 68, 397–421

stage in growing its e-commerce business, so he or she then needs a higher level of training.

3. It knows what the market needs when changes in what consumers focus on drive changes in the demand for training. In the realm of the Internet, the way in which changes in consumer behavior drive business changes goes without saying. For example, platform designers might be able to deduce the psychological needs of consumers by reviewing what consumers search for and what programs they mainly watch; these designers then guide vendors in trying to match what vendors provide with what consumers need and want.

4. It knows what the market needs by the kinds of questions that are asked in training sessions. For example, fairly high-level vendors may raise demands that are highly targeted, including supply-chain training, training in e-commerce branding, and so on, but demand generated by this path is relatively smaller. As online courses constantly improve, most vendors will be able to find the courses they need.

In developing training programs in the future, the platform will focus more on the needs that vendors propose themselves. Only by truly paying attention to the difficulties being faced by grassroots operations will the program be able to unleash their entrepreneurship. Only by exchanging places with them and thinking as they think, standing in their shoes, will the program address the problems and resolve them, and only then will it make the whole endeavor a success.

Some people ask how Alibaba can have survived and prospered through all these years, having weathered the bursting of the Internet bubble, eBay's declaration of war, and other challenges. How can it keep its head up and look to the future? Alibaba firmly believes in what it is doing. It believes that being simple and straightforward leads to being great. In a materialistic society that is immersed in the worship of money, Alibaba holds to its earliest belief, which is *return e-commerce to commerce*. Each challenge that the company takes on and overcomes is not just for show and certainly not for the sake of public officials. The company's intent is to create fertile e-commerce soil for servicing the "little trees" so that they can grow and prosper themselves. The core value concept of Ali-people—trust—runs through every action the company takes. As Ali-people say, the process of arriving at trust is far harder than the results of achieving trust. Only by gaining the trust of ever more people, however, will the company and our society have any kind of force that propels it onward and upward. In the eyes of Ali-people, each satisfied smile of a customer, each sincere word of praise, each result, each time things go as expected brings an enormous sense of accomplishment. Ali-people are most glad when they can help customers improve, whether that is in small ways to increase immediate sales or in larger things such as establishing brands. The customer is core—this is what has helped Alibaba to come through hardship and see real success.

Tmall's Department of Merchant Operations

Taobao is famous for handling a million different kinds of goods. Tmall, on the other hand, is famous for handling the best of the best. It is Asia's largest business-to-consumer (B2C) platform and the apex of China's e-commerce. Tmall has assembled most of the name-brand products of both China and the rest of the world under its roof. The key to ongoing sustainable growth of e-commerce is the sound functioning of the entire chain of the e-commerce ecosystem. As everyone inside Alibaba knows, success does not lie in any one specific link. The question becomes how to improve the management, operations, and functioning of the entire e-commerce system to create an even better space into which e-commerce can grow. Tmall's Department of Merchant Operations came into being to satisfy this need. This is a training team with considerable depth. It has its own lecturers as well as senior vendors who serve as guides in helping with business development. The core of the team is the Tmall Top Team. Its members apply a combination of both online and offline three-dimensional training methods. The aim is to provide a highly effective training platform that can improve the operating capacities of merchants and their business results. Tmall's Department of Merchant Operations does not have that many people in it—the Tmall Top Team is run by only 4 members, the training department has 20 members, and the development system has 7 or 8 members—but it is this team of not even 40 people that guarantees the smooth operation of the entire ecosystem.

What Is the Tmall Top Team?

The Tmall Top Team is composed of the top 200 merchants that make up the Taobao Mall, i.e, Tmall. This group is graded according to three criteria: (1) sales volume, which is the main criterion; (2) degree to which brands are famous, with brands being divided into international brands, first-line domestic brands, and second-line domestic brands; and (3) offline influence (e.g., some companies may be rather nondescript online but have considerable influence as well-known traditional brands with a solid base of the buying public). These things are fairly good indicators of the potential that the company might have online. In combining these three criteria, Tmall's Department of Merchant Operations selects companies that meet certain requirements and asks them to participate in setting up a top team.

For Whom Does the Top Team Devise Strategic Plans?

As first-line companies, members of the Top Team have a wealth of Internet store experience. They are familiar with the operating rules and regulations of Tmall. Because of this, when the team sends out guides to train other stores on Tmall, the results are similar to the Vendors Training Department of Tao-U. The difference is that Tmall's team focuses on how to grow specific businesses, whereas Taobao University is focused more on developing a particular industry.

The members of the Top Team are the most outstanding among the 80,000 "stores" on Tmall. As such, this team is also responsible for devising strategies for the Tmall platform itself. Tmall's wireless presales project and its online-to-offline (O2O) project have been the fortunate recipients of the team's expertise and recommendations. To give an example, in designing project procedures, Tmall's Department of Merchant Operations invites members of the Top Team in to discuss plans. It elicits their desires and needs with respect to what they hope the platform can provide them in the way of services. A plan that includes perhaps 20 to 30 items is drafted before the group meets again for further discussions. The Top Team is seen as being a consultant for the Tmall platform, as well as being the back-end support behind the release of new endeavors to the industry.

How Does Tmall Persuade the Members of the Top Team to Share Information Without Holding Back?

In comparison with Taobao, Tmall's commercial environment is more complete and sound; that is, Tmall provides a more environmentally protective ecosystem. As an environmental protector, Tmall's Department of Merchant Operations has the function of sweeping away obstructions, eliminating bugs, and formulating rules and regulations. It is only because of the incredible efforts of this team that consumers can buy things on Tmall essentially without any qualms—they know that they will not be buying fake or watered-down goods. Because Tmall has consistently regarded the e-commerce industrial chain as a complete ecosystem, its vendors quite naturally have participated in its construction. This applies particularly to the deeper levels of more specialized areas, where Taobao's online customer services providers do not get involved. This deeper level of participation requires explicit considerations in terms of sharing information.

Does sharing hurt the interests of commerce? According to the head of the Department of Merchant Operations, the actual experience of online sharing does not in fact lead to the condition paraphrased as "having the teacher starve once he or she has taught all he or she knows to the students." One key feature that distinguishes online operations from offline operations is the different nature of competition. The openness and transparency of the Internet age are making all operating plans of e-commerce platforms more open and transparent. For this reason, if only 1 percent of merchants share and 99 percent do not, things cannot remain hidden for long. What's more, trust and sharing are Tmall's and Taobao's core tenets. They are the foundation of the entire ecosystem in which every vendor participates.

Will the Tmall Top Team Lead to the Matthew Effect?

Even though the Top Team is a consultant to Tmall's Department of Merchant Operations, it is not some kind of autocratic dictator. Any potential project or plan must go through a long process of discussion and exchange before it actually comes together and gets implemented. Only when the entire body passes on it is a project actually put into motion. Moreover, the internal team at the Tmall platform has the final say on any project waiting to be implemented. This team ensures that there are no potential problems. The Tmall Department of Merchant Operations is itself the most important key to the gate.

The *Matthew effect* refers to the way the strong get stronger and the weak get weaker in any development process. In fact, though, as a platform, Tmall has never intentionally favored any single vendor or any group of vendors. Both large and small vendors participate in project discussion meetings, and voices from all sides have an equal opportunity to be heard and considered. Moreover, the main line of thinking for any project is not to protect any given enterprise or the interests of any large companies but rather to initiate new ideas.

Tmall has already made a deep impression on the minds of consumers as a superlative brand in itself, which is of crucial importance. To give the simplest example: if a consumer happens to purchase fake goods from a Tmall store, he or she generally becomes less upset about the thing itself than about the reliability of Tmall. Tmall's own trust is cast in doubt. Because of this, whenever any small vendor on Tmall runs into problems, it influences everyone, large and small alike. This leads to a decline in sales volume for all. Consequently, large commercial merchants are quite willing to help smaller vendors, whether out of self-interest or public utility. They are happy to enable smaller vendors to create better conditions for themselves. As the protector of the environment, the Department of Merchant Operations will not intentionally adorn (decorate) the environs of any particular merchant, whether large or small. Instead, it ensures that each view on the platform is as beautiful as can be and is displayed to its best advantage.

Tmall's operations are guided by the principle of creating positive competition because in e-commerce the general rule is that when one person wins, all win, and when one loses, all lose. Each vendor is a link that cannot be dismissed in the e-commerce ecosystem. Only if all vendors are focused on innovation will the entire body at large be innovative. And only if the entire body advances can conditions be created for the progress of each individual vendor.

Online Training Systems

The entire online curriculum system of Tmall can be divided into three levels. The first is for *basic merchants*, a market segment that includes mainly new stores that have joined Tmall within the past three months. This basic curriculum is broadcast in rounds and involves mutual inter-action and communication among the new participants. The second is for *specific categories of storefronts*, with Tmall giving online training that applies specifically to those categories. This training supports the development and growth of all categories with relevant cases, data, and models to follow. The third provides training on *special topics*, depend-ing on the industry or matrix within which the merchants operate. Tmall invites experts and outstanding merchants in certain lines of business to deliver courses on such topics.

Cases of Very Creative Tmall Stores

Huashengji—A New Industry that Sparks the Revitalization of Chinese Culture[7]

Huashengji is the brand name of a company that makes Tang Dynasty–style clothing. Its entire process, from design to selection of fabric to dying is imbued with Chinese aesthetics. The resulting products do not blindly follow Western trends in fashion, nor do they completely copy the original style of ancient clothing. Each aspect of the clothing, each stitch and thread, is marvelously inventive. These garments may not have an enormous market, but they enjoy a highly distinctive position in the market, one that calls to mind the national traits at the heart of the Chinese people. Huashengji is at the forefront of a movement by which commerce sparks cultural development.

Tmall has a number of other clothing brands that hark back to cultural themes. One calls for a return to nature and a self-sufficient lifestyle and is called South-of-the-River Clothing, Southern Style. This company advocates a return to ancient ways, to elegance and simplicity. The market niche that these styles are positioned to attract is clothing for young women, but their unique quality also has the effect of expressing excellence within the Tmall Commerce City.

---

[7]Huashengji's website is http://huashengji.tmall.com/.

The dynamic way in which clothing has developed as a sales item on e-commerce has accelerated the arrival of an age of arts and culture in China. Uniquely Chinese elements are embodied in these brands. They display and revive the emotional appeal of art and culture via the medium of clothing.

Cherry: Forging a New Industrial Chain

Cherries are a specialty kind of fruit that was produced originally in the United States. The flavor of the cherry quickly deteriorates after the cherry is picked, however. Because it is hard to estimate the market for such a specialty item, and because quality declines in the course of a long sales process, retailers are reluctant to carry the item, and sales figures traditionally have been disappointing. Once e-commerce developed, however, a new marketing model was adopted for this fruit. While it was still on the tree, the fruit was sold via the Internet to customers who placed orders. Depending on the order quantity already in hand, retailers then order the fruit from exporters. The moment it is picked, the fruit is shipped directly to consumers. This not only preserves its freshness but also avoids the high cost of warehousing.

Powdered milk from New Zealand has adopted a similar sales model. As soon as New Zealand's fresh powdered milk is put on a ship, China's e-commerce opens up channels for taking orders, and consumers begin to buy. The moment the powdered milk reaches China, it can be shipped directly to consumers.

Because of the existence of Tmall, people who enjoy eating specialty cherries and people who are worried about the quality of their powdered milk no longer need be concerned. They no longer need to import powdered milk on their own. From the perspective of the food industry, therefore, the development of e-commerce has facilitated the marketing of high-quality goods.

Custom-Made Clothing

Traditionally, having clothes made to order could take half a year before one received the finished goods. Going through e-commerce, however, and particularly through the consumer-to-business (C2B) platform of Tmall, the entire process can occur within 15 days. Say that a customer takes a fancy to something modeled in the weekly magazine *Roman Style*, for example. She can order it online and receive the clothing within two weeks. In the past, companies would first model things in a flagship store as their marketing strategy and then shift the clothing into normal retail outlets. Finally, if it did not sell offline, they would offer it on the Internet. This way of thinking has been completely overturned. The new method is a presales model of marketing that incorporates the back end of the supply chain. It radically lowers the costs of the enterprise while also giving customers more complete satisfaction.

Antszone[8]—Setting Up a Highly Original Brand

Antszone is a brand of men's clothing that harks back to a retro form of London style. To manufacture the clothing, the company uses only factories that produce for international luxury brands. When the brand was being established, the company spent some 10 million RMB on digital marketing. The positioning of its target market niche is fairly high end. In contrast with traditional brands, it has its own clear-cut advantages because the requirements of the production and supply chain of traditional brands are quite demanding. For example, they require the highest-quality materials and ease of selection while at the same time low warehousing costs, which puts many different parts of the supply chain at risk. Antszone uses localized design rather than hiring expensive designers. This not only meets the needs of the market but also saves a large amount on labor costs. At the same time, the company cuts the piece goods by itself, which ensures the quality of the fabric and also saves on the high cost of having to directly purchase ready-made piece goods. Slack seasons in the supply chain do not have too much of a negative impact on e-commerce. By positioning its products as low-cost alternatives, Antszone has the advantage in competing against major brands.

---

[8]Antszone's website is http://antszone.tmall.com/.

Tmall's 90-Day Virtual Training

Tmall's Department of Merchant Operations plays the role of strategic planner and a high-level consultant to merchants on the platform. Using statistical data on past transactions, the department can analyze the future development path of any given business and thereby assist in the growth of both new businesses and midlevel businesses. Each entity that has either just entered or plans to enter the Tmall platform is placed in the *test operations growth system* of new merchants and participates in three months of training. This training takes many forms. It includes direct broadcast of audiovisual material, online curriculum material that can be self-selected, and offline interactions. Class times are organized for 300 merchants at a time as an individual class. Each class has a class leader who is responsible for organizing all the operational links of the process and for providing individualized assistance to each class member. Such assistance includes visiting the stores on a rotating basis and providing online advice, with different emphases for each stage of development.

In the first month of training, the emphasis is on basic structure and the inner workings[9] of the entity. This portion of the training includes deciding on product structure, pricing strategies, product descriptions, and design and display of the storefront. The second month focuses on basic promotion "knacks" of the business and how to operate the storefront. This includes the fundamentals of using selling tools, activity planning of the storefront, forging singular products, and interpreting basic data. In the third month, the knowledge community that the "professors" provide becomes enormous. Absorbing and digesting the information takes considerable time and effort. After the course is concluded, Tmall's Department of Merchant Operations organizes tests to measure results. Vendors who do not rise to the mark lose the opportunity to enter into and reside on the Tmall platform. This high barrier to entry allows Tmall to maintain its high level of excellence.

Naturally, once new vendors come onto the platform, they still go through an initial training period to help them acclimate to the environment more quickly. During this process, teaching guides go into more depth on how to connect up with other merchants in other countries. They evaluate the stage of development that merchants have achieved

---

[9]Translator's note: The phrase in Chinese is *inner qigong,* "internal exercises to benefit the organism," which is a kind of buzzword.

and where any issues may lie, and then they come up with an overall plan to resolve issues and help merchants to move forward.

The Primary Merchant Training System

Tmall's Department of Merchant Operations plants a development assistant into the Tmall back office or back-end platform for every vendor. This so-called development assistant is a transaction analysis tool that looks at historical data. Its main methodology employs data comparisons. By comparing the data of a given merchant with data on other merchants, the development assistant uncovers the crux of issues and how to deal with them and then recommends appropriate parts of the Tmall training curriculum. The data comparisons are constantly updated, so the degree to which knowledge is transformed into greater functionality is quite high.

Tmall's Department of Merchant Operations now continues to move the merchant into deeper levels of operating procedures. The merchant's growth model begins to be crafted for a more finely differentiated market niche, so different types of merchants follow different tracks of development. This allows the training curriculum to be more precisely targeted to specific needs. At the same time, the online customer services providers of Tmall's Department of Merchant Operations send out "Diagnostic Notices" on a regular basis to each merchant and provide feedback after the merchants have implemented any changes. The merchants themselves evaluate whether or not the recommendations have been helpful. The enthusiasm with which merchants respond to feedback is what motivates the team in Tmall's Department of Merchant Operations.

Primary-considerations merchant training is a training system that centers on what are called *sectors*. Tmall's Department of Merchant Operations needs to link together all categories of sectors and, on a periodic basis, design guidance classes for primary considerations. Merchants are specially grouped according to characteristics, and their conditions are evaluated so as to move their training in the direction of "platformization." This then allows for the resolution of a much greater number of similar issues. The primary-considerations efforts of Tmall's Department of Merchant Operations are focused in this direction.

The Top Assault Team is the highest-level "business institute" to conduct skills training within Tmall. This team brings together the most outstanding talent, including visual designers and people engaged in marketing and promotion, clothing-profession managers (CPM), back-end and customer services managers, and so on. People who serve as lecturers in this institute are all highly experienced *category professionals*. For major vendors who sell well-known brands, Taobao online customer services providers also provide onsite services to encourage and establish long-term strategic partnerships.

Differences Between Tmall and Taobao

The Taobao platform currently services a massive number of vendors, that is, on the order of 6 to 8 million. The industry categories included in this community are highly diverse, and there are thousands of variations on how to develop more finely segmented industry categories. Because of this, the platform itself is like a loosely organized free market with a relative lack of supervisory control and guidance. In contrast, Tmall has consistently held to the principle of concentration. The Tmall platform services around 80,000 vendors and is positioned to guide extremely important brands toward markets. First, Tmall places strong emphasis on restricting the number of product categories and on quality control. When too many of a given category of goods appear on the platform, the platform itself intervenes to prevent large numbers of similar vendors from engaging in low-end price competition. Second, Tmall absolutely will not allow for counterfeit or watered-down goods. The moment it discovers any kind of inferior product, it dispenses extremely severe punishment. This is one of the primary ways in which Tmall's Department of Merchant Operations serves as a guardian of the environment and fulfils its responsibility to help merchants grow.

Taobao's Department of Vendors Development

Serving as backup protection for grass-roots vendors

Like Tmall's Department of Merchant Operations, Taobao has a Department of Vendors Development. In Taobao, this is actually also called the

Department of Vendor's Operations. Using the terminology of its highly qualified staff, what this department aims to do is cultivate an environment that is most suited to the survival of grassroots shops. The idea is that in times of increasingly fierce competition, such as today, vendors first have to find a way to survive before they can begin to talk about innovation. Only then will they have enough real strength to innovate.

Taobao's Department of Vendors Development includes the following six main divisions: basic services, transaction services, tools services (such as decorating the shop, placing illustrations, and so on), evaluation services, quality-control (standardization) services, and notification services. Each division handles its own duties and puts its efforts toward helping Taobao vendors survive and grow.

It is not hard for those who frequent the Taobao site to have the sense that Taobao is increasingly chaotic, with new sites popping up like mad. On the eve of the 11.11 Shopping Festival in 2013, each individual category of goods had dozens and sometimes even hundreds of shop brands from which customers could select products. A multiplicity of products aims to incite consumers to buy. As with promotion events, marketing efforts are highly creative and successful. One can flip open any Alibaba Research Institute data report and see that batch after batch of statistics reports good news. By June 2014, the number of vendors in the category of annual sales of under 100,000 RMB had increased by 60 percent, the number of vendors with sales between 100,000 and 1 million RMB had increased by 30 percent, and those with over 1 million RMB in sales had increased by 33 percent. Now at the single-million level, a double-million sales target plan on Taobao can be expected soon.

In May 2012, Taobao had 5,964,460 online vendors. Once the site was reformulated, publicly announced figures disappeared forever, but in the course of interviewing Taobao staff, we learned from internal sources that the current number is now around 8 million. Given that the platform embraces everything, it is impossible for Taobao to be as refined and as strict as Tmall. It cannot have a handle on each and every vendor that either intends to reside on the platform or already has taken up residence. The Department of Vendors Development in Taobao therefore has to formulate rules and regulations that are more universal and flexible in how they are handled, as well as being more human oriented. That is, the department has to provide services that are aimed more at typical shopkeepers. It also has to "wash out" single traditional products that are redundant in order to enable those that are truly creative to prosper and to allow the truly innovative vendors on the Taobao platform to grow.

In 2012, Jack Ma emphasized two points in a speech at China's National E-commerce Conference. First, he said that Taobao would be reducing intermediary links and allowing vendors to have direct contact with channels. Second, he said that the company would be training 1 million vendors with annual sales volume of over 1 million RMB. This is where the double-million plan came from, as mentioned earlier. In January 2013, as Jack Ma had confirmed that he would do several months earlier, he decisively split up the Alibaba Group into 25 separate business groups. This second reorganization of Alibaba's structure elicited widespread guessing on the part of the outside world. Did Jack Ma's so-called reducion in the number of intermediary links indicate that Alibaba was going to be delegating authority further down the line, that is, relinquishing some control? Was the reduction of the role of third-party platforms going to lead to a rebuilding of trust between buyers and sellers? Would supervisory regulation of stores be stricter or looser? What was Taobao hiding when it dreamed up this series of reforms? Given the massive number of vendors, was Taobao really intending to release control, allow for more freedom?

Let us move closer to the Department of Vendors Development, which is so intimately connected to the growth of entrepreneurs, and see what it all means.

What Is the Department of Vendors Development Up To?

Located in the International Building on West Lake in Hangzhou, the Department of Vendors Development occupies more than half of one entire floor. As Ali-people move briskly through the halls, there is always a race to grab any empty conference room. The heat of the action is not any less than the heat of a scorching summer day. It is still July 2013, still half a year away from the 11.11 Shopping Festival. Members of the Department of Vendors Development are already discussing their plans. They are coordinating the participation of various vendors, formulating price regulations, and handling a myriad of major and minor details. In accepting an interview (for this book), Fei Qing mentioned that the kinds of things the department has to handle are so diverse and multitudinous that it is almost impossible to sort them out minutely, but their ultimate goal is the same as that of Taobao's vendors—to set up a "high-efficiency, environmentally protected" ecosystem. It is to get beyond the traditional kinds of price wars with their contorted pricing and break through the defining limitation of "no traffic means you die." It is to help vendors create all kinds of bright spots that catch customers' eyeballs and that improve the efficiency with which vendors interact. The department has never allowed itself to become bogged down in the marketing models of traditional business. It aims to create an online marketing space that is consistent with the creative needs of grassroots entrepreneurs. What Taobao hopes to realize is not a third-party platform, made by itself, that takes care of everything and manages everything but rather to help the market carry out orderly regulation of itself.

People who like Taobao will easily discover that discounts are the "sharp weapon" of the great majority of small and microvendors when they want to spur sales. Certain brands that established themselves early on and are now of considerable size, such as Weidu Clothing and Qi Gege, do not practice discounting, whereas the branded flagship stores that first developed offline are also an exception to this rule. The unending price wars of most vendors, however, not only force smaller entities to lower what are already quite low costs, but they also force new stores to confront tremendous risk. Everyone madly tries to make a quick hit by marketing specially priced packages of things and engaging in other sales promotions. They hope to make money off sheer numbers of hits. As the number of vendors on the platform keeps increasing, however, using price alone to stimulate sales is not sufficient to keep a small vendor alive, let alone enable him or her to be profitable over the long run. Online operations do not have to pay rent, but vendors nevertheless cannot expect much income if they do not promote their goods. Discounts and promotion fees lower the profitability of most of these online stores.

The Zhejiang Yiwu Institute of Industry and Commerce has produced generations of talent. Wang Jiaying, who has been described as one of the 10 most successful Internet merchants, graduated from this institute.

Most of the students there were born into business-oriented families. In this fertile land in southern China, generation after generation has produced at least one or two exemplary businesspeople, and generation after generation has managed small family workshops. The most commonly seen practice is for the grandfather, grandmother, and an older sister or two to pitch in to the work together. In today's market economy, however, the sweet smell of success is harder to attain. Many small workshops do not rake in the profits that might have been anticipated. As the cutting edge of small businesses get into the realm of e-commerce, a large number of businesses follow on right behind. Older Sister may have started a small Internet shop selling knickknacks, and she may have spent an enormous amount on sourcing product, logistics, and handling inventory so that her monthly income comes to less than 3,000 RMB. The famous Yiwu Institute is not at all lacking in such people who sell small knickknacks. What Older Sister therefore has to do, quite naturally, is to cut her prices until she can hardly breathe. At the end of her tether, all she can do is spend her remaining money on purchasing good reviews. Having "burnt" her money, she, like other pitiful vendors who do not have a clue about business, pulls out of Taobao. Meanwhile, a new wave of entrepreneurs pours in. The cycle repeats itself, seemingly without end.

Manager Lu has a company with fewer than 30 workers. In 2012, its gross income was less than 20 million RMB. In looking at the accounts, Lu sees that the money seems to come in and go out all right, but unfortunately, it turns over only a few times a year, and as a result, Lu still has not earned any profit. Everyone had told him that the clothing business enjoys explosive profits. Often, you can price a piece of clothing at two or three times your cost. If you look more carefully at the costs, however, you become dumbfounded. In this business, average promotion fees take up 10 to 15 percent, and then there are the costs of warehousing rent and utilities and the salaries of staff, plus all the miscellaneous fees. If you cannot control your inventory rate to 10 percent or lower, then you absolutely are experiencing a loss.

Lu says, "All you can try to do is hold on. If the annual operating income of a self-branded company of the grassroots type is not over 30 million RMB, it is fundamentally impossible for it to make any kind of sizable profit." It may sound easy to make 30 million RMB, but can a bystander even imagine what hardship went into that figure? For shop owners who lack experience in large-scale operations, essentially everything has to be learned from scratch. Lu's company has already paid out several million by learning lessons the hard way. Having a grasp of the supply chain is not something one can learn in a day. Some 90 percent of companies that sell clothing are killed by having too large an inventory. The safest method is to operate in small quantities and turn over more quickly, but the problem with this is that the most direct way to lower costs is to scale up to larger orders and keep a larger inventory. Taobao's small-time vendors frequently complain that it is hard to survive. Once you start to think about it, you can see the reasons behind it.

As business on Taobao becomes harder to do and small vendors complain that they cannot survive, medium-sized vendors complain that they can survive but cannot make any money. This is the kind of situation that motivates the team members of the Department of Vendors Development. Innovation and reform are not necessarily something one does intentionally. Instead, they are forced on one by the environment. If the Taobao platform does not innovate, does not reform, does not listen hard to the voices of tens of millions of Taobao vendors, it will find it hard to realize any kind of long-term healthy growth. As the saying goes, "The rising water can lift your boat, but it also can overturn your boat." Behind the string of Taobao's astonishing statistics is a host of problems and loopholes that have to be dealt with. If they are not dealt with, and Taobao's stores find one day that they have no place to "live safely and securely," consumers also will find that they no longer have the fastest and most effective way on Earth to purchase goods.

In short, the great ship of Taobao looks terribly grand and mighty, but if it loses the support of its vendors, it is no more than a fragile reed floating on a vast ocean. It can be swamped by a wave at any time and go under. The day vendors depart is the day the wellsprings of the company's business dry up. To ensure sustainable development, it is imperative for Taobao to engage in innovation and reform. How this takes place then becomes the question. The chief inspector of the Business Development Department, Zhan Lu, says that all the departments of the Taobao platform and vendors communicate with one another to varying degrees, but from a macro perspective, there is still the issue of whether the platform's role should be one of control or just keeping things in order. He feels that at the present time there is too much control and too little just keeping things in order. He feels that the company's current perspective is not looking out far enough to the future, that there is too much emphasis on the near term and on short-term profits. This is why reforming the rules of the game has now been put on the agenda at Taobao.

In 2013, having deliberated on the matter, Taobao began its revolution. It was a revolution addressed at changing itself. Zhan Lu says that the company is currently in the midst of trying to set up completely new rules of the game with increasingly no participation by Taobao online customer services providers at all. Everything will be handed over to the market to determine. Taobao itself will serve as a high-efficiency controller, but not the kind that handles everything, large and small, not a nursemaid. Taobao will only be responsible for setting up systems and formulating the systems that govern the platform. It will provide the tools and the open data. Everything else will be handed over to vendors to do.

In announcing the reform that Taobao would be undertaking in 2013, the term *loss of control* came up. The reason for this was Taobao's decision to gradually extricate itself from the nursemaid-type of management. To cut the excessive amounts of money merchants were blindly paying to buy advertising positions, to curb the endless price wars, and to keep vendors from paying too much to improve their search engines, Taobao decided to undertake major reforms. At the same time, relaxing controls over traffic (quantity of flow) and over rules and regulations represented almost a kind of suicidal behavior because it should be recognized that traffic is Taobao's primary source of income at this stage.

The reason for putting such major determination behind carrying out these reforms can only be that Taobao had discovered its own inadequacies. Zhan Lu tried to analyze the reasons for the company's "overstepping authority" in terms of control as well as "lacking control." He notes

It may be because we were KPI driven. Faced with the need to produce business results, everyone naturally focused on efficiency. They put their efforts and emphasis on whichever vendors could help us generate GMV [gross merchandise volume] results. However, they overlooked the vendor community and vendor's

structure, including vendor reactions in recent years. Real atten-
tion on vendors has in fact declined. Such things as punishments
for breaking the rules, taking cases to court, can't be called real
innovation. It is definitely something we have been absent in
doing for a long time. We need to make up for this a little.

The goal of "reaching 2 million storefronts within three
years" may at least be getting closer. By 2014, Taobao may reach
1 million storefronts, with each conducting an annual volume
of over 100,000 RMB in business. At present, however, there
are only some 400,000 storefronts. The entire business plan of
the Taobao platform will now focus on overall structure and
the soundness of vendors, which will help to stimulate overall
sustainable growth. I myself believe that doing these things this
year is pretty much the baseline. I hope that by revamping our
awareness, we can accomplish things to buttress our position.
The first step is listening closely to what vendors have to say.

On July 17, 2013, several dozen typical Taobao vendors gathered in
a restaurant on Wen-er Road in Hangzhou, where they held two days
of closed-session meetings. They discussed new marketing strategies
and ideas and tried to create effective channels of communication with
responsible people in the Department of Vendors Development. The Taobao platform may have provided them with an opportunity to found a
company, but it did not create a whole set of diversified mechanisms that
allowed them to grow. Taobao's Annual Report had pleasing growth
statistics that relied on some of the stronger large vendors and on a
constantly increasing stream of entrants into the vendor community, but
were these new entrants truly seeing any growth?

"If we do not rely on discounting to spur sales in the future, will
there actually be any selling points that we can use to ensure adequate
traffic?" Store owners are wracking their brains trying to figure out ways
to sell. Some proposed selling a year's worth of ready-made clothes up
front and then each month, at the prescribed time, sending sanitary
napkins to the lady who had ordered the set of clothes. Some proposed
sending out small free gift items together with purchased goods as a
way to establish a firm and friendly tie with customers. Some proposed

creating a full set of traveling equipment, including a tent, nightgown, mirror, sunscreen, and so on, so as to reduce the amount of work a traveler had to do before a trip.

The *Economic Observer* selected over 100 Taobao small and micro vendors for purposes of conducting a survey. The survey discovered that 90 percent of the vendors had been in business for fewer than three years, whereas 60 percent had been in business for fewer than two years. Nearly 30 percent had been in business for less than one year. These figures clearly indicate that most entities in the "cradle" of Taobao are mere infants. It will take quite some time before they establish their own credibility and credentials. This presents new demands on Taobao as it seeks to help vendors grow.

Helping vendors grow is easy to say and hard to execute, however. Vendors are bound to take different routes as they develop, given their different sizes, lines of business, business concepts, and ideas on how to sell. One single department cannot handle it all. As Zhan Lu explains, Taobao hopes that it can communicate more closely with vendors and understand their demands in three ways: (1) opening the channels for greater traffic, (2) setting up rules and regulations for transactions, and (3) conducting customer evaluations. It then can undertake more individualized reform of its own services. Taobao is the cradle for entrepreneurs—particularly for those who exemplify the phrase "Small is beautiful." Each new grassroots storefront manager setting up his or her shop on Taobao will face a host of difficulties as he or she develops. This is particularly true in the "baby stage" of development, so the role of the cradle becomes that much more important. For the short term, the Department of Vendors Development is focusing on several basic-type projects, including opening up (releasing) the appeals process of vendors' basic rules and regulations, on fully rolling out the vendors' basic authentication, and on integrating its operating platform with vendors' basic products.

What Kinds of Things Is the Vendor Development Team Actually Able to Do?

Zhan Lu says that there are three things the team should seek to accomplish in helping vendors to grow. First, the team should improve Taobao's operating rules and regulations and clarify its appeals channels and its system of penalizing vendors for misbehavior. As the saying goes, "Without a measuring device, you can't measure the circumference." Without any rules (measuring devices) on Taobao, one cannot know where the boundaries of proper behavior lie. If Taobao intends to have millions of vendor-citizens living peaceably within its "kingdom," it has to formulate laws for that kingdom. It has to reward good behavior, punish misbehavior, and make it very clear where the lines lie. Only an environment that promotes upright behavior can nurture shops that are creative and unique. As it draws together the opinions of all vendors, therefore, Taobao also must constantly improve and refine its own rules and regulations. Otherwise, as shops increase in size, some dragons will unavoidably rise up among the fish. Taobao has a kind of "tiger blocking the way" to such things as vicious price wars among vendors, as well as keeping them on track in terms of fraudulent behavior. As Fei Qing, of the Department of Vendors Development, has said, "In order to gain more traffic, some small shops selling women's clothing incorporate the names of well-known brands into their own names so as to make the consumer think that those brands are allied with their own. As the consumer uses the search engine to find those brands, he [or she] is misdirected into the wrong storefront. This damages the reputation of storefronts that use brand names properly, and it illegally takes a share of the market of those branded products. At the same time, it increases the frequency with which consumers believe they are being cheated. It even destroys their trust in the entire Taobao platform. Opening up an 'appeals channel' that can be used effectively is what everyone is hoping for." However, as Zhan Lu points out, "The current method of taking in appeals does not follow any clear and prescribed process." Right now, fairly traditional methods are used, such as making a telephone call. As problems multiply, however, it may well be that Taobao cannot make timely responses to all the calls, and many opinions cannot get a timely response.

Because of this, in the second half of 2013, the team opened up an "Appeals Entryway" for all members that categorizes misconduct into 12 different types. Actions required before Taobao is able to initiate this appeals service include a whole series of actions such as training staff, setting up procedures, interfacing products, and so on, as well as setting up the actual mechanisms for making appeals. Handling appeals is new territory for Taobao. In the second half of 2013, it worked with the Standards Department to push the effort forward. Staff members attempted to make the appeals process more human oriented by setting up a bridge for direct communication between sellers and buyers. Moreover, by resolving some sellers' issues, such as infringement of rights, they moved toward a more standardized (regularized) Taobao platform, eliminating unscrupulous stores and suppressing vicious and antimarket competitive behavior.

Second, Zhan Lu says that the team should seek to ensure that authentication of vendors is a transparent and thorough process. Vendor authentication was something that was first proposed in 2012. It started with *Alipay A-type authentication*. Every consumer who paid for a transaction via Alipay had to use his or her own *household registration number* to guarantee authentication.[10] In 2012, the Vendor Operations Department carried out authentication of 100 percent of new vendors, which lowered the cheating and swindling behavior of vendors by between 60 and 70 percent. When new vendors now register to be on the Taobao platform, they first encounter *authentication mechanisms*. These are something akin to abiding by the rules and regulations of the platform, so accepting them should be fairly easy. However, long-term vendors on the platform have no such requirements. Implementing the same procedures with them in too precipitous a fashion might incur negative feelings. What Taobao has done, therefore, is to adopt an incremental method of sequential authentication. During the interview with Zhan Lu, he mentioned that the company hoped that authentication would cover 60 to 80 percent of existing vendors by the second half of 2013. The next step will be the vendor authentication and market-entry procedures for B-type market groups. When 60 to 80 percent of C-type vendors are authenticated, they can be certified as B-type vendors by following B-type authentication procedures.

Third, the team should create products that enable the smooth operations of vendors. These can include such applications as white-listed lists of names, black-listed lists of names, vendors' market-entry procedures, information sending, and so on. These can be embedded in Taobao's management products.

---

[10]Translator's note: Status verification number = household registration number.

Zhan Lu noted that the department is considering three other breakthroughs and innovations, in addition to the preceding three that are on a more basic level. The first is to loosen the constraints of certain rules. As e-commerce has developed considerably over the past few years, the Taobao platform has undertaken numerous additions and deletions and polishing procedures. Despite all of these, the ever-changing market produces an endless stream of new issues to deal with. To resolve these issues in a timely manner, newly added rules and regulations are not always perfect or have not been through a testing process. For example, the membership fees that members pay to list as a vendor should be adjusted, and the authentication of existing vendors should be completed, as well as all kinds of more stringent demands on new vendors. As time goes on, the onerous weight of too many rules and regulations may well add to vendors' costs, making them lose faith in the platform altogether. The team is currently intending to comb through all the Taobao platform's various rules and regulations to help vendors grow. It intends to see if there is any potential for relaxing some rules. It intends to do everything possible to create cordial relationships between the platform and vendors. By taking advantage of this good news, vendors can feel that Taobao is warmly inclined to their well-being. The number of new vendors has increased sharply in the past two years, but accompanying this rise has been an increase in the number of vendors with "evil intentions." Standardizing the rules and dispensing punishment are concerns that Taobao is highly focused on as the next step. In terms of being both concerned about and firm with vendors, this year Taobao also intends to conduct an experiment with new vendors. Online products will be integrated with offline training, with the intent of enabling vendors who have just come onto Taobao to understand just what kind of company the Taobao platform is. They should understand its rules and regulations and learn some basic operating and marketing skills so that they are equipped with advantageous tools.

The second innovation is to make certain breakthroughs in channels of communication with vendors. Currently, there are already fairly diversified channels that enable the platform to communicate with vendors, including an internal e-mail system, the information center, and others, all of which are widely used. However, given the mixed nature of the channels, there are often redundancies in how information is collected and managed, which lead to low efficiency and high costs. The Department of Vendors Development therefore is now putting its efforts into consolidating the existing channels into one communications platform.

The third innovation is to create an overall trends-analysis product that looks at vendors' structures and the distribution and direction of flow lines. The thinking right now is to design a product that will see whether or not there is a correlation between the internal structure of Taobao's vendors and matching trends in traffic. This idea is currently being discussed with the B1 Commercial Intelligence Group and the B1 Market Group.

All these things, the three basic efforts and the three potential breakthrough ideas, are an indication of the core values of the Department of Vendors Development. Because Taobao aims to be a superlative manager with a high degree of professionalism, because it is putting its efforts into helping grassroots vendors be innovative, it must first become a successful innovator itself. So far, it has done this and is continuing to work at the process. It is highly attentive to every microchange to do with vendors, is concerned about setbacks and obstacles that vendors face, and is glad for each time they innovate and are successful. Taobao resides in the same space as vendors and is codependent on them.

What Is the Greatest Challenge to Growing Vendors?

The Department of Vendors Development on the seventh floor of the Western Lake International Building is bustling and full of people every day. From morning to night, people work like a hive of diligent bees. As a department with the most intimate connections with vendors, it also is a department that faces unprecedented challenges. Zhan Lu says that the greatest of these is to ensure that people from different departments struggle together toward the same goals. The ideal situation would be to have a balance between short- and long-term goals. Nevertheless, members of the team often feel a strong sense of being pulled in one direction.

"We are a horizontal-type department, which is to say that we have lateral connections with all the different teams in the company, customer service, network security, sector categories, rules and regulations. Within the department we also have lateral connections. So we are in a fairly good position to communicate effectively on behalf of the needs, or the hopes, of others. We can get hold of the key points other people are making and meld the key issues of different departments together to create an engine that pushes the network forward as a whole."

At the same time, the demands on people are quite high in terms of their ability to coordinate communications and their capacity to organize projects. This year, the department hopes to conduct training of project managers and to upgrade the capacities of Taobao's online customer services providers.

For the Taobao online customer services providers in the Department of Vendors Development, the sense of accomplishment they get is often not the same as such providers in other departments. The services they perform do not have an impact that can be seen directly on the bottom line, as with other types of projects. Although all are doing work that relates to the fundamentals of the business, many times those in the Department of Vendors Development feel that they cannot "raise a pole and actually see its shadow." This is not to say that when the online customer services providers issue a "war report" or when an issue regarding an appeal and punishment for breaking the rules is completed in terms of quality that it will have an effect on GMV. It is hard to predict with any accuracy which vendors will produce the most notable influence. Therefore, the sense of accomplishment and the motivating force of the online customer services providers come first from changes on the vendor end of the business.

Zhan Lu says, "I place very specific demands on my own team members. My expectation is that each person, each and every month, will have an in-depth conversation with a vendor, whether that is by telephone or meeting in person. One key aspect of the way we manage vendors is the need to have a very good understanding of them, know how they are getting along, what they are thinking." By relying on this highly personalized type of management, the Taobao online customer services people in the Department of Vendors Development and the vendors themselves are gradually growing closer together.

*Does the Department of Vendors Development Engage in Special
Support for Certain Groups of Vendors?*
Generally speaking, the Taobao Department of Vendors Development
Group does not explicitly go out to support this or that group of vendors
or buyers. In the early period of setting up the Taobao platform, in order
to support the independence and self-reliance of small vendors as they
established their businesses, in its "early sprout" stage, the platform may
have tended to guide traffic in a certain direction.

The Department of Vendor Development also provided vulnerable
groups with special treatment, including disabled people and single
mothers. For example, for a period of time, it opened up a unique
domain just for them. In doing this, the platform was seeking to encourage more people to found their own companies. It continued to engage
in this public-service-like behavior for quite a long time. Through preferential market-entry procedures, rules and regulations that lowered the
barriers to entry for certain groups, opening up channels of information
transmittal for vendors, designing a more detailed platform, and so
on, Taobao set its sights on enabling more entrepreneurs to enter the
e-commerce age.

*A Case Study Regarding an Innovation of
the Department of Vendors Development*

The Tao Mark
*Many Taobao merchants do not have any concept of the importance
of brand protection. The Department of Vendors Development
recently launched a new project called the Tao Mark Project, aimed
at helping vendors to forge their own brands. Each vendor is given
an opportunity to rebrand itself, but it cannot duplicate anyone else's
name. Taobao is going to set up a connecting tool that starts with the
name of the storefront and then enables direct passage on through to
the store. This is based on each individual Tao mark that buyers and
sellers establish. Vendors have exclaimed that this is a marvelous
thing to do, the most basic way to enable vendors to lead peaceful and
happy lives. There are several reasons for designing this project.*

First, it is hard for vendors to promote their own brands on the platform. This is true especially for small brands that were born online. Those that are highly inventive and of excellent quality may well run into counterfeiting, plagiarizing, and so on, making it hard for them to operate properly and indeed to survive. Even the best storefronts need fertile soil to grow, so the Tao mark is intended to serve as a kind of fertilizer for that soil.

Second, consumers can easily find that "fish" and "dragon" brands are all mixed together on Taobao. That is, in making their selections, they may choose something that seems to be similar on the outside but is a product of inferior quality. When this goes on for long, it degrades the confidence that consumers have in the products. This is why stores must do all they can to protect and preserve their own marks and their own brands.

Third, the naming of storefronts is not standardized in any way. Some are highly elaborate in that they string together the names of several other well-known brands in order to catch the attention of search engines. They use this as their ID (registered status). This can be very inconvenient for consumers when they are trying to buy the originals.

Fourth, intellectual property protection that has antipiracy applications embedded in it is needed. Functions should be carried out in a more digitized way, with sales in real time with authenticated old customers, with individualized search, and with systemic differentiation among categories of products and labels (brands), functions that address the interests and likes of consumers and that can segment them into finely differentiated markets. This involves a communications channel that allows vendors to connect with and influence buyers, for example, Wei-tao, WeBlog (China's blog site), purchasing carts, and so on.

A Samples Room

In the words of Yu Yan, the concept of a samples room is even more marvelous. Prior to this, vendors were often stumped on how to categorize their products to attract the most traffic. To resolve this, Yu Yan is in the process of experimenting with a method whereby vendors can get around this kind of traffic issue. She hopes that Taobao will be like other houses in the future, in that consumers can select products by looking at samples in a sample room and then, based on the number of the product, go to a warehouse to pick up their goods.

With a samples room, the things the vendor has to deal with are simplified. The vendor must consider ways to make his or her own part of the samples room more attractive. This can be done by the vendor himself or herself, or the vendor can hire others to do it, including Taobao. In the end, the consumer sees his or her "treasure" in the sample room, which thereby relieves the vendor of struggling with the question of how to categorize products so as to get the most traffic.

Platform Strategies and the Long-Tail Effect

Long-Tail Effect
Many members of the Alibaba staff believe that the Taobao model is a kind of long-tail model. How is this long-tail effect manifested in the e-commerce industry? Before getting to the main menu, let us give you a few appetizers and first describe the fundamental concept behind long-tail theory.

Most readers will have heard of the *80/20 principle*. This 80/20 rule also has been called the *Pareto effect* because it was first suggested by the famous nineteenth-century Italian economist Pareto. Later it became one of the main concepts in the field of management sciences. At the outset, Pareto was attempting to use the 80/20 rule to describe and explain certain features of social structure. Later, in the course of doing further research, he discovered that almost all economic activity conforms to this law: 20 percent of the core customers contribute 80 percent of sales volume, 20 percent of stellar products contribute 80 percent of profits, and so on. However, unlike the offline traditional way of doing business, Internet-based marketing and sales are exhibiting a more extreme variant of this law, namely, the *98 percent rule*.

Unlike the 80/20 principle, this new phenomenon may be completely unfamiliar to most consumers. The general theme is the same as the 80/20 rule, and it has provided quite some inspiration to many in e-commerce. Think back to your order forms for things back on the 11.11 Shopping Festival: How many were conventional items, and how many were dark horses? Yi Xuan is a second-year college student in Xi'an. She says that she personally likes clothing and jewelry that has an ethnic character to it, but it is hard to buy the originals in markets. From the Taobao-U website, however, she discovered a page that specifically promotes ethnic items. As a result, she was able to purchase a number of items of ethnic clothing that have been much praised by her classmates. However, if such a small-scale site is located in a second- or third-tier city, it will undoubtedly be forced to close down fairly soon. The reason is that there is not that much market demand. It is hard to overestimate the concentrating effect of demand on e-commerce platforms. Many so-called nonmainstream vendors have found a niche in which to survive on e-commerce platforms. As an academic research report looking at book sales on Amazon described, "98 percent of the first 10,000 books on the best-seller lists sell one copy every quarter of the year."

Unlike sellers of the dark-horse type of ethnic garments mentioned earlier, people selling hot items have never had to think much about how to sell them. With a limited number of racks and a limited number of windows, the only intelligent thing to do is to give space to the most popular items. To get ready for the arrival of the 11.11 Shopping Festival, many vendors redecorated their storefronts. They put explosively hot items in prominent positions. In research on the market for Internet sales, scholars use the term *superstar effect* to describe this phenomenon. It represents a kind of concentrated consumer model; that is, a few items are extremely desirable and occupy the greatest share of sales. However, most of us need more than just hot items. Each person's taste has areas that differ from the most popular commodities on the market. What's more, the more options we have in choosing different things (niche products), the more we are attracted to self-benefiting things. As production technology develops, the percentage of self-benefiting goods will swiftly move up in the index ranking. High-efficiency digital publicity, massively powerful search engines, and the way in which broadband has penetrated life to an extreme degree are coming together to form a kind of force that improves information on products and allows for greater choice in e-commerce markets. This provides opportunities for very specific products to be discovered and purchased.

The explanation of the long-tail effect is actually a part of the *economics of abundance*. When bottlenecks between supply and demand begin to disappear and all products become available to people, an economy will naturally experience the long-tail phenomenon. If you take enough nonhot items and combine them together in one place, in fact, you can create a large market that could be described as the equal to the hot-items market. Kevin Laws, a venture capitalist who has served as a consultant to the music industry, puts it succinctly: "The greatest wealth can then be generated from the smallest kinds of sales."

We can think of our sector of the economy as being a vast ocean with hot items sticking up like islands above the surface of the water. We can also think of lower operating costs as a kind of lowering of the level of the water itself or as a retreating wave. As the water recedes, new land is revealed. It was there before but hidden under the surface. The richness and diversity of the world under the water are far greater than that above the surface. That richness is composed of *niche* products.

After describing the long-tail effect both directly and via analogies, we would now like to see what this theory implies by tracing it back to its roots. Chris Anderson first created this term of art *long tail*. His article entitled, "Long-Tail Theory," published in the October 2004 issue of *Wired* magazine, quickly became the most quoted article in the history of the magazine. Anderson arrived at three major conclusions. First, the long tail of product categories is much longer than we imagine. Second, there are now effective means by which we can develop this long tail. Third, once all *niche* products are grouped together, they can create a very sizable major market. The long tail actually refers precisely to those dark-horse products that have been overlooked and that are looking for a sales platform that is appropriate to their needs. Once they find that platform, they bring together astonishing demand statistics. This theory has given new hope to platform designers and Taobao store owners. Store owners have perhaps long known that there is not much benefit in blindly pursuing hot items. Only by grabbing onto a different kind of demand, the more individual demands of different consumers, can they achieve any kind of breakthrough (Figure 3.1).

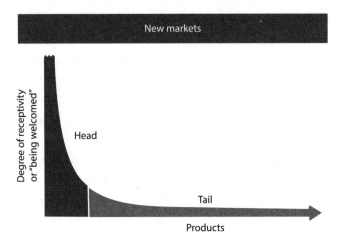

FIGURE 3.1 *The long-tail effect.*

New Markets

By being sold on the Internet, more of such *niche* products can satisfy the diverse preferences of consumers. Therefore, they have the potential to surpass the stellar products marketed via traditional channels. Both supply and demand play a role in generating the formation of the long tail. On the supply side, the main factors include increasing the accessibility of products as well as their diversity. All kinds of products are filling the Internet's essentially unlimited shelf space for products. The way products are made to order and the fact of digitization have radically lowered both production and retail costs. Enterprises involved in this unlimited shelf space have already realized one of the principles of creating sufficient critical mass—a very large number (the number of products in the tail) times a relatively small number (the sales volume of each product in the tail) still equals a very large number. What's more, this very large number can only get bigger. The efficiency of these myriad scattered sales is that they are low cost. Because there is no rent for shelf space on the Internet, the more *niche* products are sold, the greater is the benefit. Profits are no lower than and can even be greater than those of more popular products.

A flourishing tail market can provide an astonishing number of products and can provide customers with far greater options from which to choose. Successful devices to consolidate the tail need not only dark-horse products, but they also need hot products. If you are positioned only in the head territory of products, you will soon find that customers have many more needs that you cannot in fact satisfy. If you only have tail products, customers lose their way because everything you provide for them to choose from is unfamiliar. Products must range across the entire spectrum of diversity. They should extend from the most popular products with broad appeal to specific goods with very narrow appeal. Only then can information be organized in such a way as to indicate a path that has meaning for all people, namely, a path that explores the tail.

On another note, allowing for total spontaneity in choosing hot products may not necessarily be appropriate for all people. Product segmentation and then remixing may be a more successful strategy. Umaer Hake calls this *microchunking*, that is, dividing a particular area of content into different components (*microchunks*) so that all people can use whatever methods they choose to consume it or, alternatively, mixing the content together with other things to create new content. We have already seen this trend in highly segmented products and branding. An example would be how a certain shop on Taobao sells iPhone5s. This is done according to the Internet provider (either Unicom or Telecom), according to the cell phone color (e.g., gold, deep-space gray, or silver), by the menu available on the cell phone (i.e., selections from 1 to 7), by the internal memory of the phone (e.g.,16G, 32G, or 64G), by services (e.g., insured by Nationwide warranty, one year warranty, or remote service), and so on. These are all listed out as possible combinations. Each new combination can use different transmission networks and can come into contact with different customer groups. If the number of items is numerous and demand for each is low, this reflects the fact that consumer demand is fragmented because the customer base of the Internet is, in itself, fragmented. What's more, user demands change very quickly (equivalent to the fragmentation of time). As a result, Internet purchasing generally displays certain characteristics: small quantities, diverse varieties, large range, and enormous capacity (virtual shelf space). Alibaba has already given birth to an e-commerce market that is on the order of 1 trillion RMB. Within five years, this is expected to reach 10 trillion RMB. The Taobao platform alone has over 6 million vendors. It has 100 million individual user visits. This is much greater than the traditional market— for example, the famous market within China called the YiWu Small Commodities Wholesale Market has only some 60,000 booths.

On the demand side, the main factors include the wealth of online information about products, including consumers' evaluations and recommendations, as well as the powerful search and selection tools available on e-commerce websites. In slow markets, you have to guess in advance what things are going to be best-sellers and promote those. In flourishing markets, all you need to do is throw a product out there and let the market itself decide on what to buy. The distinction between a filter performed in advance and a filter performed after the fact lies in the distinction between forecasting and evaluating. The latter is always going to be more accurate than the former. The great advantage of the Internet is that it can make use of the evaluating capacity of group intelligence. Because of this, it harbors unlimited amounts of information. The Internet can grade things into levels or classes on an objective basis, and it can evaluate things subjectively through descriptions. This makes it easier for people to compare the advantages and disadvantages of products and transmit their likes and dislikes to others.

Long-tail e-commerce truly sees consumers as living flesh-and-blood people. With a large-scale custom-made system, consumers no longer need to bow before mass-commodity products that are all the same. What the wave of individualism is in fact revealing is the emergence of consumer power. The individualization of products and services and their enrichment, the more effective allocation of resources (green-ification and conservation of resource consumption), exploiting the potential of consumers, and so on all have been stimulated. Instead of being large scale and standardized, demand is becoming individualized and high value. The satisfaction and enrichment of individuals are, in themselves, generating greater personalization. They are making things more human oriented. However, simply supplying more varieties of product does not change demand. Consumers must have ways to find the kinds of products in which they have a special interest or need. A whole series of tools and technologies can now effectively take care of this, from automatic recommendations to ranking of products. These filters can push demand toward the end of the tail.

Widely used Internet user response systems allow consumers to share their feelings about and experience with Internet-based purchases. These have therefore expanded the use of public opinion and made it more automatic. However, research has discovered that the role of public opinion is not unified when it comes to different trendy products. The public does not speak with one voice. Theory from the early period ([11]Bakos 1997) predicts that public endorsements on the Internet will help consumers to find dark-horse products and so will order their preferences. Online product responses and endorsements have been seen as an import factor on the demand side. They can lower the search costs of consumers for *niche* products. Because of this, most of the research into long-tail theory believes that public opinion can influence the transmission of information and therefore can lead to the formation of long tails on the demand side. Analysis makes it clear that the endorsements system as an ordering mechanism in determining taste does help consumers to get product information from people with similar preferences and therefore reduces the degree of sales concentration. Empirical evidence indicates that Amazon's endorsement system leads to a more even distribution of sales. One of the most important methods of online user reviews as a way to measure public-opinion effect is to be found in recent empirical research. It is being regarded as an important element on the demand side. For example, [12]Clemons and colleagues show that positive evaluations of new products can help the rapid sales growth of those new products on the market. [13]Duan and colleagues show that online user evaluations have an ever greater and more positive influence on *niche* products.

Ranking popularity can amplify the effect of verbal transmission of positive responses by many times over. In traditional markets, products that are highly similar are stacked up on shelves with very little differentiation. Unlike those markets, Alibaba's selection tools have functions that are clear and simple and can help customers to make a choice. These

[11]Bakos, Y. Reducing buyer search costs: Implications for electronic marketplaces. Management Science, 43, 12, December 1997, 1676–1692.

[12]Clemons, E., Gao, G., and Hitt, L. When online reviews meet hyperdifferentiation: A study of the craft beer industry. Journal of Management Information Systems, 23, 2, Fall 2006, 149-171.

[13]Duan, W., Gu, B., and Whinston, A. B. Informational cascades and software adoption on the Internet: An empirical investigation. MIS Quarterly, 33, 1, December 2009, 23-48.

include ranking according to personal preferences, ranking according to sales volume, ranking according to reliability, ranking according to newness, ranking according to price, and so on. This recommendation information can potentially become a large and powerful marketing tool. From user evaluations to detailed specifications, information on products can respond to consumers' questions effectively and also can prevent them from giving up and not buying because of doubts and concerns. In helping to win the trust of consumers, it is important to explain the source of information that is being supplied. Clear explanations can help consumers to make use of the system. Transparency can help to establish trust, and the costs of transparency are quite low.

User ratings are the reflection of collective concepts, and they themselves can be quantified so as to make it easier to compare products and divide products into categories. These tools can organize a multiplicity of complex product types into proper order. They can help the consumer to make choices, and they can also help the store owner to try to figure out what consumers might want to buy in ways that are less arduous. Alibaba's platform has a dynamic grading system of stores. Specifically, it includes descriptions that correspond to certain grades, including grades for service attitude, speed of executing orders, and delivery of product and a percentage rating that compares the store with others in the same industry. The user evaluations of Taobao customers are often highly intelligent and incisive, some with rather flowery descriptions, but the most import thing is that other users believe these evaluations. Added together, the time and effort that customers put into these are unlimited in value. Customers are the ones most familiar with their own needs. Through online responses, these are transmitted to the production decisions of e-commerce.

Compared with traditional enterprises, the products supplied by e-commerce entities are low priced but excellent, which has greatly expanded surplus value for consumers. To save on costs, many retail stores on the Alibaba platform use their existing inventories to expand e-commerce markets. The variety of products put on the Internet is far greater than what can be put in traditional stores. It is far more efficient to concentrate product offerings on the Internet than it is to spread products out over the shelves of several hundred retail outlets. Moreover, different people may be willing to accept different price levels, what microeconomics calls the *characteristic of price elasticity*. There are many different reasons for this, including a customer's income and the amount of time he or she has to spend on shopping. In a bountiful market that is spatially unlimited, changeable pricing may become a powerful tool. It helps to maximize the value of the product as well as the scale of the market. For example, Taobao has a discounted pricing system for holidays (such as the 11.11 Shopping Festival), and Juhuasuan has a group purchasing price system. In a fiercely competitive market with plenty of diversity, prices tend to move in line with costs. Given the laws of a digital economy, however, costs can only get lower.

The Role that Alibaba's Platform Plays in Creating a Long-Tail Effect

As described earlier, long-tail theory is where the essence of an Internet economy resides. The prerequisite for long-tail theory to work, however, is scale. Only when buyers and sellers, as well as the variety and numbers of available products, reach a certain scale will long-tail theory be effective. Adequate scale then draws in consumers looking for the products that they need, and an e-commerce platform is perfect in being able to realize these functions. First, a platform is effective in making something attractive and popular, and it need not put out a lot in costs to do it. Second, a platform can serve as both a vehicle and a radiating force for other products that are being sold. The best way to fully realize the power of the long-tail effect, therefore, is to use an Internet-based sales platform such as Alibaba.

The very marrow (core) of a successful platform business model lies in creating an excellent ecosystem that has powerful long-term growth potential. It should have precise rules and an operating system and mechanisms that are all its own. It should be effective in stimulating mutual interaction among all groups or communities that reside in the system in order to achieve the scenarios that enterprises on the platform hope for. Looking out across enterprises that have rebuilt their industrial structures, we generally discover that the key to their success was to set up a beneficial platform ecosystem that links together two or more groups (communities) and that distorts and even destroys the existing industrial chain. The moment one community in the platform ecosystem is strengthened by increased demand, the demand for the other communities grows along with it as well. A positive cycle is therefore gradually set in motion. Through this platform exchange, all parties on the platform stimulate the unrestricted growth of all the other parties. The original strategic objective is gradually achieved, including the increase in scale and the improvement of the ecosystem, to the point that even opposing competitors participate in dismantling and rebuilding old industrial structures and refashioning a new market pattern.

At the initial stage, e-commerce platforms represented a confluence of information, financial, and human flows. Alibaba, Taobao, and Eachnet were some of the earliest e-commerce platforms. At the outset, e-commerce evolved out of simply separating information into different categories. Jack Ma put the information of enterprise Yellow Pages up on the Internet. He later discovered that in looking up information, customers lacked the ability to investigate the credit or trustworthiness of both sides of an exchange. As a result, evaluation systems and integrity systems were born and then gradually improved upon. With the birth of Alipay and the process of going through a third party who guaranteed the exchange (an escrow service), the buyer's risk was greatly reduced. The introduction of Internet banking then greatly improved the convenience of payment. Even large-sum transactions could go through channels outside of banks given the presence of security guarantees for transactions. With the increase in the numbers of "netizens," the virtual platform of e-commerce improved the grade levels of stores via the evaluation system. This made the transmission of information more convenient as well as more accurate. At the same time, the appearance of third-party escrow tools (guarantee of transactions), namely, Alipay, guaranteed flows of money, completing the growth of the first stage of e-commerce.

The core substance of the middle stage of e-commerce lay in warehousing and logistics. In China, the rise of speedy delivery services was an enormous help to retail sellers on the Internet. At this same time, the rise of Internet retail businesses brought tremendous volumes of business to delivery services, leading to extremely fast growth of that industry in China over the past decade. The cooperation of e-commerce platforms and express delivery companies created a service that could track order numbers at any time and any place. Online customers could look up the status of their orders whenever they wished, which provided them with an even better experience. However, as the volume of business increased, various problems emerged in express delivery services. Goods were damaged, lost, or delayed; delivery personnel had bad attitudes; and poor delivery services affected the mood of consumers and weakened their confidence in buying things via the Internet. Sales volumes then came up against a wintry dormant period. As the crisis deepened, negative evaluations poured forth, sounding out alarms to those creating platforms. Senior management at Alibaba also recognized that it was absolutely imperative for the company to build a logistical system itself. After this, Jack Ma invested 1 trillion RMB in forging what was called the *Cai Niao delivery system*.[14] This opened a new page on the development of e-commerce platforms.

The staff of the Logistics Department of Alibaba in Hangzhou has confirmed their belief that the core part of the middle period of e-commerce platform development related to warehousing and logistics and, moreover, that the purpose in developing warehousing and logistics was to truly close the circle and complete full-package service, the "whole dragon," for both sellers and consumers. The purpose also was to avoid the negative impact of outsourcing any part of the cycle to others.

The aim of this current higher stage of e-commerce platform development is to refine the categories of the platform and to enable more precision services. Segmenting industries in a more refined way relates to an in-depth search across the entire industrial chain. Done well, it can further lower the operating costs of stores. Moreover, it is more targeted than simply synthesizing all services across the entire platform. Information transmission is more accurate, shipping and handling are faster, and targeted customers are clumped into more useful categories. A vertical platform can realize greater interaction among more finely segmented customer-group markets that are both online and offline. It can unify the handling of the warehousing and shipping of the supply chain. It greatly lowers the costs of promotion, as well as warehousing and shipping, and promotes the upgrading of the industrial chain.

---

[14]Translator's note: In English, this is known as China Smart Logistics but also as the Zhejiang Cainiao Supply Chain Management Co., Ltd. It is a logistics information platform operator.

The core substance of this reconfiguration is *big data* and the way that data endows the system with greater functionality. Big data accumulates large quantities of information on merchants and consumers. It is thereby able to overturn the original model of basing sales on the amount of production and instead can transform it into a model of basing production on the amount of sales. After in-depth analysis of big data, the producer can understand more clearly how to match his or her production to what consumers want. This greatly lowers the amount of excess (unsold) goods that are both produced and held in inventory. Meanwhile, greater functionality, that is, the ability to use the intelligence of the system itself, equates with higher efficiency, less time wasted, and simpler operations, all of which lead to lower costs. Greater functionality enables the system to maintain high quality and outstanding service.

As we have always described it, creating a platform is a totally absorbing task. Platform designers are the generals on the field of markets. From a higher vantage point, they see further than others, and they determine the victory of the battle long in advance. Nobody can forget the sense of exultation on November 11, 2013, when people assembled in the great hall of Taobao Town as sales volume surpassed a record figure yet again. Staff could not hide the excitement and emotion on their faces. Alibaba had again earned a plateful of money. In theory, a platform has an advantage that cannot be duplicated by other lines of business. On the one hand, it is located on the high end of the industrial chain. Not only are returns plentiful, but the positioning allows for tremendous autonomy and a beneficial vantage point in competition. It can call the shots, and no one dare not comply. On the other hand, the business model of a platform enables all involved to be winners. As a result, the longer it operates, the greater is its value.

However, as consumers eye the tremendous revenues of Taobao with envy, we must recognize that the operations of the platform are in fact facing serious dangers and obstructions. It is in fact quite hard to build successful platform strategies. First, prior to selecting a platform strategy, you must ensure that you have the capacity to accumulate a massive number of users. To be number one in the number of users in a large market not only requires exceedingly strong products but also fortunate market conditions in terms of strong demand and marketing and promotion procedures that are effective. Second, the enterprise selecting its platform strategy must be able to provide its users with massive "stickiness." Any company intending to operate a platform must be a service-oriented enterprise, and moreover, it must service the rigid demands of users. There are in fact very few of these kinds of service entities, and competition is intense. Finally, as an enterprise selects its platform strategy, it needs to have a business model that cooperates with others in winning, "First you, then me." This so-called platform is actually built for others; it is built to enable other people to make money. Only if relationships among those operating on the platform are mutually reinforcing can the platform itself continue to exist and grow big and strong. A well-functioning platform not only requires an acutely intelligent sense of business, but it also requires the desire to create well-being on the part of all. The reason Alibaba has been successful in its platform strategy is that it relies on a culture that puts service above all. At the outset, its initial significance lay only in being a transaction platform where everyone could get together and conduct business. People participating in transactions then asked the platform to provide it with a certain degree of value, with things that were on the nature of confirming qualifications, providing authentication, managing, providing insurance, and so on. It then transformed into becoming an integrity platform. This represented an elevation of the transaction platform. In recent years, the anticorruption movement that Jack Ma has championed has been dedicated to preserving this attribute. Integrity is the key to changing the transaction model and to profitability by unearthing the potential of the Internet effect in consumer markets. The Taobao platform links up sellers and buyers, whereas the participation of third-party applications software vendors enables the platform's mechanisms to be more complete. Since entering the market in 2003, Taobao conducted 8.02 billion RMB in transactions within two years. It grew at a rate of over 700 percent. In 2006, Taobao's transaction volume reached 15 billion RMB, and it occupied the premier position in the market with a 65 percent market share. In 2010, the total sum of transactions conducted on the Internet in China "stormed the pass" by breaking through 1 trillion RMB. Taobao's market share in that was over 80 percent. While we enjoy the sight of these dancing figures, we should also take care to analyze them in a level-headed and rational manner.

What tricks has Alibaba latched onto in order to enable it to storm one pass after another? What precisely has it done to pluck the fruit of such astounding success?

The book *Platform Strategies* points out that there are two main categories of network effects that operate in platform models. One is the *same-side network effect* and the other is the *cross-network effect*. The same-side network effect refers to how a particular group within all users begins to affect others within the group when scale reaches a certain size. The cross-network effect refers to when the increase in size of a particular group of users has an influence across the platform by increasing the effectiveness with which other groups are able to use the platform. Platform enterprises design mechanisms that are intended to stimulate positively reinforcing cycles via these network effects and thereby to increase effectiveness. To avoid network effects that work in the opposite direction, mechanisms must be set up that filter users. The most basic way to do this is to authenticate the user's identity. Alibaba requires each user to register for an account number with a true and valid identity. This is effective in improving the reliability of platform services. In addition to identity authentication, another method is to have users become authenticators of one another. This mutual-evaluation mechanism is worth promoting because the results of combined opinions generally have the force of public trust behind them. The mechanism by which users grade stores on the Taobao platform is intended to enable sound transactions and the ability to differentiate between outstanding and inferior products. It is done to coordinate more precise pairing of needs and serves as an important reference for people's decisions on whether or not to carry out a transaction. Meanwhile, those who are being graded can create their own publicly acknowledged brand depending on their own individual energy and efforts. Moreover, in individual markets (or in two or more markets), they can position themselves with respect to customer groups more precisely, and they can target customer groups more precisely. The strategic driver of a platform is its ability to provide each element in the group with unique value. Whoever becomes the focal-point community in the ecosystem depends mostly on the way platform enterprises position themselves and the resources they command. From the beginning, Taobao has positioned itself as an aggregator of millions of small merchants and sole proprietorships. As a result, it has created an ecosystem with a tremendous variety of product options.

As representative of one platform model of e-commerce, the Taobao system has effectively used the advantages of the Internet to earn money by taking in annual platform usage fees from merchants and advertising fees. The enormous number of users on both Taobao and Tmall and the enormous base of merchants have basically created a natural monopoly in this particular realm of Internet effect. The others, Tencent, Jingdong, DangDang, and Amazon-China, have some revenue from their platform businesses, but they have vastly fewer platform advantages than the Taobao system. In terms of the architecture of its basic infrastructure functions, Taobao is already using an open-system pattern. The users of the platform already conceive of themselves in ways that are not limited to "buyer" or "seller." A great diversity of identities can realize their own business value on the platform, including consumers, retail shops, value-added services, shippers, e-commerce pay providers, commodity providers, brand-holding entities, and freewheeling individual businesspeople. As the saying goes, the ocean's vast capacity can accommodate hundreds of rivers. In the embrace of a very rich and diverse business ecosystem, all have gradually grown powerful together. In the course of growing its platform, Taobao has scrupulously abided by the principle of only providing basic infrastructure and not trying to do everything. The whole business of logistics could bring in several tens of millions in revenue to Taobao, and indeed, it is a large source of profits for Taobao, but Taobao does not undertake the business itself. Instead, it opens the business to partners with whom it cooperates. This is not done to strike a pose but is a rational business decision. Taobao's policy makers are taking into consideration the fact that Taobao might well be able to do everything, but it cannot do everything well. If it tries to do all, it will provide second- or third-rate service. The platform itself will not be first rate and, consequently, will not succeed in "growing a single blade of grass." Taobao can only be a first-rate service company by being open and enabling the best companies to survive through competition. It can only be the model for the industry (and have a model effect) if it truly asks users to vote with their feet by providing traffic.

As Chen Weiru, author of *Platform Strategies*, points out, the reason merchants and consumers are willing to carry out trades on Taobao is that it extracts very low fees from merchants. This requires that the platform be highly cognizant of the needs on both sides of transactions. For example, Taobao provides microlending services. It understands that merchants have funding needs but are unable to get money under the existing banking system. As a result, it has dealt with this issue in a strategic way.

The very essence of platform strategies, as per the success of Taobao, lies in creating an ecosystem that allows for win-win benefits in many different ways. This enables members to enjoy the benefits while the platform itself gets bigger and stronger. As Chen Weiru describes it, the key path to success for platform enterprises lies in providing the greatest benefits to all kinds of customers and satisfying the greatest number of needs. This is the only way a company can remain on untakable territory in the midst of competition and industry restructuring. Platform models have precise rules and regulations that are unique to themselves and that can provide effective incentives for the mutual interaction of all different kinds of groups (communities). The moment one begins to grow as a result of increased demand, the demand for the others increases along with it. In this manner, a positively reinforcing cycle is established. By communicating with one another via the platform, all parties assist in stimulating the unlimited growth of other parties. Through selecting the right platform model, it is possible to move to greater scale, improve the ecosystem, deal with competition, and even dismantle and restructure current industrial structures, including refashioning the overall pattern of China's market.

CHAPTER 4

CLUSTERING INNOVATIONS THAT STARTED WITH 1688.COM

XIANG SONGLIN

Enterprise operating models have changed dramatically with the diffusion and constant upgrading of information technologies, and competitive strategies have changed along with them. A large number of companies now use e-commerce to conduct transactions among the main entities of their supply chain. As a new form of supply-chain management, e-commerce has become a key weathervane for understanding supply-chain innovations. E-commerce is also one of the main variables affecting a company's operating results.

As Internet applications and the use of e-commerce become more universal, a new form of market competition is emerging that takes advantage of the ways in which full-channel supply chains of e-commerce enterprises are changing and being restructured. Such changes shift the services model in a digital direction, fully accessible on the mobile Internet and fully compatible across multiple platforms. They spur the creation of a more finely segmented market and a membership economy with the aim of increasing the efficiency of such business models as consumer to business (C2B). They aim to achieve a shift from supply-chain management methods toward highly effective ways of cooperating with others.

This chapter starts by looking at the restructuring of the supply chain of agricultural goods and e-commerce. It looks at the innovations

Note: The pronunciation of 1688 in Chinese is similar to "a-li-ba-ba"—hence the name of the company's website for the Chinese public. In addition, the syllables as pronounced in Chinese are homonymous with getting rich.

of China.taobao.com at a more closely defined division of labor and logistical innovations, as well as at demand innovations with greater fragmentation of production. It looks at the international division of labor and Internet trade. It explores how the Ali ecosystem can provide greater functionality for customers with respect to supporting their creations, marketing, and production. It looks at how Alibaba can encourage enterprises, especially small and microenterprises, to make use of the important role that innovation in supply-chain procedures can play.

China.taobao.com and Innovative Integrations of Supply Chains for Agricultural Products

Agriculture is the basis of China's economy. Issues relating to the trade in agricultural goods, together with how to increase farmers' incomes, have always been of primary concern to the Chinese Communist Party and the state.

One of the hot topics among both theoretical researchers and those who formulate policy has been the potential for e-commerce in agriculture. The questions are how to make use of e-commerce platforms to restructure the supply of agricultural goods in the country and how to improve market activity so as to increase farmers' income. Farmers are more familiar than anyone with the unique attributes of agricultural goods. E-commerce is now giving these farmers a stage on which to play out their dreams as *grassroots entrepreneurs*. Not only have farmers improved the operating results of agricultural production, but they also have changed the supply-chain model for agricultural products. These things are playing an important role in invigorating the market and improving incomes.

Establishing China.taobao.com

Although quite a few people engaged in e-commerce are selling agricultural products, the management model governing the overall supply chain for agriculture remains backward. In 2013, Min Yu and Anna Nagurney[1] compared the supply-chain management of agricultural products and that of industrial products in a research project. Agricultural products are subject to weather, decompose quickly once picked, and are highly regional in production, so not only are their market prices more volatile but their supply chains are also relatively less stable. At the same time, agricultural products are generally used for food, which means that freshness and food safety are of concern. These things do not generally apply to supply chains in the industrial arena.

The Alibaba Research Institute looked into the question of using e-commerce in traditional industries (including agriculture) at the county level. They found that businesses that were handling agricultural products on the Internet encountered various bottlenecks, production quantity issues, and natural conditions that prevented them from growing further once they had reached a particular stage. Meanwhile, buying food on the Internet is not yet comfortable for most people because of food safety concerns. Keeping agricultural products fresh presents special demands on warehousing and shipping, and the cold-storage facilities are limited in China.

All these problems have hindered the development of the supply chain for agricultural goods. How to make use of rapidly developing trends in e-commerce to stimulate faster growth of traditional industries, and particularly agriculture, has become a vital topic of discussion in e-commerce circles. The establishment of China.taobao.com is providing a new path to this end. It is helping to restructure the supply chain for agricultural products and promoting a way for farmers to earn more income.

China.taobao.com is part of Alibaba's key strategy to restructure local (provincial) commerce and spur regional economic development. Alibaba's deployment of resources in the agricultural sphere can be seen in Table 4.1. China.taobao.com is based on the Alibaba network platform. It is supported via partnerships with provincial governments and

---

[1]Min Yu and Anna Nagurney, "Competitive Food Supply Chain Networks with Application to Fresh Produce." *European Journal of Operational Research* 224(2):273–282, 2013.

the commercial companies that are under the jurisdiction of provincial governments. It enlists the participation of Internet businesses engaged in specialty foods, processed agricultural products, and tourism in the operations of each local platform of China.taobao.com.

TABLE 4.1 *Alibaba subsidiary companies and departments that relate to agriculture*

SUBSIDIARY COMPANY	DEPARTMENT	BUSINESS GOAL
Central Business Unit (CBU)	The CBU handles wholesale distribution of agricultural products within China via the website operations department, the operations department handling different trades, and the agricultural channel.	Wholesale for domestic agricultural products
International CBU (ICBU)	The ICBU handles international wholesale distribution of agricultural products. This is accomplished by the information platform, by extended services, and by agricultural categories.	Wholesale for international agricultural products
Taobao	The new agricultural development department	Exploration of an e-commerce model for "green," or ecological, agricultural products
	China Specialties Project within food categories	Creating markets dedicated solely to regional agricultural specialties
Tmall	Food and agricultural products	Online retail of these products
	Vendors' businesses and services	Developing services that relate to agricultural products
	Logistics–Planning–Express Delivery Station Project	Deploying rural networks that foster agenting businesses in agricultural products
Juhuasuan	Fresh-food category	Online retail of fresh food
Alipay	Department for new rural affairs	Providing convenient payment and financing services in rural areas

Source: http://club.1688.com/threadview/34070876.htm.

Company, Department, and Lines of Business

CBU: Website Operations Department, Industry Operations Department, agriculture channel, wholesaler of domestic agricultural products

ICBU: Information platform, in-depth services, agricultural categories, wholesaler of international agricultural products

Taobao platform: New Agriculture Development Department, exploring e-commerce models for green ecosystem products

Taobao platform: Food categories, China specialties categories, forging a China local specialties professional market

Tianmao: Food categories, selling foodstuffs and agricultural products

Tianmao: Business Development Department, services for stores, services for helping operations to do with agricultural products

Tianmao: Logistics Department, "Scamming" Department, "Trash" Department, post-box items, rural websites, growing the business of serving as a purchasing agent

Juhuasuan: Live and fresh products category, selling live and fresh agricultural products

Alipay: New Countryside Affairs Department, rural payment by ordinary people, and rural financial services

By the second half of 2012, a number of provincial China.taobao.com "halls" had been set up, including Xinjiang Hall, Sichuan Hall, and Guizhou Hall. The governments of other provinces then quickly lined up to cooperate with Alibaba and set up local halls of their own that promoted their local features and displayed the unique flavors of their foods and locally grown products. By the end of 2013, eight different provinces had set up such specialty halls with Taobao, including Hubei, Sichuan, Shandong, Xinjiang, Guizhou, Anhui, Shanxi, and Taiwan. In addition, over a dozen county- or municipal-level *China.taobao.com halls* had been set up by the end of 2013. As more and more localities are registering such platforms on Taobao, one can sit back and use one's mouse to peruse the offerings of a veritable banquet of Chinese delights.

Constructing and developing this project relate to the way many departments in Alibaba are attempting to contribute to China's "New Agriculture" endeavor. The Alibaba Research Institute prepared a report entitled, "White Paper on E-commerce Relating to Agricultural Products (2012)." Statistics in this report indicate that completed e-commerce transactions for agricultural goods in 2012 came to 19.861 billion RMB, which was an increase of four times over the 2010 amount (Figure 4.1). Looking at specific categories, the largest volume of business was done in three categories, the first relating to traditional nutrition, called *bolstering* (including honey and other bee products, swallows' nests, mushrooms,[2] and Chinese caterpillar fungus); the second, vegetable oils, rice noodles, dried goods, and seasonings; and the third, tea. These had total annual sales volume in 2012 of 6.141 billion, 3.453 billion, and 3.416 RMB, respectively.

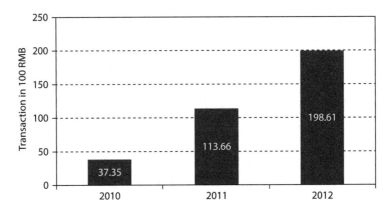

FIGURE 4.1 *The trend in transactions relating to agricultural commodities on Taobao, including Tmall (unit = 100 RMB).*

In terms of trends, the category growing at the fastest rate includes live and fresh products (seafood and other aquatic products, fresh fruits, and so on). In 2012, this category grew by 42.06 percent over the previous year. Tea was the main item in terms of agricultural sales volume on Taobao in 2012, with daily sales reaching 7.22 million RMB. Different kinds of dried meat and fruit ranked second, which traditionally had been popular sales items on the Taobao platform. Such things as honey and other bee products also maintained high growth rates, with sales figures reaching new heights. Fresh fruits and seafood and aquatic products had a breakthrough year in 2012, becoming the fastest-growing agricultural product of all. Eggs, milk, and various grains are still in a startup stage

---

[2]*Lingzhi*, or "glossy ganoderma."

and have not yet seen a significant increase. Such animal products as swallows' nests and deer antlers are showing negative growth rates because of the strengthening of animal protection concepts.

Despite this growth in the trade of agricultural products via e-commerce, problems are still quite pronounced, including the phenomenon of buying high and then not being able to sell. Since the second half of 2012, most parts of China have run into a soft market for both vegetables and fruits. Not only did this severely hurt farmers, but consumers were still paying high prices when they went to buy fruits, vegetables, and other agricultural products. The main reason for this seemingly contradictory problem is the existence of too many links in the distribution chain and large losses owing to waste.

Studies show that vegetables go through four to six different links in the chain to get from the field to the table of a consumer. Each additional link adds to costs. On top of these are various kinds of taxes and management fees. The excessive costs of the distribution chain are the direct cause of finding things hard to sell. At the same time, because cold-storage facilities have been slow to develop, vegetables sent anywhere but locally face such uncontrollable factors as weather changes, being held up along the way, and so on, which lead to enormous waste.

A major issue for the government, enterprises, and the public itself therefore has become how to restructure the supply chain for agricultural goods to reduce these problems. As e-commerce has developed, the government and the public are increasingly participating in restructuring of the agricultural supply chain. Everyone is looking for opportunities to link up the resources they have in hand with the "New Agriculture." Prior to this, high distribution costs, food safety issues (including unsound certification procedures), and low cooperation in supply chains were all problems for agriculture. Now, however, as participants are increasing, these problems are being dealt with to a substantial degree. For example, the Lenovo Holding Company set up an Agricultural Investment Affairs Department specifically aimed at expediting investment in and preferential treatment for fresh produce.

Even though problems surrounding the links of agricultural trade are legion, Alibaba, too, hopes to use local specialties to stimulate consumer demand for agricultural products. To do this, in 2012, the Taobao platform set up a New Agriculture Development Department and launched a channel for developing an agricultural ecosystem. It was exploring a production model for e-commerce in green agricultural products. Tmall also organized business resources to provide more professional support and services for the 4,000 sellers of food products under its banner. Juhuasuan[3] also hopes to provide opportunities for Internet selling of large quantities of live and fresh agricultural products via group purchasing.

The enormous business opportunities that lie behind agricultural products contribute to the seductive appeal of e-commerce and restructuring supply lines. According to Alibaba Research Institute figures, the sales volume of agricultural goods on all Ali platforms reached 28.4 billion RMB in 2013, and in 2014 it was up to 48.3 billion RMB, a 70 percent growth comparing with a year ago.

The massive agricultural products market has been providing not only a solid foundation for Internet purchasing but also an unprecedented market opportunity for local governments. China.taobao.com platforms were created to take advantage of this, and they have already played a major role in restructuring the supply chain of agricultural goods.

Innovative Role Played by China.taobao.com in China's Agricultural Supply Chain

In fact, this project started back in 2010. While nurturing a large group of Internet businesses and helping them get registered on the site, Taobao kept exploring how to use its own best advantages to stimulate the growth of e-commerce sales of agricultural goods. The general idea was to do this through aggregating products, for example, through China.taobao.com. Later, for various reasons, China.taobao.com was set aside. Not until April of 2012 did Taobao's Foodstuffs-Category Team take it over, and only then was it put back on the agenda. The operating model that gradually developed was called the "1+1+1 model," namely, government plus service operators plus the Taobao platform.

[3]Translator's note: Juhuasuan is an online group-purchasing marketplace. It specializes in such techniques as flash sales so that customers pay less for products because of the large volume being purchased by the group.

It should be noted that this China.taobao.com project was needed as a way to make progress in applying e-commerce to agricultural goods, but it also was an experiment in restructuring the entire supply chain of agricultural goods. The way the halls were managed by three integrated entities meant that the advantages of each one could be put to good use. Government could apply its advantages in supervisory regulation by being the one to endorse product certification regarding food safety. That is, it could ensure compliance with quality standards of food products. Service operators could promote and publicize the specialties of their own local areas and improve the systems that serviced the supply chain for agricultural goods. The Taobao platform could set up an agricultural products database and a domain for managing vendors. On the basis of its overall traffic, it could draw flow into the distribution of agricultural products via a greater use of e-commerce.

From a certain perspective, you could say that these three, in addition to the online stores dealing in agricultural goods, formed the main entities for also growing e-commerce via China.taobao.com. More important, their efforts to restructure and develop the supply chain were an indication of future trends in applying e-commerce to agricultural goods.

1. China.taobao.com Helped to Consolidate the Industry

The local China.taobao.com spurred the growth of a more concentrated supply chain. Industry consolidation is happening in essentially all fields of global industry, but it is particularly important when it comes to developing agriculture.

Classical British economist Marshall was one of the first people to describe the phenomenon of industry consolidation. He tied this to the theory of differentiation of industries. He believed that externalities were the primary cause of industry consolidation. Industry consolidation could allow enterprises to enjoy the benefits of externalities and the economies of scale that resulted from the common influence of technology diffusion, professional personnel, and investment in intermediate products. French economist Perroux pointed out that the theory of maximum growth is helpful in explaining the phenomenon of consolidation. He pointed out that as industries consolidated, a dominant industry served as core but had a linked and spreading or involving effect on other industries.

This attracted other resources into the sphere of consolidation, stimulating further economic growth in that area.

Similar effects can be seen in China. Although China.taobao.com focused mainly on selling agricultural goods via the Internet, the growth of these sales also helped to consolidate the industry and spur regional economic development. We can get a glimpse of this from the example of Sui Chang. Sui Chang County is located in the southwestern part of Zhejiang. A mountainous topography covers 8.83 percent of the region's total land area, and this unique natural environment has resulted in a number of high-end Sui Chang specialties, including various mountain-grown teas and vegetables that are famous both inside and outside China. People started selling these products on the Taobao platform in 2005, but it was done in a fairly incidental and ineffective way. To spur industry consolidation and use the advantages of a group to develop local e-commerce for agricultural goods, the Party Commission of Sui Chang County, in conjunction with the Bureau of Commerce and Industry and several local entities, set up the Sui Chang County Internet Association in 2010. This association positioned itself as a service entity. It was mutually interactive and self-governing. Its aim was to realize information sharing and mutual resource assistance among member stores of the network and product providers.

In order to find larger markets for Sui Chang's agricultural products, the government of Sui Chang County cooperated with the Alibaba Group. In January 2013, it opened China.taobao.com Sui Chang. The operator of this platform was the Sui Chang County Internet Association. This platform primarily displays specialties produced in Sui Chang and attracts already existing Sui Chang online stores in as "residents." It has adopted the concept of "staying warm together as a group" and also has been able to take advantage of industry consolidation in spurring the development of the region's economy.

Data indicate that between January and August 2013, after China.taobao.com Sui Chang went online, its average monthly sales volume was much higher than the volume of all stores in the previous year (Figure 4.2). Internet consumers can purchase any specialty product produced in Sui Chang by entering the Sui Chang platform. At the same time, this concentrated approach to e-commerce has been extremely effective in spurring local economic growth. The gross domestic product

(GDP) of Sui Chang County has gone from 2.6 billion RMB in 2004 to an astonishing 7.67 billion RMB in 2013. The percentage of Internet-based retail sales to total retail sales has gone from 2.91 to 9.42 percent. The percentage of Internet sales volume to GDP has gone from 0.58 to 2.39 percent (Figure 4.3). E-commerce has become an important force behind economic growth in Sui Chang County.

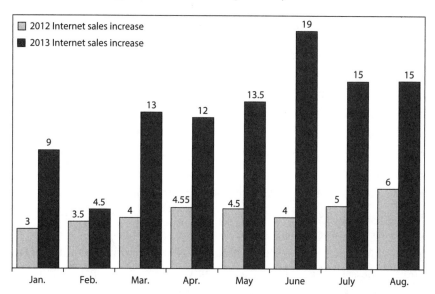

FIGURE 4.2 *Volume of Internet-based sales after the Sui Chang platform went online compared with 2012 (unit = 100 RMB)*

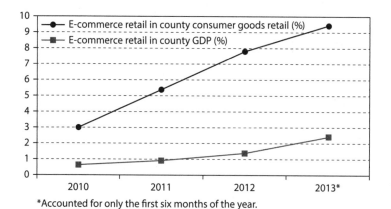

*Accounted for only the first six months of the year.

FIGURE 4.3 *Comparison between the share that Sui Chang e-commerce retail sales hold in terms of total GDP versus the share held in total retail sales of consumer goods*

China.taobao.com not only has spurred the concentrated development of e-commerce, but it also has facilitated the innovation and growth of an e-commerce group type of supply chain. German economist Rolf Sternberg[4] conducted research on industry concentrations in three geographic areas of Germany and discovered that there was a very strong internal inclination or link among the group of manufacturing companies, suppliers, competitors, and research institutions in each area. The growth of the entire group served to stimulate supply-chain innovations.

Although Sternberg was the first person to suggest this concept of group-style supply chains, the concept also was formally proposed within China by Dr. Li Jizi in 2006. He combined the theory of industrial groups and supply-chain theory and incorporated the effects of Internet development. As the market becomes one cohesive unit and the Internet develops, regional industrial groups and their supply chains will work in both horizontal and vertical coordination with a range of enterprises and thereby enjoy an advantage in market competition. Enterprises within the group will both compete with and cooperate with others in the group. They will share in the advantageous links of their own self-value chains while at the same time enjoying the advantageous links of other manufacturers and businesses. This will play a role in developing new products more quickly, as well as enabling dominance in new markets.

The supply-chain management and innovations of group-style e-commerce can be seen on China.taobao.com. In the Sui Chang platform, the Sui Chang County Internet Association has organized more than 30 training events of various sizes at which more than 3,000 attendees have received training. The purpose has been to prevent any problems from affecting the entire supply chain of the process, from sourcing resources to organizing Internet products to selling. At the same time, the association also has helped suppliers (such as cooperatives, agricultural households, and so on) to do research and development (R&D) on new products and has improved the success rate of these new products in the market. This kind of training and cooperation have directly propelled the development of e-commerce group supply chains.

---

[4]Rolf Sternberg, "Innovative Linkages and the Region-Theoretical Assumption vs. Empirical evidence." 1953. The paper is cited in an article posted on web.cenet.org.cn/web/kfyj/index .php3?file=detail.php3&nowdir=&id=19012&detauil=1.

By June 2013, among 1,473 Sui Chang online stores, 164 were dedicated solely to supply, and 41 were solely providing services, including shipping, express delivery, banking, operations, photography, and website design and creation. The innovative group-supply-chain system that gradually formed within Sui Chang County not only provided a greater number of jobs for both urban and rural residents but also persuaded more people to take up e-commerce as a profession. As a result, various forms of e-commerce began to flourish, which made the entire ecosystem healthier and also increased group formation within the supply chain.

2. China.taobao.com Helped to Restructure the Supply Chain and Overcame Situations in Which Smaller Farming Households Were Excluded from the Business

This area relates to the issue of supermarkets versus small farmers. Research has shown that restructuring and consolidating the supply chain are conducive to improving efficient trade of agricultural products. In 2002, Dutch scholar Gigler and colleagues[5] defined restructuring the agricultural products supply chain as improving and consolidating each link in that chain to minimize costs and achieve greater harmonization of the whole process. Quite a few countries have been trying to improve their agricultural products supply chains through policy design and corporate planning. Through strategic alliances, contractual forms of cooperation, and joint ventures, they are trying to take the industry in a vertically integrated direction.

Since 1995, the Chinese government has adopted policy measures designed to promote the restructuring and growth of the supply chain of agricultural products in order to build a wholesale market system and to make the wholesale market more "corporatized."[6] It has been fostering professional associations, forging rural brokering teams, and cultivating the growth of leading ("dragon-headed") enterprises. The government has confirmed the legal standing of farmers professional cooperatives. It

---

[5] J. K. Gigler et al., "On Optimization of Agri-Chains by Dynamic Programming." *European Journal of Operational Research* 139(3):613–625, 2002.
[6] Translator's note: That is, more run by corporations as opposed to government entities.

has tried to optimize the regional distribution of agricultural products by promoting such concepts as "one township, one industry" and "one village, one product." The goal is to achieve an optimized restructuring of the supply chain of agricultural commodities and to improve benefits to all the entities involved.

Both developed and developing countries have seen the swift growth of supermarkets. Along with this development, more and more consumers are purchasing fresh produce from modern retail stores, including such supermarkets. Supermarkets and other large-scale retail outlets are regarded as a driving force for optimizing and restructuring agricultural product supply chains. In this context, in 2008, China's Ministry of Commerce proposed the concept of linking up agriculture with supermarkets. It began an experiment to have farmers interface directly with supermarkets.

Behind this supermarket revolution lies another issue that needs to be explored, however, namely, the issue of whether or not farming households are in fact in danger of being marginalized by the process. Although there is still some controversy over this issue, the fact is that in such countries as South Africa and Nicaragua, in which supermarkets dominate the agricultural commodity supply chain, small-scale farms have been excluded from the list of suppliers. Small farmers in fact have very little chance of supplying goods to supermarkets. The reason for this is that as competition becomes ever more intense and consumers become more demanding, enterprises have ever more stringent purchasing requirements on the agricultural goods they purchase. Through vertical integration, they are gradually forging value chains with very high standards. Another aspect of this is that small farming households are not suited to the development trends of agricultural product supply chains because of problems relating to public services, funding, policy, management, and other considerations. They are therefore withdrawing from the agricultural commodity supply chain. In the process of restructuring and maximizing the situation via a policy of linking up farmers and supermarkets, therefore, such things as quality control and safety standards may well limit the degree to which small farming households can participate.

The emergence of China.taobao.com platforms helps to avoid the problems that small farming households face in such situations. The same quality-control requirements do not exist on the platforms in the way that they do in the supply chains for agricultural goods that are dominated by supermarkets. The demands made on enterprises coming onto the platforms are also not very high. Any seller of agricultural commodities who meets certain rules and regulations can enter into business on the platforms and market best-seller specialty products. Every year in Sui Chang County, a large number of young people decide to take up e-commerce as a profession. Because of this, the variety of agricultural products being sold on the Internet in Sui Chang is constantly increasing. Nuts, tea, and even fresh produce are now taking up a considerable percentage of sales. Starting in 2013, moreover, the trade in fresh fruits and vegetables increased to the point where it now is the leading product in Sui Chang's e-commerce business (Table 4.2).

TABLE 4.2 *A list of agricultural products sold on the Sui Chang e-commerce platform. This illustration shows the diversification of agricultural products sold via the Sui Chang e-commerce platform between 2010 and the first half of 2013. As can be seen from the table, the Sui Chang e-commerce platform has been extending the variety of local products that it sells on a retail basis.*

YEAR	MAJOR CONSUMER GOODS SOLD
2010	Traditional neutrinos goods, nuts, fresh foods
2011	Traditional neutrinos goods, nuts, grain-oil-tried foods, house plants
2012	Traditional neutrinos goods, nuts, grain-oil-tried foods, house plants, tea-alcohol-other soft drinking stuff
2013*	Traditional neutrinos goods, nuts, grain-oil-tried foods, house plants, tea-alcohol-other soft drinking stuff, fresh foods

*Accounted for only the first six months of the year

The Sui Chang County Internet Association has set up an agricultural commodities retail platform on the Internet that has provided a fast-track channel for agricultural producers, including cooperatives, as a kind of "e-stimulus." Local cooperatives have sources of high-quality products but lack the experience and personnel to deal with e-commerce. By connecting with retail outlets on the Internet, they have a fairly low-cost way of selling their goods. This has vastly accelerated the e-commerce dealings of traditional companies that process agricultural goods.

3. China.taobao.com Platforms Are Helping to Ensure Consumer Safety Guarantees for Agricultural Commodities

Agricultural commodities must go through many links in traveling from the field to the table, including production, processing, shipping, and so on. At each stage in this process, they are subject to the risk of food safety considerations. The more complex the supply chain of foodstuffs, the more frequently food safety issues arise. This has led to a problem that the entire globe is facing, namely, the public loss of confidence in food safety. To ensure that the trade in agricultural goods remains alive and well, one of the main considerations has been to create conditions that guarantee food safety.

China.taobao.com platforms are putting all their effort into ensuring the food safety of products that consumers purchase on the Internet. Relatively speaking, however, Alibaba has much less authority in this regard than local governments, who are responsible for the strictness of regulatory requirements on local specialty products. Because of this, Taobao and local governments are cooperating with one another to enable local governments to regulate the safety guarantees for local specialty products and then put their endorsements on products to guarantee food safety.

For example, the county government of Sui Chang has promised to increase food safety regulation in terms of personnel, budgets, policies, and space in order to expedite the development of local e-commerce. In 2013, moreover, Sui Chang County invested 3 million RMB to build an agricultural commodities testing center in an all-out effort to ensure the safety of foodstuffs. After the Sui Chang platform went online, a set of control mechanisms was implemented to ensure quality control. These are described as government + farming households + cooperatives + Internet store associations + Taobao platform. The Sui Chang platform is also beginning to establish standards for the processing of local specialty products. It is using such methods as onsite examination, ensuring real-name certification, spot testing of processes and filing case records, ensuring tracking of sources, alliances with insurance companies, and requiring the deposit of a guarantee. This is to ensure the safety of all three links in the process: presale, during sale, and postsale. Within China, therefore, China.taobao.com platforms have forged a whole new food safety mechanism for the agricultural commodities supply chain.

Outsourcing the Logistics and Cooperative Innovations in Supply Chains

Given the development of information technologies, it is becoming harder and harder for companies to deal with market competition by means of either vertical or horizontal integration. Instead, division of labor and cooperation in the supply chain have gradually become the keys to how companies work together.

Cooperation in the supply chain occurs when companies share the same goals and are pursuing mutual interests. To arrive at win-win solutions, a portion of the supply-chain process is granted to other enterprises. Cooperative supply-chain arrangements can achieve a number of objectives, including the introduction of new technologies, the development of new markets, an expanded scope of goods and services, and economies of scale. Such arrangements can help to lower the inefficiencies that may be caused by integrated administrative control when a company operates solely on its own and becomes overstaffed or when a market stops working properly. They can thereby reduce unnecessary risk.

On the Alibaba platform, supply-chain cooperation among e-commerce enterprises is extremely dynamic. Essentially all Internet stores outsource the circulation of products to third parties to handle all logistics. This kind of division of labor and cooperation as applied to the supply chain not only improves the efficiency of e-commerce operations but also creates a positively reinforcing cycle within the Ali economic ecosystem.

Furthering Specialization and Outsourcing Logistics:
To improve its ability to harmonize logistics and the functions performed by logistics, at the very outset, Alibaba struck up strategic cooperative relationships with a range of services within China, including the postal service and various delivery companies. By means of unified ordering systems and improved service standards for the delivery of packages, Alibaba upgraded the experience of consumers who buy things on the Internet. The strategic cooperative agreements between Alibaba and a whole list of delivery companies were a way to achieve a division of labor and also mitigate the consequences of self-interested policies in the initial period

of such a division of labor. As time went on, however, the efficiencies of both the platform and logistics companies improved with experience. Standards for shipping platform-generated goods improved, as well as the skills and actual execution of delivery companies. The supply chain relating to the delivery of e-commerce goods developed and fostered innovation in a beneficially reinforcing cycle.

The manner in which Alibaba pushed forward development of its logistics supply-chain management system was not in response to any one company's mistakes or problems. Instead, it was to resolve issues that led to some products not being saleable on the Internet because of problems with supply-chain logistics. To deal with these issues, Alibaba forged agreements with logistics companies (goods circulation companies) on such things as the design of order forms, handling procedures, customer responses, and so on. Together these partners came up with simple standards to be used by all. This spurred the corresponding development of the logistics industry[7] and improved overall management of enterprise supply chains.

These changes and improvements in the overall environment for logistics systems, in turn, stimulated further refinements in the division of labor among logistics companies. The result was a better operating environment for the logistics industry as a whole as well as for Internet operators. For example, constraints relating to cold-storage facilities had prevented frozen goods from being sold directly on the Internet. On July 2, 2013, Tmall announced that it would be providing cold-storage services as part of an experimental program in delivering fresh and frozen foods. Coverage would start in Shanghai and then spread to 26 cities in which e-commerce was particularly thriving, including Beijing, Shanghai, Guangzhou, Shenzhen, Hangzhou, and Tianjin. By relying on business-to-business (B2B) cold-storage city-to-city shipping, Tmall would go "the last kilometer" in realizing delivery to homes. To the greatest extent possible, it was shortening the supply chain and reducing the time it took to get fresh fruits and vegetables from field to table.

---

[7]Translator's note: Western readers should know that goods circulation prior to reform in China was organized by different levels of government. Logistics, as Westerners know it, did not exist. To a certain extent, this is still true in some industries—which is why Alibaba's innovations in this area are so important. In restructuring how business is run, Alibaba is really contributing to establishing China's new logistic system.

*Refining the Division of Labor and Innovation in Cloud-Warehousing
and Cloud-Logistics*

The concept of detailed division of labor can be traced back at least to
380 BC, when Plato described how specialization and the division of
labor could improve social welfare and also how the division of labor
was the foundation of a monetized market. Adam Smith's classic, *The
Wealth of Nations*, gives us the most profound insight into the subject,
however. Smith believed that the division of labor represented the most
powerful engine driving advances in the forces of production. Any skills
used by different sectors of the economy and any highly refined labor
force in fact represented a division of labor.

The theory of the division of labor was first applied to the sphere of
international trade. Various schools of thought explaining the phenomenon of a division of international labor have gradually developed by a
list of economists. These theories and economists include the theory of
comparative advantage by David Ricardo, the theory of factor propor-
tions by Heckscher and Ohiln, and the doctrine of cooperative international division of labor by Kiyoshi Kojima. With the rise of transborder
analysis, such neoclassical scholars as Rosen, Becke, Xang, and Yew-
Kwang Ng came up with further ideas. They attempted to rethink many
theories in the field of economics in their belief that the division of labor
improved and evolved with higher efficiencies in business transactions.
According to their analyses, such efficiencies allowed for higher levels
of labor division. The division of labor within enterprises carved out its
own independent standing, which then allowed for greater cooperation
with other enterprises. The resulting further division of labor allowed for
higher production efficiencies.

Division of labor theory also can explain the phenomenon of outsourcing on the Alibaba platform and the outsourcing of the supply chain
of e-commerce enterprises. They are the consequence of a division of labor
and improved efficiencies in business transactions.

In terms of the supply chain of e-commerce, the three great processes,
or *flow streams*, are the flow of information, the flow of money, and the
flow of goods. These are the foundation on which the whole circulatory
process of e-commerce functions. With specific regard to Alibaba, the
company's B2B platforms and the Taobao platform focus on information

flows, whereas Alipay focuses on money flows. Because it has no business focusing specifically on the flow of goods, however, this link in the process is completed by offline logistics companies. Buyers and sellers process information on supply and demand as provided by the Alibaba platform, but the actual transactions and links in the process of circulating goods are handled by others. Having different entities handle the division of labor among the three different flows of the supply chain is itself a way of meeting the demands of an agreement-based division of labor theory.

Japanese economist Kiyoshi Kojima analyzed the process by which production is specialized. He pointed out that relying exclusively on the principle of comparative advantage has the potential to lead to monopolies and overconsolidation in the process of greater division of labor. This then affects the stable development of a harmonious form of division of labor and trade. Specialized production therefore should abide by the principle of an agreement form of the division of labor. By agreement, certain parties should focus on certain goods and services while granting the right to deal in other goods and services to other parties. This then enables a tremendous reduction in the production costs of all goods and services. It plays a role in improving the efficiencies of the division of labor and in expanding the volume of business transactions.

The ways in which Alibaba uses the advantages of its own database platform are also helpful in refining the division of labor in e-commerce and in developing the e-commerce supply chain. Cloud warehousing and cloud logistics use the comparative advantages of division-of-labor specialization and the ongoing innovations in logistics systems.

Classical English economist David Ricardo believed that a division of labor does not necessarily have to be built on the basis of absolute advantage. By being based on comparative advantage, it can still stimulate the growth of trade and the growth of economies. The natural endowment in factors theory points to the sources of comparative advantage even more directly in that both trading partners focus on the relative abundance of factors in either goods or services. By mutual exchange of more abundant factors, they can mobilize the advantages of specialized division of labor and obtain comparative interests in the process.

In contrast to third-party logistics companies, Alibaba enjoys comparative advantage when it comes to e-commerce data. Using its own data advantage to cooperate with logistics parties and to exchange related services is a process fully in accord with the requirements of natural endowment in factors theory. Based on this, the use of cloud warehousing and cloud logistics is a new approach to resolving problems related to the e-commerce supply chain and the handling and shipping of goods.

Cloud warehousing is a new warehouse-management strategy. Under the existing model, e-commerce companies possess their own (virtual) warehouses. Once they receive orders, they send goods in their warehouses to the warehouse of a third-party logistics enterprise, which, in turn, ships the goods to customers. This greatly increases the superfluous links in the process and extends the time required for delivery. When alliance-type models are used for third-party arrangements in particular, goods are transshipped several times, adding to the problem. In contrast, the cloud warehousing model consolidates all resources of society. Alibaba's warehousing system provides an open socialized (mass) service platform for buyers and logistics enterprises, as well as for other independent e-commerce websites. Looking over the long term, as it matures, cloud warehousing will provide an extremely convenient and efficient way to improve the shipping and handling of commercial goods for both consumers and businesses.

In concert with cloud warehousing, Alibaba's *cloud logistics* plan is currently an experimental model that lies between direct operations and the alliance model of how to handle logistics. It carries out management in the direct-operations mode but at the same time provides a platform of consolidated information for public use. It works by combining oceans of information, categorizing it, and sharing it between the enterprise and the customer. In ensures that different companies' products are divided up according to order information within the warehousing system and shipped out efficiently.

A combination of cloud warehousing and cloud logistics can effectively coordinate information flows relating to the various links in logistics and the actual shipping of goods. By controlling the core links in the entire process—that is, warehousing links—noncore links related to shipping can be outsourced to break through logistic bottlenecks.

Given China's current state of logistics systems, which are imperfect, this Alibaba strategy has far-reaching significance. By being in charge of the core forces of goods circulation and thereby being able to improve the entire supply chain, once China's goods circulation system does improve, then outsourcing nonessential links to others will allow Alibaba to find effective ways to break through logistics bottlenecks. In terms of the entire business of e-commerce, this will enable Alibaba to play the role of navigator for key "dragon-headed" enterprises as their businesses grow.

Because of this, cloud computing and cloud logistics will be able to meet the demands of e-commerce enterprises, logistics enterprises, and normal users in terms of the information required as goods are being shipped. It will detour around the unnecessary time and space requirements that stand between production factors and the ultimate consumer. It will handle the information requirements of all the different links generated by the processes of manufacturing, shipping, packaging, packing, warehousing, processing, reassembling, and final delivery. By going through a logistics information platform, information can be transmitted quickly and accurately to everyone on the goods circulation chain. This includes production enterprises, logistics companies, agents, and customers. The process will allow for improvements and ongoing innovations in the management systems that apply to the logistics end of e-commerce enterprises.

Production, Segmentations, and Innovations in Servicing

In addition to the way in which the entire logistics chain is independent of Alibaba, as e-commerce has developed and data have become more open, quite a few e-commerce merchants are also outsourcing many things to third-party service companies such as Independent Software Vendors (ISV). These companies handle such things as the design and refurbishing of stores, the completion of certain operations, photography, data analysis, and so on. Such e-commerce service companies are emerging as the result of a finer division of labor in the industry but also as a result of the need to outsource fragmented or disaggregated production and services.

Going from Being "Big C" to Being an E-commerce Service Company:
The Innovations of the E-commerce Vendor xltt.taobao.com

The Internet brands–management company established by Feng Jieqi is an e-commerce company that is engaged solely in providing services to other e-commerce companies. Many people may not immediately understand what this means. One way to explain it is this: after May 20, 2011, when Lamborgini registered on Taobao Commerce City, it made a single sale priced at 6.488 million RMB. This was the single largest transaction in the history of Taobao. The behind-the-scenes planner of this entire episode and the manager of the entire process was the Internet branding company founded by a woman named Feng Jieqi.

When Feng Jieqi was a college student, like most young women, she liked to surf Taobao and buy things online. She would recommend things that she liked to other people. As these occasions became more frequent, she began to think of starting an online store herself. Based on accurate positioning of her idea and on hard work, she quickly became a prize-winning seller, crowned with such titles as "triple-crown winner" and "five-star winner." Her company, xltt.taobao.com, gradually led the ranks of Taobao's cosmetics brands.

As online competition increased to a white heat, however, Feng Jieqi confronted pressure to transform her model, as did most cosmetics stores. The key dilemma was whether she should continue to be a channel for selling many other brands or should she become an e-commerce service provider herself. As she was considering her options, the Taobao platform held a Taobao convention entitled "Century Cooperation" in August 2010 aimed at lining up partners with whom it intended to cooperate for a century. This gave xltt.taobao.com the chance to become a Taobao Partner (TP).

Services for e-commerce operations include daily operations, receiving customer orders, brand promotion, shipping of goods, and so on. If a service company is able to encompass all operations and take on all procedures, it is regarded as something like a "tugboat for the market." Based on more than five years of experience in operating a Taobao store, Feng Jieqi set up a company called the Shanghai Internet Luxury Brands Management Company, Ltd., or Shanghai Luxury for short. This became one of the few first "tugboats" in the market.

Starting a company is never smooth sailing all the way, and the newly established Shanghai Luxury was no exception. Although innumerable trials had made xltt.taobao.com a TP, customers did not appear in droves. Just as Feng Jieqi was worrying about how to promote her company, Maybelline came knocking on the door. This company became Shanghai Luxury's first customer.

Maybelline is a well-known cosmetics brand. It had long tried to use e-commerce to promote and market its beauty products. It had cooperated with a well-known advertising company to do this, using such management services as website design and operations, but actual sales were not impressive. Feng Jieqi also had retailed Maybelline products online. Based on the sterling reputation of xltt.taobao.com, she had served as an agent for the company and had sold a considerable amount of its products. When Maybelline started looking for a partner, Feng Jieqi used her acute sense of the market and immediately saw a business opportunity. She went to the homepage of the official flagship Maybelline store and began to make a number of constructive recommendations on how to improve it based on her many years of experience in buying cosmetics herself on Taobao. A senior person at Maybelline listened to her recommendations and immediately invited her to agent its store operations. Feng Jieqi did not disappoint the company. The first day after the revised Maybelline flagship store uploaded its new site, it completed 50 major transactions, which improved its Internet-based sales results considerably.

After this, Feng Jieqi resolved to carry through with her idea of becoming an e-commerce service provider. Holding to the idea of having a core business in designing brand strategies, she added two "wings" to the business, namely, creative design and services that enabled the "e-ification" of companies, that is, making companies e-commerce ready. In single-site fashion, she provided "tugboat" services for brand-name companies that involved selling, customers, and logistics. She became a specialized e-commerce company dealing in all-round "tugboat" services. In the short space of a few months, Shanghai Luxury had provided services to dozens of well-known brands in China and had assisted in the creation of numerous e-commerce "miracles."

Production Segmentations and The Emergence of
E-commerce Service Companies

The transformation of xltt.taobao.com from being a "Big C" to being a company that services e-commerce was one manifestation of the thinking behind a fragmented production process. It was very much in alignment with the economic development trend of outsourcing services.

Since the 1990s, the *fragmented production model* arose out of the experience of international trade trends. The scholars first proposing the concept, Jones, Kierzkowski, and Lurong,[8] described it as "separating out the production process and deploying it in different spaces." Based on this, American economists Dixit and Steiglitz, Helpman, and Krugman[9] analyzed the levels of fragmentation from various perspectives, including monopoly competition, scale economies, demand, and the size of the market. Meanwhile, other economists, such as Falvey, Shaked, and Sutton,[10] analyzed the vertical division of labor in a disaggregated production model from the perspective of factor endowment, technological advance, product improvement, and so on. All these approaches involved disaggregating or fragmenting the production processes of enterprises and then positioning them in different spaces in order to achieve cost advantages and economic efficiencies. All these approaches were helpful in explaining the disaggregated production activities and the outsourcing of services in the economy.

Whether or not a company chooses to use its own production in the supply chain or to outsource its needs depends on how transaction costs compare with production costs. If internal production costs are higher than external transaction costs, the enterprise will tend to opt for outside suppliers. It will not undertake integrated production all by itself. The

---

[8]R. Jones, H. Kierzkowski., and C. Lurong, "What Does Evidence Tell Us about Fragmentation and Outsourcing?" *International Review of Economics and Finance* 14:305–316, 2005.

[9]A. Dixit and J. Stiglitz, "Monopolistic Competition and Optimum Product Diversity." *American Economic Review* 67:297–300, 1977; E. Helpman, "A Simple Theory of International Trade with Multinational Corporations." *Journal of Political Economy* 92:451–477, 1984; E. Helpman and P. Krugman, *Market Structure and ForeignTrade.* Cambridge, MA: MIT Press, 1985.

[10]R. Falvey, "Commercial Policy and Interindustry Trade." *Journal of International Economies* 11:95–111, 1981; A. Shaked and J. Sutton, "Relaxing Price Competition Through Product Differentiation." *Review of Economic Studies* 49:1–13, 1982.

reason enterprises choose a supply-chain management model that splits things out instead of integrating them internally is that outside suppliers can handle the investment in this part of the process more efficiently. For people running companies, the core lesson when it comes to managing the supply chain is to ensure that relationships among suppliers are handled properly so that the advantages of each resource that is used serve to improve the efficiency of the supply chain as a whole. This then enables the company overall to meet market competition and serve the requirements of consumers.

On the Alibaba platform, the fact that numerous e-commerce merchants outsource services to third-party service providers is also the consequence of weighing their transaction costs against the costs of production. Transaction costs are pervasive throughout daily life and production. However, in the school of *New Institutional Economics,* as its founder Ronald Coase saw it, traditional economics and organization theory operate under the hypothesis of ideal conditions. They completely overlook the existence of transaction costs. Coase felt that the most important thing about transaction costs is that they help an enterprise determine whether or not cooperation is more of a surefire thing—whether taking advantage of cooperation will lower the risk of operating activities or not. To lower risk, the enterprise must be willing to go through some kind of authority (such as another enterprise) to help it allocate resources.

American economist Oliver E. Williamson summed up the decisive elements in transaction costs succinctly. He felt that two different kinds of considerations determine transaction costs. The first is *transaction factors,* including uncertainties, the use of assets for a single purpose, frequency of transactions, and so on. The second is *human factors,* which can be summed up as the limited rationality of people and their consequent opportunistic psychology. Deciding on transaction factors and the constant revision of contractual terms is determined by the degree to which assets can be used for a sole purpose, to the uncertainties of market exchange, to the frequency of transactions, and to human opportunities. The more inflexible assets are, that is, the greater the degree to which they can be used for one purpose, the greater is the reliance of both sides on the transaction. If one side breaks the contract, this leads to enormous risk for the other side. To avoid this risk, as well as the uncertain market environment owing to opportunism, if both sides in the game adopt trust-ing cooperation, this saves on transaction costs for both sides.

The complexities and volatility of market environments bring uncer-tainty to all transactions and influence the stability of the cooperation of both sides, increasing the risk of breach of contract. Because of this, a trust relationship must be established as either a promise or a contract to reduce the influence of interference by market conditions, as well as changes in consumer preferences, differences in the information both sides have, the degree of trust not being comparable, and so on.

The frequency of transactions is related to the cost of transactions. More frequent transactions imply a greater number of contracts, which necessarily add to the cost of those contracts and the cost of exchanging those contracts. At the same time, however, it reduces the cost per con-tract. Because of incompatible information, different transaction entities may possess different information, which lessens the opportunities for both sides to reach agreement and leads to higher transaction costs.

When transaction costs begin to influence transaction activity, the enterprise may choose to adopt a different form of cooperation, one that is more in line with the needs of the supply chain. To lower transaction costs, after a reduction in forces and a reduction in its levels of structure, an enterprise may find that the market itself is a better substitute for the enterprise in performing certain functions of administrative man-agement. Outsourcing the supply chain is one cooperative method by which the market substitutes for layers of operations in an enterprise. This cooperative method then becomes an agreement relationship based on a joint assumption of risk and mutual sharing of information within the context of a supply chain. Both enterprises share direct goals and common interests. Their aim is to lower inventory levels and the overall costs of the supply chain, to strengthen communications and exchange among members, to preserve the routine nature of handling cooperative relations among enterprises in the supply chain, and thereby to enjoy a better position in the market—that is, greater competitive advantage, better financial conditions, higher-quality goods, higher turnover, better customer satisfaction, and better business results.

Within an e-commerce environment, the reason an e-commerce merchant chooses to outsource certain services to third-party providers and not undertake to do everything itself is also that it wants to save on transaction costs and improve efficiencies in the division of labor. Division of labor has always been the main factor determining growth of the forces of production and social progress. Meanwhile, transaction costs have a decisive influence on the level of the division of labor. A significant issue is how to lower internally generated costs. Externally generated costs are generally inflexible—it is hard to change them—whereas internally generated costs are more artificial. With advances in science and technology, some internally generated transaction costs can be reduced by adopting more advanced technology, renovating systems, and so on. The third-party service providers on the Ali platform are the result of both technological advances in the Internet and the need to reduce internally generated costs.

A survey undertaken by Tmall Commerce City indicates that there are already over 100 e-commerce entities on the Tmall platform that provide outsourcing services to e-commerce companies. Among the 50,000 merchants on Tmall and the 70,000 brands that are registered on the platform, more than 40,000 are considering outsourcing services. One online clothing store, headed by a woman from Henan named Zhang Yanyan, indicates that the use of outsourcing has proven extremely convenient. Internet merchants can outsource almost any part of the entire process. Yanyan personally frequently uses Internet agenting, information systems, and "paying by clicking" software for optimizing the search process. It saves her time and effort and is not expensive.

The degree to which assets can be used for just one function is another important reason that online stores choose to use third-party services. This so-called sole use indicates the degree to which an asset can be shifted to another use and the degree to which this lowers its production value. Highly specialized assets imply a large amount of hidden costs. Once these hidden costs are separated from their original function, their predetermined connection to transactions, they fail to have much value at all. Instead, they can be extremely damaging to the factory or the business, resulting in major losses. In other words, the assets in which a company has invested are not in themselves liquid or marketable. The moment a contract is ended, the investment in that asset is hard to recoup. The original purposes of the investment are hard to shift to something else.

*Roles of Opening the Data in Spurring Innovations Among
E-commerce Service Providers*

As China's largest online sales platform, Alibaba officially announced in 2010 that it would be opening its data to the entire world. Merchants, enterprises, and consumers would be able to enjoy its oceanic amounts of raw data. Given the complexities of the data and security issues surrounding use of the data, Alibaba would carry out this release of data based on certain principles and according to defined levels of data. It called this kind of service the "magical realm of data."

The opening up of data and use of the "magical realm of data" transmitted quite clear innovative signals to the outside world. This is so because the development and competition in e-commerce are highly similar to those of large-scale markets. In the initial stages of market operation, all the market has to do is put order in the ranks of shops, then divide them into categories, and ensure that each shop pays rent, management fees, and so on. As the market matures and competition becomes more intense, and as the market itself begins to manage things more intensively, when each more detailed management system is instituted, it is accompanied by stricter implementation, and a brand effect begins to take hold. After this, the market transitions to all-out competition among brands. By this time, competition is no longer based on how much one has to pay in rent but rather on comparing the value added of each kind of service.

At present, competition in the e-commerce arena has not yet reached the bitter levels of competition in large-scale markets. It has, however, passed beyond the initial stage and entered the ranks of branded competition. The presentation of a policy to open up data to others was a signal that the market had begun to enter the deeper levels of service competition. From materials made public to date, this open-data policy mainly provides the following service functions: it provides data on enterprises from a number of different perspectives, including market research analysis, store analysis, consumer analysis, sales results analysis, and website improvements. This helps enterprises to peruse trends in industry developments at any time and focus on the market shares of brands. It helps them to understand in a timely manner the concerns that consumers have about products so that the market can respond quickly. In an all-around way, from different perspectives, it allows enterprises to understand consumers and carry out highly effective and precisely targeted sales efforts. With no trouble at all, enterprises can see the ranking of brands and the ranking of popular products.

Beyond doubt, the target customer of this open-data service is commercial enterprises. Its design and operation are clearly aimed at this market segment. Commercial enterprises can carry out market strategy analysis based on how they manipulate the open data. They can use actual statistics to support their marketing and product-restructuring efforts—decision makers in enterprises now have actual data on which to base decisions. At the same time, given the various kinds of data in the "magical realm of data," decision makers can basically determine what is most popular and fashionable in the market and thereby propose targeted business operations. The provision of open data, moreover, can stimulate service providers and logistics providers in the supply chain to provide better service. Naturally, as compared with similar data provided by other third-party organizations, the advantage of Alibaba's "magical realm of data" lies in the accuracy and timeliness of the data. The reason is that Alibaba's official data can accurately and in a timely fashion reflect the characteristics of its own enterprise, which gives the data much higher value as a point of reference.

With the opening up of data and the emergence of e-commerce servicing companies, the industry of e-commerce services saw explosive growth. According to statistics provided by the Alibaba Research Institute, in 2012, China's business volume in e-commerce services, the actually completed transaction value, came to around 200 billion RMB. This was an 83 percent increase over the previous year. This supported around 1.2 trillion RMB in Internet-based retail sales and 8.4 trillion RMB in e-commerce transactions altogether. The explosive emergence of all kinds of third-party service companies could be attributed to Alibaba's strategy of mobilizing an open-data policy. Deputy CEO of the Alibaba Group and Director of the Alibaba Research Institute Liang Chunxiao has noted that the market for Internet-based retail services is the fastest-growing component of the China e-commerce services ecosystem. In 2012, transaction volume in this area came to 15.2 billion RMB, an increase of more than 200 percent over the preceding year. This volume was due to having ever more abundant targets for services and ever more diversified ways of providing services, including IT services, guided-purchasing services, operations handling, outsourcing of customer services, training, and so on.

As the deputy CEO of Tmall has explained, "Eighty-five percent of the vendors on the entire Taobao platform are working in coordination with the help of e-commerce service tools." In addition to sales and promotion tools, a number of other services are being provided. Many other third-party servicing companies provide businesses just coming on to the Internet with website design, management services, photography services, customer servicing and order taking, data analysis, logistics, and customer-service training. These e-commerce services companies play two main roles in helping e-commerce enterprises as well as managing their supply chains. First, they use an open e-commerce cloud work platform to provide businesses with deeper levels of third-party applications so that such businesses can have a handle on market demand more quickly. Second, they provide a mobile end-vendor work platform called *Qianniu* for different levels of people in a small or medium-sized vendor organization, including management. This relates to the entire process of the work chain, from products to transactions to selling, membership, human resources, and accounting. It covers all end users, including iPhone, android, cloud cell phones, iPad, and so on. The backup is supported by an e-commerce cloud service called *Jushita*.[11] All these things support the development of a customer supply chain. Finally, targeted at the Tmall and Taobao vendor services platform, depending on their own role, they provide more precise and accurate purchasing guidance and recommendations. The platform carries out multidimensional guided purchasing depending on categories. Considerations include vendor rating level, credit rating, the store's operational links, lines of business, and so on. Based on all considerations, the platform offers custom-made professional services that can precisely meet the needs of vendors.

I am confident that China will have the world's largest e-commerce services industry in the future given this open-data policy and the speed with which services companies are growing. This will help to improve

---

[11]Jushita was founded on July 10, 2012 by Tmall together with Alicloud and Wanwang Network for establishing an open working platform for e-commerce. It brings together the entire resources of the Alibaba Group to achieve "cloud+SAAS model", and create unlimited business value through resources and data sharing and interoperability. SAAS is abbreviation of software-as-a-service.

the operating results of e-commerce and the supply-chain-management systems of enterprises.

Demand Analysis: Consumer-to-Business (C2B) and Online-to-Offline O2O Innovations

Prior to the appearance of demand-chain management, traditional supply-chain-management models mainly went as follows: branded company (production R&D company) → all levels of agents → all retail stores → consumers. This kind of supply-chain system, which was dominated by the branded company (or production company), was the prime culprit of high inventories.

The reason was that in the process of transmitting information along the chain, the information was often delayed or faced a whiplash effect and became distorted. That is, information about the actual demand of the ultimate customer in the supply chain was constantly exaggerated as it traveled up the chain, leading to overstocked inventories of the enterprise and superfluous production. It happened as follows: first, the retailer estimated consumer demand and ordered goods from the wholesaler. The wholesaler ordered goods from the distributor. On the one hand, this generated delays. On the other hand, it also exaggerated quantities. To ensure that customers' full needs were met, and to deal with uncertainties, the wholesaler was forced to have more on hand in inventory than the retailer. The result was that information about demand was constantly exaggerated as information was transmitted, and the information became severely distorted. The lack of fidelity to original figures led to high costs for the entire supply-chain system and low operating efficiencies.

A second reason for high inventories is that communications between the vendors and suppliers took place at periodic trade shows. In this process, agents often would use local sales estimates in determining order quantities. However, because the supply-chain links were not effectively supported by IT, market information often would be inaccurate. Fairly large disparities occurred between forecasts of what the market might be and the actual needs of consumers. Production and final sales then began to move along different tracks, causing severe problems.

In China, many industries still rely on retailers downstream to provide them with information on market demand and not on the end-user consumers themselves. This kind of supply-chain model, which relies on feelings and individual experience to select products and order goods, is one of the causes of China's overstocked inventories. To reduce inventories and realize the goal of being lean and less asset encumbered, many e-commerce businesses are fixing their sights on the growth of individualized, custom-made production and flexible production.

From Clothing to Furniture: The Innovation of Individualized, Custom-Made and Flexible Production

Case Study 1: IWODE

IWODE was founded in 2006 by a Chinese student who had studied in England and returned to found an e-commerce business focused on custom-made clothing. All clothing companies dream of making only as much product as customers need and having as little inventory as possible. They hope to do this by having a greater brand spillover price effect. Nevertheless, creating a development model by which clothing companies have zero inventory and light assets has been very slow in coming. The main reason is that there is always a conflict between individualized and flexible production to satisfy customers and standardized production that can operate on any kind of scale.

Case Study 2: "All Handmade," Yan Huajie and Story-Pitaowang

The handmade customized products of Story-Pitaowang are a classic example of both agile production and individualized made-to-order. "Each stitch tells your own story," as the company says, and this motto also describes the desire of entrepreneurs to create something new. Unlike other entrepreneurs, Yan Huajie created this brand to satisfy a need that was not being met—she could not buy handmade cases for cell phones in the market. This unmet demand also provoked her to implement her innovative ideals. Unlike the usual made-to-order business, Story-Pitaowang's individualized made-to-order business is not limited to a few different products in a few different colors.

Depending on the consumer's choice of patterns, leather materials, and accessories, the company can provide more than 20,000 different types of goods in different combinations. Its offerings include a range of products that goes from phone covers and covers for notebook computers, to wallets, to leather bags—the possibilities include anything one might need.

Creating leather items that are unique to the individual consumer is Story-Pitaowang's specialty. Once consumers select a particular pattern or design, they can then choose colors from more than 60 leather samples, as well as the straps or handles, the words they want embossed on it, and so on. Consumers can satisfy their own needs as well as their own sense of aesthetics. The company has an 80 percent rate of returning customers due to this extreme focus on individualized made-to-order products. Many of these returning customers either use items for themselves or give them as gifts to others, which contributes to the company's word-of-mouth reputation.

Case Study 3: Wang Xiaorao and Shizuniao's "Free Custom-Made" Business

The brand known as Shizuniao (translated as "the bird from ancient time"), created by Wang Xiaorao, takes individualized custom-made production to a new level. It enables the consumer to reach his or her ultimate desires in custom-made design. As someone who studied dance and the arts from an early age, Xiao Xiaorao has her own ideas about individualized custom-made design. She divides the market into two segments: deep-seated custom-made and half-ready-made. The so-called deep-seated variety of custom-made requires a custom-made approach throughout, starting from the selection of materials. High-end women's clothing, for example, requires a degree of quality that is completely above and beyond the demands of the public at large. The finished product has to impart a unique taste which belongs solely to that individual consumer. In contrast, half-ready-made products are created on the basis of already-made things that then have individualized elements added to them. From this perspective, the mainstream of ready-made shops on Taobao is currently providing half-ready-made items. As consumer demand becomes ever more "rational," however, deep-seated custom-made products will become the mainstream. This will then require a restructuring of resources and firms in the e-commerce business, given all the various steps in the process of creating "completely made-to-order." Such restructuring will include the materials, items used in the assembly of complete products, partially assembled components, and so on. Clearly, this kind of deep-seated production cannot be done on a massive scale, which is what allowed Wang Xiaorao to recognize a business opportunity. The brand she established, Shizuniao, aims at the goal of creating greater freedom in custom-made choices by disassembling the production process into different segments.

Case Study 4: Shangpin Zhaipei: Custom-Made Furniture of the New-Homeowners Network

Shangpin Zhaipei is a furniture company that was founded in 2004 with the aim of creating a completely new kind of production process. (The company name means "top quality furniture that fits your home.") It combines an ability to let consumers themselves design things digitally with the use of the internet for sale of the actual furniture. Its production uses software in the upstream process of computer-controlled parts manufacturing, but the model extends to the downstream process of how consumers experience the results. The moment this digitally controlled custom-made furniture concept came out, it began to influence the entire home-furniture industry. Despite the severe contraction of the home-furniture industry overall in 2008, due to the financial crisis, Shangpin Zhaipei maintained its strong performance, and the company continued to grow at a rapid pace.

In early 2009, the opening of the New-Home Network of Shangpin Zhaipei marked the prologue of the impact of e-commerce on the furniture industry. Sales of home furnishings shifted from media portal platforms to e-commerce-based platforms. The strong alliance between Shangpin Zhaipei and Alibaba led media to declare that the age of web-based direct sales of made-to-order furniture had arrived.

This signified that consumers nationwide could now easily and quickly access the service of made-to-order furniture via the New-Home Network. In the process they also could enjoy a 40 percent discount off the normal market price.

The Importance of Analyzing Demand with Regard to Individualized Made-to-Order Production and "Agile" Production

In 2007 the American scholars U. Jüttner, M. Christopher, and S. Baker (in "Demand Chain Management Integrating Marketing and Supply Chain Management," *Industrial Marketing Management* 36, 2007, pp. 377–392) noted that private companies are paying more and more attention to the diversified demand of consumers. Nevertheless the existing supply- chain theory cannot meet the needs of these companies, since they now must evaluate new ways to organize production and management. This means we must construct a completely new supply-chain system that is aimed at satisfying the individualized demands of consumers. The new demand management that is being introduced seems to have grabbed hold of the key points of coordination with traditional supply-chain markets. Demand management can provide companies with a new form of supply-chain design that is based on consumer-generated demand of a uniquely defined sort. It is in this context that we now have the emergence of what is being called demand analysis, or demand-chain management.

The appearance of consumer demand analysis is related to the arguments that have long been put forth about marketing theory and documentation on experiential research. Back in 1990 A. Kohli and B. Jaworski (in "Market Orientation: The Construct, Research Propositions, and Managerial Implications," *Journal of Marketing* 54, 1990, pp. 1–18) pointed out that whether or not companies can create greater value for consumers is critical to whether or not companies can achieve the operating objectives they set for themselves. How do you provide consumers with greater value? In the past theory always emphasized putting priority on developing management systems that govern the supply chain. Supply-chain management did indeed help realize the goal of providing consumers with greater value. In 1982 R. K. Oliver and M. D. Webber (in "Supply Chain Management: Logistics Catches Up with Strategy," as cited in M. Christopher, ed., *Logistics: The Strategic Issues*, London: Chapman and Hall) had already come out with the idea that enterprises should establish growth strategies by focusing on setting up supply chains, but the actual implementation of such plans by private companies happened only in the early 1990s. At that time people's understanding of supply-chain management mainly had to do with the relationship between suppliers and consumers. It involved having a coordinated response between upstream and downstream supply chains in order to create greater value for the ultimate market of a company's ultimate products.

Prior to the 1990s innovations in the supply chain generally were initiated only by fairly large-scale enterprises. These generally were already in command of a number of stable supply channels and sales channels. Because of that, some smaller companies meanwhile started to occupy micro-segments of the market. Using their ability to take advantage of specialized division of labor, they began to move into certain parts of the value-added chain. Since large, dominant companies held control over most value-added parts of the supply chain, the innovations of small- and medium-sized companies were only applied to making partial improvements in either products or processes. They did this successfully in these limited areas, unearthing the potential of existing markets. This made it hard for traditional supply-chain models to meet ongoing needs of enterprises for growth. However, eventually enterprises were forced to reevaluate their entire supply-chain management system.

There have been two general schools of thought when it comes to reevaluating supply-chain management systems. One favors lean supply chain management. The other favors the flexible and nimble, or agile, type of management. The first school emphasizes the real-time aspects of managing suppliers. It focuses on "using fewer materials to produce more products." The aim is to reduce inventories and reduce waste in production processes. The second approach emphasizes being agile and tough. It calls for upgrading supply capabilities in order to meet the changing demands of consumers more quickly. In 2000 M. Christopher (in "The Agile Supply Chain: Competing in Volatile Markets, *Industrial Marketing Management*, 29, 2000, pp. 37–44) noted that lean supply-chain management must have an accurate grasp of consumer demand. On that basis it asks suppliers to provide materials and carry out mass production in batches, in order to meet consumer demand in the market. The nimble style of managing supply chains is just the opposite. On the basis of differentiating consumers, it satisfies the differentiated needs of consumers by working in reverse in how it asks suppliers to provide materials. Although both of these supply-chain management models require adjustment in relationships with suppliers in order to meet market demands, the demands on the two are completely opposite to one another. M. Rainbird (in "Demand and Supply Chains: The Value Catalyst," *International Journal of Physical Distribution and Logistics Management*, 34, pp. 230–251) contends that in the lean style of supply-chain management, the key factor determining success or failure relates to the "just-in-time" nature of supply, particularly when brand loyalty to a company's products is high and consumer demand is qualitatively consistent. Nevertheless it is hard to realize consistent demand in the real world. Not only are there differences in demand among different consumers, but any given consumer may change his or her demand at any given time. Companies should therefore do their best to discover these differences in consumer demand and base their supply-chain decisions on them in a nimble or agile manner. The aim is to make the consumer feel that he or she has received greater utility in the course of consuming the product. Put another way, if there are differences in consumer preferences, merely trying to reduce inventories and avoid waste as a supply-chain management strategy will not fundamentally improve the level of consumer satisfaction. That approach to supply-chain management also makes it hard to resolve the problem of low efficiency, which you may find in corporate operations that have been going on for a long time.

Despite differences of opinion regarding management theory, there is broad acceptance of the idea that the process of market exchange serves the purposes of increasing utility to consumers. In 1997 R. Woodruff (in "Customer Value: The Next Source for Competitive Advantage." *Journal of the Academy of Marketing Science*, 25, 1997, pp. 139–153) defined the "utility of consumers" as being the satisfaction that consumers derive from products, or, more specifically, the subjective feeling that consumers have about their own preferences regarding the product, their evaluation of its unique qualities, and the degree to which it satisfies their consumption goals after they have used it. This definition incorporates things experienced in the course of consuming something, as well as differentiating the end results and purpose in using a product. It incorporates the need for a company to provide consumers with value-added utility in a product. Even more important, A. Parasuraman (in "Reflections on Gaining Competitive Advantage through Customer Value, *Journal of the Academy of Marketing Science*, 25, 1997, pp. 154–161) feels that consumer utility changes in a dynamic way so that not only are there differences among the preferences of different consumers, but the same consumer's demands are also constantly changing. Because of this a company must know how to differentiate each consumer's preferences and must be proactive in anticipating and changing along with those changing preferences. The power of managing consumer relationships lies in accurately understanding and influencing the factors that make consumers modify their subjective values. (This power is derived from information on both the market and consumers.) Companies must discover the differentiated needs of different groups of consumers (by segmenting the market or consumers), and they then must transform this segmented information into actual products or services in order to satisfy differentiated demand (whether that involves making products to order or developing services). Via market channels, companies then market the products they have created to consumers, in order to keep improving consumer response (which is done via pricing, trademarks, communications, and upgrading of products). Given all of this, in 2004 A. Zablah, D. Bellenger, and W. Johnston (in "An Evaluation of Divergent Perspectives on Customer Relationship Management: Towards a Common Understanding of an Emerging Phenomenon, *Industrial Marketing Management*, 33, 2004, pp. 475–489) defined this kind of management of consumer relations as a demand chain. That means developing and using market information so as to carry out an investment strategy for managing consumer relations that helps create and sustain maximum profitability.

Even though various aspects of demand may be fairly new concepts, in recent years a number of scholars have conducted in-depth research on the subject which has been accompanied by considerable debate. W. Selen and F. Soliman (in "Operations in Today's Demand Chain

Management Framework, *Journal of Operations Management*, 20, 2002, pp. 667–673) feel that the demand chain is a method of handling and coordinating the relationship with consumers. It starts with the ultimate consumer of a product, then moves back in the reverse direction to the source of the materials to be used, and the suppliers. Similarly T. Vollmann and C. Cordon (in "Building Successful Customer–Supplier Alliances," *Long Range Planning*, 31, 1998, pp. 684–694) feel that the demand chain starts with consumers and later extends to the entire supply chain. S. Baker (in *New Consumer Marketing*, Chichester: John Wiley & Sons, 2003) has expressed the opinion that there are fundamental differences between demand-chain management and normal garden-variety supply-chain management. Demand-chain management requires adjusting the orientation of the supply chain so that consumers are the starting point of the supply chain and not the end-point of the whole process.

So far as a company goes, its performance in the market is the result of how well it satisfies the demand of consumers. Because of this, enterprises must carry out restructuring as necessary, must acquire an understanding of consumers' wishes, and must transmit consumers' demands to those producing the products. D. Ketchen and L. Guiniupero (in "The Intersection of Strategic Management and Supply Chain Management," *Industrial Marketing Management*,33, 2004, pp. 51–56) and others noted in 2004 that once demand is blended into the supply chain, it is easier to see how suppliers hope to make a contribution to improving utility for consumers. It is easier to see how the demand chain concentrates the specific utility of a variety of consumers. A process that increases results for consumers is the direction in which effective management of supply chains should develop.

With the growth of information technologies and e-commerce in China, many enterprises on the Alibaba platform have begun to experiment with the central task of managing consumer demand. In order to satisfy diversified consumer demand, their development strategies have been instrumental in pushing forward a whole new age in the development of supply-chain management systems, one that is based on the demand chain. One can imagine that the main orientation in the future will be trying to differentiate consumer demand as well as to create supply-chain management systems that are designed to improve the utility of consumers. This chapter addresses the subject only in a limited way, by looking at the newly emerging C2B, and O2O parts of the Alibaba platform as representative of the trend. In the following paragraphs, a simplified discussion and analysis of these topics is presented.

Consumer-to-Business Innovations

Consumer-to-business (C2B) is a business model in which consumers (individuals) also create value by working together with companies via the internet. This model allows consumers to share in the use of Big Data. Businesses profit from the willingness of consumers to name their own price, or contribute data, or provide links to their products, while consumers profit from reduced-price products, direct payment, flexibility, and so on.

In 2012 the C2B advance-sales model that Alibaba pioneered brought a ray of light to the problem of overstocked inventories in China. In invisible fashion this model began to ameliorate what had become a dire situation. The so-called C2B supply-chain model in fact takes consumer demand as its starting point. Its end point is satisfying that demand. As a concept it encompasses the convergence of consumer demand that is enabled by e-commerce platforms as well as the restructuring of corporate supply chains that is being done in order to provide convenient services to both sides. C2B also encompasses the various services provided by service providers, including logistics, information, finance, and so on, as well as the transaction services provided by intermediary organizations, including legal assistance, design, pricing, consulting, and trades. Information on demand is first generated by the consumer. Through e-commerce platforms it moves in a reverse direction as it is transmitted to retailers, agents, branded companies, suppliers, and intermediaries. In a short period of time this information can assemble quantities of consumer-demand information from individual consumers. This then can provide companies with concentrations of large volumes of orders. After receiving these orders, companies may optimize the results—select those that they choose to supply with product, depending on whether they want to start at the end, the middle, or even the beginning of the supply chain. They can define and lock in consumers more accurately, which allows them to prepare product in advance, to clear out inventories, to manage their upstream supply chains more efficiently, and to lower production costs, logistical costs, and inventory costs to a very great extent. The C2B supply-chain model can therefore satisfy the individual demands of consumers, but it can also lower inventories to the maximum extent possible for corporations. It can safeguard the seller's profits while also realizing a win-win situation for all.

Many companies in China are facing a crisis in how they manage inventories, due to their extremely large amounts of overstocked product. The garment industry is one example. In the first three quarters of 2012, the total value of inventories held just by companies that have been listed on the market came to RMB 73.07 billion. One well-known brand even revealed that the value of its inventories has risen to the enormous figure of RMB 25 billion. Data from the National Bureau of Statistics show that in the first ten months of 2012, China's garments and accessories industry had realized a mere RMB 70.81 billion in total profits. This seems to confirm the rueful comment made by factory managers of garment companies who say that they work hard all year, but the results of their efforts simply lie around in warehouses. The third-quarter results of the nine large listed companies that manufacture male clothing (Canudilo, Saint Angelo, Joe One, Sept Wolf, Canal Scientific & Technological Co. Ltd, Giuseppe, Sinoer, Busen, and Trands) show that every one of these nine companies valued its inventory at over RMB 100 million. The combined value of the inventories of these companies came to RMB 3.862 billion. Meanwhile such well-known branded companies as Lining, Meters Bonwe, and HeilanHome have an even more prodigious problem. The value of the inventory of one company, HeilanHome, already represents 56.82 percent of the total assets of the company, and the value of another, Meters Bonwe, is 49.55 percent of total assets. Such massive amounts of inventory create an intolerable burden on cash flow. At any moment, they can lead to the risk of severing the financing chain. In contrast to this is a new practice: Starting in the fall of 2012, domestic garment-manufacturing companies created brisk sales by giving steep discounts and employing other means to dispose of goods at reduced prices. Many brands even entered the strange and awful cycle of listing on the market and then just discounting goods, casting them off "even as the tears flowed." All of this was undertaken in order to moderate the extreme problem of overstocked inventories.

The moment C2B was released, it was warmly welcomed by the market. Again, to take the garment industry as an example: the quantity of goods in inventories in all retail market channels is enormous. Just taking a portion of that and shifting it toward e-commerce channels has undeniably been effective in improving the competitiveness of companies in the market. This has been done in part by shifting the model toward custom made products for new items. Companies first make a sample item of clothing, then put it on display on the internet. Once orders come in, the company then organizes wholesale production. At the same time, C2B supply-chain management can shorten and speed up the entire chain of product supply–production–sales. Baoman can serve as an example. Taking advantage of the "miraculous" sales on the 11.11 Shopping Festival Day in 2012, this company was able to carry out the entire production cycle in a mere seven days. After a very precise and accurate reckoning of the quantity of orders that came in, the company mobilized the production process all the way from cotton to fabric to dyeing, as well as marketing and sales. During this process, its factories lowered their capital utilization ratios and their costs of inventories, marketing, and sales. On the new items they achieved a zero-degree level of inventory risk. Moreover, the retail sales also satisfied the targeted demands of specific consumers, while simultaneously enabling individualized made-to-order and agile production. Manufacturing for sales that are made in advance also provides a way for the public to participate in the process of design. Industry does not just provide a few products to the public and say, "Take your choice." From the perspective of experiential economics, consumers are more willing to participate in this kind of activity, while they concurrently guide actual enterprises into producing products that can actually be sold.

Looking at the sales figures, the thing that consumers want most right now is individualized made-to-order products. Peacebird can serve as an example. This firm first put a question-and-answer form of questionnaire on the internet and gathered in data on consumers' likes and opinions regarding craftsmanship, packaging, and so on. At the same time it made use of the image of the A-li raccoon so well known to Ctrip.com users in custom-making limited-edition products. After that it carried out individualized custom-made production. The original idea had been to do small-batch production, but the market response exceeded expectations by so much that the company had no choice but to do volume production. Another company, JOMOO, also based decisions on a subcategory of net users in developing new products to meet special demands.

It should be pointed out that individualized custom-made manufacturing does not exclude or replace standardized production. In many people's minds, C2B is just individualized made-to-order production aimed at targeted groups of people. In fact, that covers an important part of the great wave of C2B, one that has relatively high profits, but does not represent the whole thing. C2B does not rule out demand that is held in common, and indeed a fair percentage of goods can still be produced in a standardized manner and circulate in the market. However, despite being standardized, the C2B manifestation of such products is different from those previously made in the industrial age of commerce. The greatest difference is that the method by which individualized demand is satisfied starts from the perspective of the consumer. It does not start, as in the past, from a wild guess at what demand might be. It does not stem from a "close-your-eyes type of design, and a gambling kind of R&D." In the garment industry, when winter clothing is put on the market, companies are already beginning to issue spring apparel. This stems not from any real understanding of what the consumer wants, but purely from a guessing and driven kind of behavior. This is precisely what has led to the major defect in the large industrial-style economy, a defect that can no longer be sidestepped. Under the low-efficiency model by which production and marketing mutually interact, high inventories for some products and high levels of sold-out goods for others can easily coexist. Excessive marketing— even aggressive, malicious marketing—is prevalent. Fundamentally it becomes very hard to avoid contradictions between marketing and production.

If you take out the highly individualized products that are made to order, how do standardized products get produced under the C2B model? First you have to look at how much participatory power and guiding authority consumers have, when it comes to such links in the process as defining and designing products. Suppose an enterprise makes contact with 50 million users. Out of those, it "unearths" demand that is held in common among 5 million users. It then creates 5 million products for these users. From the users' standpoint, the products are already individualized, but from the manufacturer's standpoint, the production is still fairly standardized. At the same time the company may well organize completely different product groups for another 500,000 users, and, among these, 50,000 of them may be completely individualized and made-to-order.

In terms of outward appearances, the enterprise has sold the same product to 5 million people, but the C2B model has been an extremely good choice for reaching the market. In the traditional industrial age, a company might undertake such things as market surveys, questionnaires, random sampling and so on, all of which were low-efficiency routine practices. Or people might just produce products in a standardized way and try to promote them while covering their eyes and praying that they might turn out to be bestsellers. In contrast to this appproach, the C2B model allows a company to achieve circulation of products with a zero-retention rate in inventory. Meanwhile the B2C model in the industrial age meant that you had to go through channels, and each and every level of sales had to achieve the same sales quantity, the same 5 million. The moment one level failed to sell everything, inventory piled up. In contrast the minute you had a bestseller and sold out, you then had a product shortage. When the company sold 5 million items using the C2B model or the old standardized model, the results might look the same, but the driving concepts and the driving models behind the results are completely different.

C2B is therefore a fundamental change in the logic behind commerce. Its core idea is that the consumer drives the entire process of commercial activity. In comparison to the B2C model, which is a derivative of the traditional industrial-economy age, and which is large scale, standardized into production lines, and cost-oriented, the C2B model is driven by consumers. It takes consumer demand as its starting point, and it moves in wave fashion one by one along the links of the supply chain, but passing backward in a reverse motion toward the producer.

O2O Innovations

O2O (online-to-offline or offline-to-online) is a different innovation in demand management that is based on the diversified demand of consumers. It is a multisided platform business model that links up online users and offline businesses. Exchange of information between online and offline blends online-resources with the offline real economy. This enables the real economy to become an extension of the digital world, by using it as a channel. This practice helps offline commerce to unearth and attract customers who are online. Consumers, meanwhile, can sift through online products and services, complete payment, and then go to a "real" store to complete other purchasing. This model was first applied to the B2C strategy at Walmart. After that it became familiar to all as a web-based form of group buying. Right now O2O e-commerce and social-communications networks are closely connected with mobile end-users. In addition to net-based buying groups, other commercial forms have appeared, such as mobile preferred treatment, individual recommendations, and so on, based on the value-added service of the position. Enterprises engaged in O2O e-commerce are too numerous to list. In addition to such outstanding companies as Foursquare, dianping. com, and lashou.com, there are also Facebook, Twitter, Alibaba, TenCent, and Baidu—the "crocodiles" in the field that are ferociously getting into the action. Transaction volume is increasing at an extremely fast pace.

On the Alibaba platform, companies that use the O2O model to manage their supply chain include Linshimuye and Taobao's ifeng.com. After seeing a pattern online, the user can go offline to carry out his order. What's more, as e-commerce is seeping into every possible entry point, and into the daily lives of people, traditional lines of business are facing an enormous challenge. The furniture industry can serve as an example. As B2B and B2C e-commerce models were successfully penetrating such traditional business categories like garments and food products, the furniture industry could be regarded as one of a minority of traditional industries that had not yet "put on the cloak" of internet business. This can be attributed to two different tiers of causes. First furniture requires higher-cost inputs compared to such traditional industries as food products and clothing. It is heavier, and its logistical costs are therefore greater. In addition furniture being sold through e-commerce lacks the ability to provide direct perceptual understanding. For consumers buying furniture on the internet is necessarily "a game of chance." Second furniture products emphasize the experience and quality of the furniture. Actual stores can provide that experience in a direct way; to a much greater extent, they can stimulate a buyer's desire to own the piece.

In order to expedite the process of a consumer's getting product information online, send an order, pursue a transaction, and share the experience with others, and at the same time to allow consumers to go offline to a real store and physically experience the product or service, Alibaba has put major effort into supporting and encouraging the O2O e-commerce business model. This not only breaks through the sense of distrust that a consumer can get in the course of buying things digitally, but it also reduces the physical and psychological costs to the consumer that can occur by simply going into a store and buying something.

Offline "real" stores face the problem of having to be local for local consumers. In order to provide consumers with a better way to find the locations of real stores, and to push forward the development of the O2O business model, Alibaba has put massive investment into purchasing Gao-de (Autonavi.com) software. After Alibaba invested in Gao-de, the strategic cooperation of the two has focused on building basic infrastructure as a kind of entry point for the business, which means using the mobile internet positioning and services for improving daily living. They have launched broad-based, in-depth cooperation on a number of levels, including digital design, map engines, product R&D, cloud computing, advertising and promotion, and commercialization. All of this is to provide users with greater services and more options.

Map services are an important entryway for the entire O2O supply chain. Inside China, among the three giants in the internet—Alibaba, TenCent, and Baidu—only Alibaba lacks a high-quality map resource.

If Alibaba intends to find a breakthrough point with the O2O model, the most critical thing for the company right now is to put more time and effort into this mapping service. Gao-de Maps has as much as 21.6 percent of the Chinese cell phone market for map accounts, and using O2O can promote and provide the necessary coverage for the map business. Dominating this mobile internet entryway will undoubtedly be critically important in defining the pattern of how O2O develops in the future.

Alibaba had in fact begun to deploy its resources in the mobile internet sphere some seven years ago. It not only was the earliest company to get involved in O2O, but its "deployment chain" is also the longest of any enterprise. Specifically Alibaba allied with the hottest social-media platform right now, namely Sina's Weibo. It earned an enormous user base through dreaming about "domesticating e-commerce." As noted previously Alibaba also joined with China's leading domestic supplier in map navigation, Gao-de. Gao-de's superior assets enabled it to move more easily into the age of mobile internet. It was also highly significant in terms of extending Alibaba's primary business.

The triumvirate of Ali + Sina + Autonati has not only created a powerful alliance in e-commerce, but in the future it will provide a much stronger competitive advantage as competition in the industry heats up. In terms of portals, there is UC and Sina's Weibo; in terms of mobile digital analytical tools, there is Youmeng; in terms of online and offline connecting platforms, there are Juhuasuan and Meituan. For payment methods there is Zhifubao (Alipay). After purchasing Gao-de, the Gao-de navigation tools and massive quantities of map data have allowed Alibaba's "local life platform" to receive core support. With the "local life platform," the last link in Alibaba's O2O industrial chain will be nearing completion. In future competition in this industry, if the online and offline businesses unite, that will create an absolutely massive explosive type of force. It is precisely this kind of development model, using an improved form of O2O, that has drawn more "real" companies onto the Alibaba platform, and that is spurring the rapid growth of traditional industries as well. In the furniture industry, for example, more than 100 new firms registered on Alibaba's TMall site in just one month, August 2012. Close to one-fifth of all items now relate to the home. Nevertheless, it will take time for online influences to seep into offline business. It may still take a certain length of time before the development model of O2O garners appreciable results.

Alibaba's Innovations with Respect to International Trade

Since the start of this opening-up process, China's implementation of such opening strategies as welcoming foreign investment and developing foreign trade has propelled high-speed economic growth and social prosperity. China has become one of the fastest-growing and most accomplished emerging economies in the world. Behind this appearance of economic prosperity and expanding exports lies a hidden crisis, however, owing to uncertainties about the ongoing stability of the country's exports.

Indications of this lie in the overly concentrated structure of China's exported products. This compromises the ability of trade to withstand volatility. It can be seen in the way processing industries are the main engine for export growth, whereas target countries for these exports are insufficiently diversified. Given that China's exports hinge on the economic growth of developed countries, external shocks can easily create volatility. This current global economic crisis is a good example of how lower global growth can have a negative impact on China's exports.

One of the more controversial topics among policy makers and among economic theorists, therefore, is how to ensure the stable growth of China's export trade. As a company that develops Internet and mobile platforms, Alibaba is being very proactive in exploring its own role. Its open-style big-data system on the international trade platform has blazed a new kind of Silk Road for the new age. It is helping conventional trade, as well as the trade in services, to find a sustainable path of development.

The Role of Export in China's Economic Growth and the Impact of Economic Crises

The fast growth of China's economy is inseparable from the country's open strategy, that is, its strategy of using external resources and external markets to bolster its own economy. For example, in contrast with another of the five BRIC countries, India, in 1978, China's actual GDP was 96.6 percent of India's, but by 2009, it was 3.1 times that of India. After allowing for population differences, the actual per-capita GDP in China was a mere US$23 higher than India's in 1978. By 2009, it was 3.5 times higher. Given that the two countries are fairly close to one another in terms of resource endowment, population, and environment, China's faster economic growth is closely related to its strategy of exporting to external markets to spur internal growth.

Between 1978 and 2009, China had only five years in which it showed a trade deficit (1985, 1986, 1988, 1989, and 1993). India had only two years in which it showed a trade surplus (1978 and 1979). In this period of 32 years, moreover, China's trade surplus expanded by 381.9 times, whereas India's trade deficit expanded by 98.2 times.

China's expanding trade surplus arose from the sustained way in which exports have flourished. By the end of 2010, China's imports grew at an actual average annual rate of 16.6 percent, which was 90.9 times the rate in 1978. Given such a fast rate of import growth, exports had to grow at a faster rate to achieve a trade surplus—between 1978 and 2010, China's exports grew at an actual average annual rate of 17.4 percent, which was 115.2 times the rate in 1978. This sustained prosperity of the export trade could be seen particularly in the period between 1997 and 2008, when exports grew at a high rate of 19.1 percent, whereas imports increased only at a rate of 17.7 percent. The resulting cumulative trade surplus came to 1.3572 trillion RMB.

The consequence of this sustained expansion of exports has been that China's economic growth has increasingly come to rely on foreign demand. Since 2000, China's degree of reliance on exports has consistently exceeded 20 percent. This figure represents the percentage of exports in gross national product (GNP). At the peak of reliance on exports, in 2006, the figure was 36 percent. In 2007, however, the U.S. subprime credit crisis erupted, leading to a financial crisis that made global demand drop precipitously. This impeded China's exports, and the speed of China's economic growth fell dramatically in 2008 by 5 percent. The country's export situation deteriorated further in 2009. Using 2008 figures as the basis, exports fell by another 18 percent, and the speed of economic growth responded by falling another 3 percent. Although the pace of economic recovery has gradually picked up again, and external demand is constantly rising, as is the pace of China's economic growth, there has been no fundamental change in the way China's economic development model still relies on foreign demand.

Excessive reliance on foreign demand makes China's exports extremely prone to volatility. The vulnerability of the country's export growth to foreign shocks was apparent in this last round of financial crises. This has had other ramifications as well. China's mode of economic growth entails selling old products in massive quantities to developed countries. Not only does this give the false impression that the country is dumping products on importing nations, but it leads to intensification of trade frictions.

Take the United States as only one example. In 2008, the United States initiated 15 trade relief investigations toward Chinese products, notably higher than the average number of 10.9 such investigations per year in the period 2002–2005. In 2009, the United States issued 23 trade relief investigations, and the sums involved were a record-breaking US$7.6 billion. Not only is it hard to keep exports growing at an even pace, but constantly intensifying trade frictions are making China's original trade-driven model of growth unsustainable. If China can instead export quantities of new items to a greater range of countries, if it can expand the scope of its traded products and not just the volume, it should be able to realize a more stable export growth.

Alibaba Forges a Silk Road for the New Age

The fundamental reason for the tightening of China's foreign trade environment and the ongoing spread of and intensification of trade frictions is that export products are not yet sufficiently diversified, whereas target countries for exports are not yet sufficiently multilateralized. The fundamental ways to change this are to increase the percentage of new products among exports and to shift from selling primarily to America, Japan, and Europe to selling to most developing countries. As China's largest online trading platform, Alibaba has been proactive in exploring ways to do this. The Internet-based Silk Road that it has created is intended to help achieve faster export growth for China.

In evaluating the future of China's export trade as it faced the economic crisis and the postcrisis period, Alibaba became convinced that confidence in purchasing Chinese goods was recovering. It did this by using its overseas purchasing inquiries and indexed search engine data. It correctly forecast a rapid rebound of Chinese exports in the first quarter of 2010. This was so because, in the fourth quarter of 2009, Alibaba's platform data indicated that consumer markets in developed countries were warming up again at faster-than-expected speed, with the United States taking the lead. The fastest rise in inquiries related to purchases of Chinese food and beverages, beauty products, and personal caregiving (nursing). Purchasing inquiries made to Chinese suppliers also were increasing dramatically from such countries as Germany, Russia, and the Middle East, countries that, in the future, will make a major contribution to increasing China's exports.

As former Chief Operating Officer of Alibaba's B2B company Wei Zhe has noted, "The confidence of foreign buyers in Chinese goods is coming back, and it is possible that the overall level of foreign-trade exports may get close to the level of early 2008. At the very least, the recovery of Internet-based trade is surpassing the recovery of traditional markets."

In fact, under the joint stimulus of fiscal-stimulus policies and budgetary spending, the economies of the United States and Western European countries began to recover in the third quarter of 2009. What's more, this recovery should be ongoing. GDP in the United States has been growing above 1.5 percent since 2011, while economic recovery will remain slow. The leading indicator of the Purchasing Managers' Index (PMI) also suggests that manufacturing industries in the United States, Europe, and Japan are beginning to recover. After being depressed for 17 months, for the first time the Eurozone broke through a PMI of 50 in October 2009, which implies that the economy is strong and that people's expectations are positive.

China's customs data are also showing growth in China's export trade. In December 2009, China imported 62.16 million tons of iron ore and 21.26 million tons of crude oil. Starting on January 1, 2010, China and the Association of Southeast Asian Nations (ASEAN) instituted a policy of zero customs duties, which provided excellent conditions for a rebound in China's exports. In addition, in that single month, 3.34 million tons of steel were exported, whereas exports of unrefined aluminum, containers, integrated electrical circuits, color televisions, and household items are doing better than expected. At the same time, based on the judgment that a fall in the unemployment rate in the United States will help to provide consumer-pull demand, Internet-based orders from abroad are constantly increasing. All of this helps China's exports.

However, despite the gradual recovery in demand from international markets and improvement in the overall situation, it will still take time for people to deleverage after the economic crisis and during the postcrisis period. It will be very hard to get back to prosperity in any short time given the amount of overseas consumer debt. Based on the 4.5 million global registered users that Alibaba commands, the data of its supplied goods, and the way all countries are putting greater investment into stimulating their own trade, Alibaba holds fast to a low-barrier-to-entry model of e-commerce. Using services and technology, it intends to help small and microenterprises to get over a "turbulent springtime" and realize a situation of stable export trade growth. Alibaba's cooperation with the authorities in Macao is a good example of this.

Alibaba's Cooperation with the Bureau of Trade Investment and Promotion in Macao

During the economic crisis, in the first eight months of 2009, Macao exported roughly US$64 million in total value (in Macao's currency, 5.11 billion), with exports targeted mainly at the United States and the European Union. Depressed economies then led to a constant slide in export figures, however, causing Macao's Export Department to take proactive measures to expand trade and seek new markets. To do this, the Trade and Investment Bureau in Macao established a cooperative relationship with Alibaba in October 2009. Its purpose was to work together in promoting e-commerce to more small and microenterprises in Macao. In its initial stages, this cooperative endeavor included setting up a plan to encourage Macao's smaller enterprises to open up new international trade markets. To do this, exporters in Macao could apply for a maximum of roughly US$2,500 in assistance from the Trade and Investment Bureau to be used in purchasing Alibaba's support services for e-commerce.

The cooperation between Alibaba and Macao authorities will help to strengthen Macao's exporting ability, but through the use of e-commerce, it also will help it to expand its customer base and improve its purchasing processes and improve its competitiveness in global markets in general.

Alibaba is also cooperating with 22 Arab countries, acting as a go-between and a bridge to finding Chinese opportunities in the Arab world. It is helping to create the underlying conditions for China to be a new trading partner with Arab countries, successfully forging what it calls a "modern Alibaba Silk Road." Many trading partners from Arab countries now exist on Alibaba's global purchasing platform who not only are helping China's e-commerce break into the massive market of the Arab world but also are themselves finding Chinese products that help them make money. For example, raw meat in Arab countries is three times the price of China's raw meat. Given this large profit margin, with Alibaba's online trading platform acting as a go-between, some Arab customers are realizing that China can provide them with massive profits. They are now thronging to buy things in China, to the extent that some Chinese suppliers cannot handle all the business. Given the profit margins on importing Chinese beef and mutton, Arab traders have been able to put Chinese meat in essentially all markets in the Arab world. Some 85 percent of all mutton and beef consumed in Arab countries is now imported from China.

By threading their trade through the fabric of Alibaba, many Arab businesspeople are doing very substantial business. Not only meat, but such things as petroleum, electronics, and the export of physical labor are now large-scale businesses. As a matchmaker between the economies of China and the Arab world, Alibaba provides commercial opportunities to Arab businesspeople every day. At the same time, it provides the Arab world with the price and quality advantages of Chinese exporters. The result is a win-win model that works. This development concept of win-win solutions has enabled Alibaba to successfully establish a new Silk Road between China and the Arab world that enhances economic and trade relations and enriches economic activity. In terms of trade, this Silk Road is just getting started, but there are certainly more "treasure troves" waiting to be found by Chinese and Arab businesspeople via the Alibaba online trading platform.

Alibaba's Big-Data System Helps to Develop the Trade Both in Goods and in Services

Alibaba's big-data system is helping to expedite the growth of regular business as well as the trade in services. Looking only at small and micro-enterprises, only 5 percent of China's suppliers hold 20 percent of all export volume conducted by these enterprises. Despite the highly demanding export situation, suppliers on Alibaba's platform are maintaining their ability to keep up fast-paced growth. The context for this is the backing provided by the big-data system of Alibaba's international trade platform. Use of this system allows for more effective matching of buyers and sellers because purchasing conducted directly on the platform is based on a massive quantity of data analysis. The survival ability of cross-border e-commerce companies is much higher than that of traditional foreign trade enterprises. This effectively promotes much faster development of China's trade in goods as well as its trade in services.

Looking first at the trade in goods, in the postcrisis period, global purchasing demand has not actually changed but has shifted in the direction of smaller quantities and more frequent purchases. To take Europe and America as representative of traditional developed-country markets, the number of buyers has risen dramatically. In the past three years, American buyers on the Alibaba website have gone from 2 to 7 million, whereas European buyers have gone from 360,000 to 1.6 million. Meanwhile, each single transaction is for a much smaller amount of money. Most orders for any single transaction do not exceed US$30,000 (roughly 200,000 RMB), and transactions are concentrated in consumer products industries. This global trend, toward smaller amounts and more frequent purchases, means that buyers have to link up with suppliers more efficiently. This gradually allows the new form of e-commerce services to display its pronounced advantages over traditional forms of foreign trade.

Based on the accumulation of big data and analysis of those data, purchasing on Ali can be *direct to market*. Overseas buyers can directly issue detailed purchase requirements, and suppliers then quote prices on a voluntary basis. The two conduct online negotiations and conclude the business. In the past two years, the scale of buyers engaging in the direct purchasing markets has gone up 7 to 10 times per year.

Statistics supplied by Alibaba show that there are currently 80,000 Chinese suppliers who are active on its platform, which is roughly 5 percent of the number of enterprises engaged in foreign trade in China. However, the results of third-party surveys and research indicate that this 5 percent of Chinese suppliers is creating 1.3 trillion RMB worth of exports (including those that go through Alibaba). This is roughly equal to 20 percent of the total value of exports carried on by China's small and microenterprises. From this it can be seen that Alibaba's big-data system is playing a role in stimulating fast growth of China's commodity exports.

The trade in services is similar. In 2013, the size of China's trade in services hit a record high, with the total value of imports and exports reaching US$539.64 billion, according to China's Department of Commerce statistics. This was a 14.7 percent increase over the preceding year. Despite the constant increase in overall volume, however, China's trade in services is still a small percentage of its international trade overall. The total trade in services was only 11.5 percent of total imports and exports in 2013, and this was only 0.7 percent higher than it had been the preceding year. From the percentage of trade occupied by services, it can be seen that China's level of development is still rather backward. On a global basis, the percentage of services trade to all trade is generally 20 percent. The percentage in Brazil, another BRIC like China, is already 24.9 percent, whereas that of China remains at 11.5 percent.

E-commerce is an important component of China's trade in services, and it should open up a new territory for this business in the future. The reason for this is that e-commerce is closely tied to commercial trade at every link in the process, and commercial trade is the cornerstone of the e-commerce services business. E-commerce includes not only large-scale industry, the logistics of commerce and trade, tourism services, and so on but also e-commerce applications for traditional enterprises. It includes Internet-based purchasing and Internet-based selling, as well as such innovative forms of business as mobile-phone-based e-commerce.

The new advantages that e-commerce brings to China's services trade are as follows: first, e-commerce can dramatically reduce the costs of trading in services. Because e-commerce reduces a great number of links in the chain of business, buyers and sellers can carry on business activity directly and thereby lower transaction costs. Second, it can improve transaction efficiencies. Both buyers and sellers can adopt standardized, digitized contracts and so on. Third, it can reduce regional barriers to trade and expand opportunities for trade in services. Fourth, it can improve the international competitiveness of China's companies that engage in the trade in services.

At the same time, e-commerce has developed in unprecedented ways on the Alibaba platform in terms of service industries. Not only has it galvanized greater development of logistics and e-commerce supporting industries, but it also has spawned an emerging industry of e-commerce services. Right now, more than 170 million customers have purchased things via the Internet in China. E-commerce is already widely established in the country and is influencing the consumption behavior of both enterprises and individuals in profound ways.

E-commerce has become a key industry that China has decided to nurture in order for it to become a new nexus for economic growth. I believe that China's export of e-commerce-based services will make great progress in the future given the contributions of the rapidly growing Alibaba e-commerce services industry and the contributions of its big-data system. Export of e-commerce services, in turn, will spur the upgrading and restructuring of China's overall trade in services.

CHAPTER 5

INTEGRITY CAPITAL–BASED MICROFINANCE

DONG YOUYING

In recent years, the Chinese government has been putting major effort into transforming its institutions, a process that includes such things as making interest rates more market driven. As one consequence, the situation surrounding the funding of small business has received more attention and is changing for the better. More banking entities feel that one of their major orientations in the future should be a shift toward financial services for small business. Various kinds of entities that offer small loans are springing up and increasing the possibilities for small business to be financed. Meanwhile, the Internet, with its use of big data, is making it possible to break out of the traditional model of financial services. Microfinance is becoming a vital new force in the recognition and fostering of small businesses.

Alibaba currently has 500 million registered customers on its Taobao platform. As an additional rearguard force, it has 800 million customers registered on Alipay. It is constantly building platforms on top of platforms and creating a new experience for customers. Its differentiating strategies rely on platforms and the Internet, as well as on concentrating the forces of many microentity customers. By creating new rules so as to insert itself into the traditional realm of finance, it is constantly seeking to penetrate the core functions of the banking business. This chapter explores the integrity capital–based grassroots financial innovations of Ali Small Loans.

Grassroots Finance in the Internet Age

If you mention Alibaba in China, the names Alipay and YuEbao spring to mind for many people. New forms of finance brought on by e-commerce have blown over us all like a kind of hurricane, sweeping the daily life of millions of people into its vortex as it goes along. Many people start to understand finance as something that relates to capital and something that services capital. For example, by controlling the risks, tax consequences, and returns from asset restructuring, rich people can become even richer.

Meanwhile, the appearance of the financial crisis made people's long-festering resentments toward the financial system erupt like a geyser, which eventually resulted in an extremely large-scale resistance movement. Images of the banners of Occupy Wall Street accompanied the headlines in newspapers and magazines. Top traders and "gold collar" workers at the leading banks now suddenly became the targets of media attacks. Common people held tight to the money they had saved up over half a lifetime of hard work and wondered what to do with it. Many technologically advanced new startup companies were desperately waiting for funding but were out of luck. In this kind of system, both supply and demand lacked confidence in each other. As a result, the ability to use money and to increase value by using it was greatly reduced.

In fact, however, the essence of putting finance to best use does not lie in generating the highest profits. One of the three Nobel laureates in economics in 2013, Professor Robert Shiller, wrote in the book, *Finance and a Good Society*, that the essence of finance lies in raising money for economic activities. It lies in improving social welfare and increasing efficiency through the ability to distribute funding resources. By focusing on the well-being of society at large and by injecting indispensable life blood into the real economy, finance has the potential and ability to fashion a much broader and deeper economic prosperity for all. As many people see it, financial institutions, especially large ones, should not use finance as a way to maximize profits and seek immoral personal gain. Instead, finance should be something that works to improve the welfare of the entire society.

Essentially all scholars, not just Robert Shiller, recognize the importance of finance to the well-being of society. Many propose their own ideas on how to design systems to accomplish this. It is not such an easy thing, however, to ensure that finance truly does benefit the common person.

The difficulty that microentities face in getting financing is a classic example. This problem exists not just in China, with its multitude of microenterprises, but also in a very real sense worldwide. Asymmetrical information is one of the main causes of this funding problem for microentities. The financial institutions and governments of many countries are searching for ways to resolve this core issue, but nobody has found a highly effective answer. Now that we have entered the information age, however, the growth of the Internet and big-data applications is providing a new way of thinking about the issue.

Internet financing is not just a matter of enabling those making loans to receive higher value, of making it more feasible to control risks, and of making the process of borrowing money faster and easier. More important, it is to allow common people, those grassroots classes with no special privileges, to enter into the whole financial system. It is to enable them to have a real right to participate in that system on an equal basis. The Internet allows information to be more transparent, and it allows information transmission to break through the bounds of time and space. By drawing on the support of more complete information, grassroots classes of people can make more rational decisions, be more proactive in grabbing onto opportunities, and wield the force of finance to improve their own results.

If you want to draw on the power of finance to unleash grassroots entrepreneurship, it is essential to have "renegades" in the financial industry. Alibaba wants to be such a renegade. It does not want to smash the banks. Instead, it wants to stir up what has been a stagnant pond, challenge the traditional institutions to think in more competitive terms, and stimulate changes across the entire industry. Not only are grassroots envoys such as Ali-people thinking this way. To a certain degree, people like Zhou Xiaochuan,[1] who represent the government or official financial institutions, are thinking this way as well. They are also proposing their own ideas on emerging financial models.

---

[1] Zhou Xiaochuan was governor of the central bank of China for three terms.

Zhou Xiaochuan has said

Once these new methods appear, they will begin to challenge traditional business models. My answer to that is that this is a good thing. Competition will change a traditional industry for the better and make it grow. It will be a strong stimulus for making the industry adapt to new things. Because of that, competition will help [the traditional system] get up to speed with the times, and with the pace of science and technology. The ultimate result will be that competition brings better services and products along with it. The entire financial industry will then provide better goods and services to the real economy and to all kinds of customers in that real economy. This is absolutely certain.

To a great extent, Alibaba does not want to limit itself to being an entity that does microfinance. There are many Internet companies and financial institutions that can perform this function. Instead, Alibaba is very clear about the fact that its advantages lie with its ecosystem. Its goal is to build a microfinance services platform that provides high-quality, highly efficient, personalized services that are open and competitive. Ultimately, the aim is to stimulate the formation of a positively reinforcing cycle in the entire ecosystem of Internet interaction. It may be that at the current time it is hard to separate out some financial services technologies (such as the Ali Small Loans) from the Alibaba ecosystem, but as the ecosystem grows, its corresponding basic infrastructure will improve, and its financial force will be able to benefit more people. At that time, it will be able to unleash greater grassroots entrepreneurship.

In the information age, Internet companies are not actually using totally new methods to "play at" finance, creating eye-catching products that float on the surface of things. Instead, they are embedding the innate spirit of the Internet into financial innovations, such things as openness, equality, cooperation, and sharing. Supported by data and technology, they are making information more transparent while lowering costs and raising efficiency, thereby benefiting more people. In what follows, therefore, we will sort through the financial domain of Alibaba to see how Ali-people do grassroots financing in the Internet age through financial innovations.

Alipay: The Foundation of the Ali Ecosystem

The curtain has already come down on the 11.11 Shopping Festival 2013.[2] A total sum of 35.019 billion RMB has been paid through Alipay, creating yet another record of sales in the e-commerce age. Although some problems appeared in the first hour after retail outlets began selling, with an inability to process payments, the Taobao and Alipay technical team swiftly restored operations. They successfully met the challenge of dealing with 213 million Internet people processing more than 100 million orders on a single day and with the massive quantities of data that stand behind those numbers. Accolades came in from around the world. The excellence of Alipay's technology truly does deserve respect, but it is the impact of the thinking behind that technology that is profoundly changing our lives.

In recent years, Alipay has already become an indispensable part of many people's lives. Alipay's online payment system has made transactions safer, quicker, and easier—from consumers paying for things on Taobao to 460,000 businesses that receive the money. The system has made people's lives more convenient in many ways—from enabling people to pay their utility bills online to processing credit-card transactions. Alipay's real significance does not lie in its 800 million registered accounts, however, or in the 20 billion RMB in daily transaction volume that it can handle via some 100 million separate transactions in a day. Despite these massive numbers, the real significance of Alipay lies in its being a critical link in the chain of Internet exchanges. This is more important to producing an Ali ecosystem and enabling it to grow.

Faced with Taobao's Need, Alipay Resolves the Trust Dilemma
Ali-people often say that while they are innovating to solve problems, they cannot help but take a step forward and actually create something new. Faced with an abyss before them, that is, they will face bone-crushing defeat if they do not make the leap. To understand the origins of Alipay, we have to go back to the year in which it was born. We have to see what

---

[2]The November 11 Shopping Festival is the world's largest online shopping event.

the e-commerce environment was like back then and what Taobao faced in terms of major challenges.

The Taobao platform was established in May 2003. The main thing holding back the growth of e-commerce transactions then was a particularly fundamental problem—that of mutual trust between buyers and sellers. Buyers did not believe sellers and therefore were unwilling to extend direct payments. Sellers did not trust buyers and were unwilling to risk shipping goods. Alipay was born out of this opportunity. As Shao Xiaofeng, former CEO of Alipay, said, "In a certain sense, what Alipay did at the beginning was not so much online payment as online escrow—that is, serving as the guarantor of credit." This new financial innovation involved considerable risk, but it also reflected Alibaba's confidence in e-commerce. Both the risk taking and confidence appear to have paid off.

On October 15, 2003, Alipay put this *guaranteed transaction model* into effect on Taobao for the first time. The buyer first remitted funds into Alipay. Alipay then notified the seller to release the goods. Once the buyer received the goods, he or she confirmed release of the payment, and Alipay paid the seller. By serving as guarantor in the middle, Alipay was able to resolve the problem that had plagued e-commerce from the beginning—that of trust. Once this escrow system was set up, it ensured the formation of a consumer environment on the Internet.

The first piece of business via this escrow system occurred when a certain Mr. Jiao purchased a second-hand Fuji camera for the sum of 750 RMB. At the time, he did not use the payment method we use these days, but rather he went to a bank counter and physically paid money into Alipay's account. Later, Alipay was to abolish this bank-counter type of payment and shift instead to payment via Internet banking. This saved further on transaction costs as well as the cost of time. From start to finish, resolving the whole issue of trust was driven fundamentally by Alipay's constant innovations.

In addition to resolving this issue of trust, the very existence of Alipay enabled electronic payment to become quick, easy, and effective. Alipay's functions with respect to currency payment greatly facilitated the advance of Internet purchasing. Looking back at the history of how "currency" developed, in primitive societies, people used such things as shells and hides as vehicles for embodying value. This simplified the trouble of exchanging goods for other goods. Currency then went from being metal coinage to being pieces of paper as people constantly sought to create payment tools that were more convenient and more effective. In the age of electronic commerce, payment links that go via the Internet have replaced remittances at a counter. Third-party payment tools such as Alipay appeared to improve the efficiency of such payments (Figure 5.1).

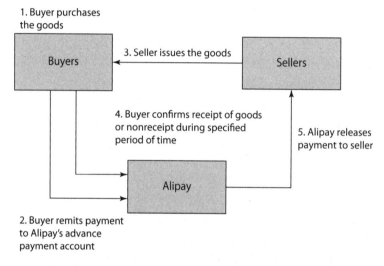

FIGURE 5.1 *Flowchart of Alipay's escrow function in guaranteeing transactions*

In the Song Dynasty, a commodity economy developed rapidly enough that the limited amount of copper currency in circulation at the time was insufficient to satisfy the demand for liquidity. As a result, people found other solutions, such as the use of iron coinage in Sichuan. Such coinage was extremely inconvenient, however, being of low value and also heavy. Buying a piece of fabric might cost 500 jin in coinage (a measure of weight that equals 0.5 kilogram or 1.1023 pounds), so payment would require the use of a cart. The world's earliest paper currency came into being as a result, called *jiao-zi*. The appearance of this paper currency was a major accomplishment in the history of China's currencies, given its ability to create greater liquidity and facilitate trade. In similar fashion, the appearance of Alipay provided a guarantor of credit for both buyer and seller and also reduced the costs of payment links owing to the need to communicate via different banks. This greatly increased the efficiency of payment and was effective in driving the development of e-commerce.

Payment via the Internet and the ongoing development of e-commerce have contributed to each other's growth. The head of Alipay's Science and Technology Department, Wan Gang, has commented, "When the Taobao platform launched Internet purchasing, it may have been supported by network technology, but Alipay was what enabled it to come out of its shell and stand above all of the many other Internet purchasing platforms." PayPal in the United States was a competitor of Alipay within China at the time. In contrast to Alipay, PayPal developed in a climate of excellent credit services in the United States, while Alipay grew up in the midst of primitive and rather wild credit conditions.

Undaunted in the face of certain risks, however, the pioneers at Alibaba forged ahead in the midst of this wilderness. Through hard work, they eventually were to enjoy the fruits of success in this particular realm. That is, Alipay went from 0 customers to 100 million customers in the first five years. It then went from 100 million to 200 million customers in only 10 months. After that, it "climbed on the express train" of both the Internet and e-commerce in terms of processing transactions. Between 2009 and 2012, the number of transactions processed via Alipay increased at 60 percent per year on average. In 2012, Alipay handled 6.23 million transactions, including around 70 percent of all online credit-card transactions within China.

During this period, Alipay also launched various business solutions that greatly improved cooperation among commercial merchants so that its own business lines have developed as a result. At present, Alipay works with more than 200 financial institutions and with some 500,000 commercial entities. It also has become a major tool in influencing the confidence with which consumers approach the Internet. In China's e-commerce, it is playing the role of certifying and enabling credit. According to the results of surveys conducted by the Zheng Wang Consulting Company,[3] 88.3 percent of users feel that websites that provide Alipay services are more reliable than those that do not provide such services. Moreover,

---

[3]http://bjzhengwang.show.imosi.com/1/company_desc.aspx.

whether or not Alipay will accept a site into its system plays a direct role in that site's degree of confidence.

As the very basis of Alibaba's ecosystem, as the outstanding body enabling Taobao's sustained growth in annual turnover, as the "bugler" calling the tune for millions of "netizens" who are marching toward the new consumer age—and as all the positive and pleasing figures tell us—Alipay fully deserves its praise. Without Alipay's ability to resolve the whole trust issue at the very beginning, customers would not have rushed to register on the Taobao site, and the habit of buying things on the Internet would not have become embedded into daily life. Millions of sellers would not have taken up residence in the Taobao system. The multitude of businesses that evolved as a result of the ability to sell via Taobao would not have come to be, nor would Alibaba itself have such positive prospects for future growth.

A Service That Enables the Public to Have a Fast, Easy, and Safe Way to Make Payments

According to Alibaba's own statistics, the success rate for people purchasing things on the Internet, from sending off an order to the seller's receipt of payment, is only around 70 percent. Thirty percent of orders are lost, whether due to payment technology problems or causes relating to the purchaser himself. Not only does this lead directly to lower turnover and loss of profits, but also it leaves consumers with unhappy purchasing experiences. This has a long-term negative impact on ensuing sales. Alipay has done all it can to elevate the success rate of payments and to ameliorate problems with payments for orders.

At present, Alipay has cooperative partnerships with more than 200 domestic banks, 4 overseas banks, and 5 international bank-card groups and third-party payment companies. It cooperates with these companies very closely. In addition to the most basic kind of bank transfer of funds from one account to another, starting in 2010, Alipay gradually linked up with more than 100 banks to promote a fast and easy pay service. In going through this kind of new technology, customers no longer need to connect with an Internet bank. As long as they possess a bank card, they can complete online payment in a fast and easy way. The promotion of this fast and easy payment technology is lowering the threshold for customers who pay online. It has greatly reduced the procedures required to complete transactions and has strengthened the security of bank accounts.

In addition to the attractions of Alipay with which people already are familiar, including quick and easy and Trojan-free transactions, in April 2013, Alipay introduced a third-party insurance institution into its business, namely, Ping An Insurance, to ensure the safety of users' funds. If anyone's account is fraudulently used by someone after using quick and easy to pay, Ping An insures them by paying for 100 percent of what they lost. Moreover, Alipay bears the cost of all insurance fees. This cooperation between Ping An and Alipay has opened up another form of insurance that guarantees that an online payment will "cross the river safely." At present, 150 million Alipay users are already making use of quick and easy payments.

As smart phones and other mobile technologies have become universal, and with the developments in Internet purchasing and applications software, the enormous wave of wireless payment is already on us. The market research group Ipsos has jointly conducted research with Alipay that makes it clear that mobile payments and e-commerce are already relatively mature and that around 80 percent of users are willing to try such new payment products as Sonic Payment.[4] Already, 86 percent of users who have been surveyed have attempted to purchase things using mobile technology. In the first quarter of 2013, the size of the transaction market for third-party payment in China reached 63.9 billion RMB, with mobile Internet payment transactions accounting for 47 billion RMB; within this figure, Alipay's mobile transactions came to around 24 billion RMB, indicating that Alipay held a 50.1 percent market share.

According to Alibaba's statistics, in 2012, the success rate of payments that were made through traditional cell phone banking channels was 38 percent. Despite this low success rate, however, Alipay's wireless paying business is growing and becoming sizable at an extremely fast pace. The number of times people used wireless to pay in 2012 was up 223 percent over the previous year, and the total sum of money transferred via this method had increased by 546 percent. The number of

---

[4]http://baike.baidu.com/subview/9803481/9933211.htm.

discrete transactions using Alipay via cell phone is now 9.2 percent of all payments made through Alipay.

In 2013, during the 11.11 Shopping Festival, Taobao Alipay payments made via cell phone reached 5.35 billion RMB, which was 5.6 times what the total had been in 2012. The transaction volume of Alipay's cell phone payments overall came to 11.3 billion RMB, in 45.18 million separate transactions, which was 24.03 percent of all transactions.

In the realm of mobile payment, Alipay's product innovations keep streaming out. In January 2013, a new product was officially released called the Alipay Wallet. This is an all new mobile customer end-user application. This so-called wallet provides an experience that transcends a real wallet. It has a variety of functions including automatic recharging of money for a cell phone account, paying bills for credit cards, paying fees for daily living, Sonic payments, discount coupons management, hand-form payments, Quick Response (QR) code, access to YuEbao, and so on. It can listen to commands spoken by a consumer's cell phone and carry out "smart" transactions. Many scanning and information recognition applications that have been used in Western countries are also being used and are enabling offline transactions and payment to become much more quick and easy.

In all these innovations, including quick and easy payment, credit payment, and wireless payment, the starting point for Alibaba is to ensure that the consumer has a safe, fast, and easy way to make payments, a way that increases the success rate of payments as well as their efficiency. It is to ensure that payment problems are resolved in order to support the growth of e-commerce.

Furthering the Growth of the Payment Industry by the Use of Technology and Competition

Payment systems within China are divided into two categories, online and offline. Online payment is carried out primarily by three parties, Alipay, Cai Fu Tong, and UnionPay.[5] The Internet payment model involves having independent entities with sufficient material strength and reputable guarantees sign contracts with all large banks. The three primary partners

---

[5] *Yin-lian*, which is China's credit-card system.

supply the transaction payment platform that interfaces with the banks' payment settlement system.

According to Enfodesk statistics, by the third quarter of 2013, third-party Internet payment platforms in China had received and transferred 1.6655 trillion RMB worth of transactions. Alipay accounted for 40.3 percent of those. This was higher than the 28.1 percent handled by UnionPay and the other third-party Internet-based payment institutions. In May 2011, the central bank of China announced the names of the first group of nonbanking institutions to receive permits to engage in the payment business. Alipay was among the 27 third-party payment enterprises on the list.

Offline payment is the traditional channel by which funds circulate and are paid in China. This method is divided into card-issuing institutions (i.e., banks), slip-receiving institutions (i.e., banks and third-party payment services), and UnionPay and settlement institutions. Of these, UnionPay is the sole settlement institution that can both issue point-of-sale (POS) machines (a POS information-management system) and be a slip-receiving institution and receive slip-receiving market income. By the end of 2011, the asset level of UnionPay had already reached 13.8 billion RMB, with operating revenue of around 6 billion RMB and net profit surpassing 1 billion RMB. In the four years prior to this, UnionPay's operating revenue increased 2.5 times, whereas net income increased nearly 10 times. With the swift development of the third-party payment industry, the many third-party payment institutions do not have to tie in to settlement agreements, however, but can work directly with banks. The cardless mobile payment business is also gradually progressing. The monopoly position of UnionPay with respect to payment settlement is therefore now constantly being challenged.

The role that banks play in this online payment system is very special, that is, the system composed jointly of UnionPay, third-party payment, and banks. On the one hand, banks are not willing to allow UnionPay to be a large-scale monopoly in settlement. They would rather see competitive resources available via multiple channels. On the other hand, the innovative products of third-party payment institutions form a competitive relationship with the payment settlement of banks. Because of this, the banking industry is also accelerating its own transformation, looking for innovation. More and more banks are beginning to focus on research and development (R&D) of Internet-based and mobile-based platforms and are speeding up their own individualized financial products to satisfy the financial needs of different customer groups. For example, they are setting up platforms that provide financial services for e-commerce.

According to 2012 surveys undertaken by UnionPay, fees for actual payment made by a nonfinancial institution to a bank for online payment came to only around 0.1 percent of the transaction amount. This is much lower than the 0.3 to 0.55 percent level within the UnionPay network. UnionPay calculates that the losses to all banks because of these low fees exceed 3 billion RMB. The cost is substantial when UnionPay installs POS machines and when banks install automatic teller machines (ATMs). Moreover, these offline channels are mostly for payment settlement. To prevent withdrawals from credit cards, slip-receiving institutions need to rigorously investigate the qualifications of merchants, and very small merchants generally do not come up to the standards required. Moreover, it costs several thousand RMB to install a POS machine. Each time a card is swiped, there is another substantial handling fee.

In contrast to this high threshold and high-cost offline payment method, online payment adheres to the concepts of the Internet—open and shared by all. An online payment environment can be built on the existing Internet infrastructure. At present, Alipay has already signed agreements with more than 200 financial institutions, forming an open payment and settlement channel. As the third-party payment market continues to develop and grow in size, the online payment environment will become even more transparent and open.

It is true that offline POS machines and ATM networks have an enormous customer base already and satisfy an enormous need. For a long period of time to come, online payment will not be able to replace these offline channels. Nevertheless, the swift growth of the online payment industry has raised levels of technology as well as competition for the entire payment industry. The core reason is that the open network of the Internet allows for lower costs and higher efficiency.

In terms of payment settlement, in 2013, Alipay executed 12.5 billion transactions, which approached the offline consumption by card swiping of 12.7 billion transactions. This swift increase in the application rate of

Alipay not only reflects the fact that online payment is an effective way to supplement China's existing payment systems but also that the appearance of third-party payment is aligned with the tide of the Internet age.

When third-party payment groups were in the midst of fierce consolidation, if one wanted to one had to rely on outstanding service and reasonable fees. Current CEO of Alibaba's Micro Domestic Business Group and former Deputy CEO of Alipay X. Yeming has noted, "Third-party payment enterprises cannot be in a competitive relationship with banks. We are a payment services provider that works together with and supports banks in elevating the experience of the customer in online banking." As long as regulators do not lean toward any one side and as long as they ensure a fair and effective market, reasonable competition on the part of all will force competitors to carry out innovations and improve the quality and effectiveness of their payment services. The tacit battle between third-party payment enterprises and UnionPay and the competition among third-party payment enterprises can help to build and maintain a kind of dynamic balance. This is beneficial not only to consumers but also to the society at large.

In March 2014, the People's Bank of China (China's central bank) issued a temporary restraining order calling for a stop to face-to-face payment services of Tencent and Alipay via virtual card products and Quick Response (QR) Code. For awhile, opinions were voiced saying that the central bank was protecting vested interests. However, at the same time, we do need to admit that there have been certain security problems in emerging payment methods, including those of QR Code. These are greatly in need of being addressed. Nevertheless, mobile payment has been launched, and the overall situation cannot be stopped. On April 9, 2014, Deputy CEO of Ali's Micro Finance Group and Chief Risk Officer Hu Xiaoming revealed that Ali Small Loans, under the leadership of the central bank, is currently in the process of formulating and perfecting payment standards for the QR Code. Whether it is the central bank, UnionPay, or Internet companies, all must find a way to protect the rights and interests of consumers through processes that are both cooperative and competitive.

Payment constitutes a necessary link among enterprises, merchants, and consumers. Only if the costs of this link are constantly lowered and its efficiency is improved can the productivity and the entire society's ability to consume constantly increase. Only then will entrepreneurship at the grassroots level continue to be sparked. This is one of the reasons Alipay and its payment links are so significant to grassroots innovation.

Ali Small Loans: Turning Trust into Wealth

After getting over one of the most fundamental barriers to entry for small business, namely, payment, Alibaba set its sights on the issue of how merchants within its ecosystem can get financing. Given their small size and limited ability to withstand risk, and because of their lack of corporate governance structures and adequate collateral, many of the merchants on the Alibaba platform find it hard to get operating loans through normal channels such as banks. Their ability to grow and even survive is constrained by the lack of finance.

Recognizing this financing need of many Internet merchants, Alibaba began to provide financial services for online merchants via Ali Small Loans.[6] This stemmed from its principle of doing all possible to serve the microenterprise. It came up with a slogan to describe the approach: "Turn trust into wealth, and make it easy to borrow money."

Difficulties of Small and Microenterprises in Getting Funding and Grassroots Entrepreneurship

As noted earlier, the slogan for Ali Small Loans is "Turn trust into wealth, and make it easy to borrow money." However, turning this motto into reality is not so easy.

Anyone can recognize the vital contribution that microenterprises make to China's economy. The best estimate is that small and micro-enterprises make up over 99 percent of the total number of enterprises in the country. They provide close to 80 percent of all jobs in cities and towns and generate over 75 percent of all entrepreneurial innovations. The value created by these enterprises comes to 60 percent of China's gross domestic product (GDP), and the taxes they pay come to 50 percent

---

[6]Translator's note: Now called Ant Micro Loan under the Ant Financial Services Group.

of total national tax revenues. Nevertheless, their inability to get funding has continued to hold them back. It is the main obstacle to their further growth, and indeed, it often threatens their existence.

Since the global financial crisis, China's microenterprises have been in a very tough situation. They are facing reduced orders even as the prices of their raw materials and labor have gone up. Intensified competition within industries is yet another challenge they face, which highlights the problem of scarce capital and the inability to get financing.

Microenterprises rely heavily on self-generated funds to pay for operations. Using one's own funds or borrowing from family and friends cannot support long-term growth, however. External sources of funds are currently limited to one singular channel: loans from banks or similar financial institutions. Barriers to entry are very high when it comes to using the stock market, debt markets, and private equity, and microenterprises basically have little hope of taking advantage of these channels for funding. Despite the fact that they therefore rely primarily on bank loans, only 12 percent of microenterprises can actually get a bank loan. Current Deputy CEO of Alibaba and head of its Innovative Finance Department Hu Xiaoming believes that the reason the other 88 percent misses out is either that they have no collateral to put up for a loan or that they cannot handle the complexities of the loan procedures. A third reason is that they are not the banks' "cup of tea."

Without funding channels, the inability to get capital often deals a death blow to grassroots entrepreneurs who have founded their own companies. Imagine if all those Silicon Valley entrepreneurs had not been able to get that first "bucket of money." How would the Internet have come about? How would companies such as Facebook have developed? It may not be appropriate to compare high-tech companies and Internet enterprises with grassroots efforts in China. Nevertheless, we cannot deny the innovative forces of China's grassroots, nor can we deny their potential to change China. In trying to release further grassroots entrepreneurship, therefore, one step that must not be overlooked is resolving the problem these microenterprises have in getting funding.

Meanwhile, among the multitude of microenterprises, those that are in the business of e-commerce often do not have offline assets or even data on their operations, so they face the same problems, if not worse, in the real world when it comes to raising money. On Alibaba, however, they have indeed amassed a large amount of data, including the amount of goods they have shipped, their sales data, their supply-chain circumstances, and customer evaluations. All of this information can be used as evidence of credit. Alibaba therefore decided to provide a financing service via the Internet using data from the Internet.

Cooperating with Banks in Providing a Bonded Insurance Loan Service

In 2002, Jack Ma launched something called Credit Access, which can be considered the first emerging sprout of an Alibaba financing service. After this, the Alibaba website amplified this by creating a Credit Access Index. This provided a quantified evaluation of the credit situation of both sides of a given transaction. By creating a system around this, Alibaba incorporated a whole set of indicators into an index that described an enterprise in terms of basic conditions, years in operation, trading conditions, and any business disputes, lawsuits, and so on.

At the outset, Alibaba was not intending to be a loan provider on its own. Instead, it set its sights on the "big guys" in China's financing industry, namely, the state-owned banks. Starting in 2007, Alibaba allied with the Industrial and Commercial Bank of China (ICBC) and the Construction Bank of China to launch an Internet-based bonded-insurance loan service for member enterprises.[7] This opened up a credit service that conformed to the resources of both sides. Members were not required to put up any kind of collateral. An alliance of three or more enterprises had to come together to go through Alibaba to apply to banks for a loan. Alibaba mainly played the role of a loan intermediary. It also supplied the credit records of the companies to banks, and it was then up to the bank to do due diligence and decide on whether or not to make a loan.

What had looked like a beautiful blueprint turned out to have numerous problems in actual implementation, however. Alibaba's cooperation

---

[7]The term *lian bao* means bonding a list of individuals or companies together for insuring someone's loan; *lian* indicates an alliance, that is, with banks, and *bao* again makes use of the reiterated idea of treasure, or *bao*.

with the banks was not as smooth as anticipated. The banks' traditional model for extending loans did not match well with the many small-scale, short-term loans required by e-commerce financing. There also was a huge gulf between the two sides in terms of loan concepts and review and approval procedures.

With respect to Alibaba's cooperation with the Construction Bank of China, people inside Alibaba expressed the following during interviews: "Of 100 enterprises we recommend, the Construction Bank may wash out 97 and approve 3. In the end, only two or three actually get a loan. We feel that this is rather inefficient, and it also provides a bad experience for customers." Hu Xiaoming has frankly admitted the differences:

> *Our average level of loans for customers right now is only some 60,000 RMB. When we talked to them, loans made by ICBC and the Construction Bank of China generally came to 2 RMB million. In our eyes, this was not loans to microenterprises. The entities we prefer are smaller since they are the real innovators, one factory, a shop run by husband and wife, or the customer might even be a retired military person. So long as he had credit, we were willing to loan him 2,000, 20,000, 100,000 RMB. This was the kind of thing we would rather do.*

Although this original grand scheme came to nothing, cooperating with China's commercial banks was to be of tremendous significance for Ali Small Loans. In the course of the cooperation, Alibaba drew more members into its Credit Access system and set up a complete credit evaluation system and risk-control system. Even more important, Alibaba found the direction it wanted to take in the whole process. Through innovating, it decided to use its own methods to provide financial services to microenterprises.

In June 2009, "Ali-loans" was spun off from the business-to-business (B2B) service and Ali Small Loans was established.[8] On June 8, 2010,

---

[8]Translator's note: Now called Ant Financial, a financial services provider.

three separate entities established the Zhejiang Alibaba Small-Sum Loan Shareholding Company, Ltd., in Hangzhou. The three were the Alibaba Group's Lian-he Fuxing Group, the Yintai Group, and the Wanxiang Group. This entity was China's very first microloan company oriented toward making loans to e-commerce.

After this, a similar company was set up in Sichuan Province based on cooperation between Alibaba and the Chongqing municipal government. Alibaba then began to provide financing services for microenterprises and individual entrepreneurs on the B2B, Taobao, and Tmall e-commerce platforms that were both of an ongoing nature and favorably priced. It used a data- and Internet-based operating model. Its core business was providing small-scale loans. Ali Small Loans, separated out as an independent entity, constantly improved on its operations and became highly specialized in providing financing for more and more people. At the same time, it kept to the marrow of the Alibaba mission, which was to unleash grassroots entrepreneurship. It constantly sought out new territory and resolved new problems, daring to be a sort of "hero on the front lines," breaking the path for others.

Small Is Beautiful: Focusing on Microfinancing Services

There are many reasons that formal financial institutions lend little support to microenterprises. Among them is that bank credit is not suited to the specific characteristics of small business.

According to the results of a survey undertaken in 2011, the operating and financing situation of 3,231 microenterprises in 36 cities could be characterized by the following four main features. First, their operating capital shortage was fairly low (64 percent had a gap of less than 100,000 RMB, 94 percent had a gap of less than 500,000 RMB, and 98 percent had a gap of less than 1 million RMB). Second, their time frame for needing financing was high (82 percent needed financing within 10 working days, i.e., completion of the review and approval procedure within that time, and 43 percent needed to get the loan within 5 working days). Third, they could withstand quite high interest rates (86 percent of those interviewed expressed the ability to accept rates that were four times the legally mandated rates). Fourth, they generally lacked any collateral. Alibaba's credit product was designed in a way to allow it to be targeted specifically at these characteristics.

1. Degree of Capital Gap Fairly Small: So Ali Small Loans Made Loans of Less than 1 Million RMB

Loans of 1 million RMB or less basically could satisfy the turnover rate of capital in microenterprises. It could meet their investment needs for internal bolstering. In contrast, the standard financial institutions universally kept loans at a level of more than 1 million RMB owing to their need to control costs. They therefore were unable to meet the needs of microenterprises on this front.

What's more, based on the principle of fast-in, fast-out, a loan model that saw fast turnover of loans allowed Alibaba to use a relatively small amount of capital and yet create a relatively large cumulative quantity of loans. In 2013, the average amount of a single loan made by Ali Small Loans was 13,000 RMB. The average amount made to a single customer was 36,000 RMB. This was far lower than the single-loan quantity that a traditional financial institution was able to make. Alibaba thus used its own advantages to make up for the shortcomings of banks.

2. Need to Get Loans Quickly: So Ali Small Loans Simplified Procedures and Sped Up the Process of Issuing Loans

Ali Small Loans operates 7 days a week, 24 hours a day, year round. It issues loans and takes in loan repayments all the time. If an applicant has his or her materials in order, the system can provide him or her with a loan within three minutes of completing the process of review and approval. This is the shortest time an applicant has to wait; the longest time, if his or her materials are in order, is seven days. The entire process takes place on the Internet. The procedures are simplified, and the applicant does not need to spend money on transportation or other such links in the process.

3. Mostly Short-Term Use of the Money and an Ability to Withstand High Interest Rates: So Ali Small Loans Adopted a Loan Model of Fast In, Fast Out

In contrast to bank loans, Ali Small Loans adopted a small-sum loan model that was fast in, fast out. In all of 2012, the average length of time that a customer "occupied" capital was 123 days. Although the interest that customers could withstand and accepted was 18 percent at an annualized rate, the actual cost of the money was around 6.7 percent.

A good example is order loans. Ali Small Loans' order loan product was priced at a daily interest rate of 0.005. On average, a customer would use such a loan for four days. At an annualized rate, the financing interest-rate cost of the loan to the customer was only 6 percent, roughly equivalent to the officially approved standard interest rate for a one-year loan.

4. Difficulty in Supplying Any Guarantee or Collateral: So Ali Small Loans Did Not Require Collateral

The credit loans of Ali Small Loans did not require any collateral whatsoever, nor did any guarantor need to stand behind the customer. For the order loan product, the applicant had to supply either the orders or the shipping receipts (bills of lading). This swept away what had been an important hurdle in making credit loans available to microenterprises. It also went a step further in simplifying the applications and review and approval procedures, and it lowered the costs of the financing for microenterprises.

Alibaba's small-sum credit loan product did fairly well in differentiating itself from standard bank credit products. It focused on a small segment of the market, namely, microfinance services, and therefore was able to extend benefits to more microenterprises that had been left on the outside of official financing channels. Because of the need to control costs, and because of discrimination against the different kinds of ownership systems of small businesses,[9] traditional banking institutions did

---

[9]Translator's note: That is, because of their being privately owned as opposed to state-owned.

not target the many small businesses on Alibaba's platforms as potential customers. These customers therefore were outside the range of vision of the official financing institutions. When talking about how Ali Small Loans positioned itself, Hu Xiaoming has said, "In the entire financing ecosystem, we only make loans that are 1 million RMB or less. We leave anything bigger to the banks. We are 'vegetarians'; we don't eat this kind of meat."

Given both cost and risk considerations, traditional banks are unwilling to touch the microfinance business, whereas Ali Small Loans explicitly declares that its upper limit is 1 million RMB. By positioning itself in a very clear-minded way, based on cloud-computing technology and a large amount of data, Alibaba has carved out an entirely new path in Ali Small Loans. By the end of 2013, 642,000 customers had received loans through this system. Ali Small Loans had issued a total amount of 172.2 billion RMB in loans.

Big-Data-Based Risk-Control System

The critical issue in providing funding for microenterprises lies in figuring out how to handle information asymmetries. The field of information economics says that information asymmetries between buyers and lenders lead to higher costs, as well as creating moral hazard and adverse selection. This influences the equilibrium between lending and borrowing, supply and demand.

Why is it that banks find it so hard to make microloans? Microenterprises have particular qualities that ensure that information is asymmetrical, whereas the traditional loan technologies of banks ensure that returns are not able to cover the risks involved. Alibaba, however, believes that it can use its big-data technologies and its cloud-computing capacity to resolve this asymmetry in information to a certain degree. By the end of June 2013, the nonperforming loan rate of Ali Small Loans was 0.84 percent, lower than the level of commercial banks in China. The product called Ali Small Loans uses Alibaba's core technology, namely, big-data technology, to improve the structure of information in an effective way and thereby maintain this relatively low rate of nonperforming loans. The unique advantage held by Ali Small Loans is that it has access to over 10 years of accumulated statistics on microenterprises on Alibaba's platforms. It uses these statistics to form a risk-control system, with preloan, midloan, and postloan links that tie in to one another.

Before making a loan, Ali Small Loans abandons its broadly open-style method of operations and sales. It instead analyzes data that have been amassed on its platforms. It differentiates among customers, selecting those on the platform that have been operating for a fairly long time and that are more reliable or creditworthy. It then bestows credit on these and issues an invitation to contract with its small loan product. Right now, more than 2 million merchants are being invested with such credit. This enables more micro-opportunities to enjoy the resources of funding and credit.

In applying for loans, customers do not need to provide any collateral or guarantees. All they need to provide is gross sales figures for the past year, operating costs, gross assets, gross liabilities, and other related financial data. Alibaba's trading platform has already accumulated a large amount of data on them relating to their volume of completed orders, volume of trades, inventory turnover, customer relations, credit record, and so on. Based on its cloud-computing platform, Ali Small Loans then "mines" these data and carries out a "washing" process. It uses big-data-handling technology, including rating cards and quantitative analysis to make a fairly accurate assessment of the ability of the microenterprise to pay back a loan and of its likely intentions of paying back a loan.

After a loan has been extended, Alibaba carries out a real-time form of regulatory control over data to do with the borrower, keeping track of volume of business, evaluations of the entity, conditions of the industry, and so on. If it discovers any unusual activity or violations of prescribed thresholds, it can automatically mobilize mechanisms that make deductions from the borrower's Alipay account. Most of these supervisory controls are handled automatically via cloud-computing systems and computers. Loan officers are only responsible for supplemental actions. With respect to loan term limits, Ali Small Loans encourages borrowers to pay back loans as fast as possible. According to Ali Small Loans statistics, the term of order-type loans generally does not exceed one week. Each individual loan generally comes to less than 10,000 RMB, but the frequency of loans is high. Some vendors take out order loans practically every day.

In addition, Ali Small Loans has set up a corresponding credit-restoration system that allows enterprises to restore a good credit rating. If they themselves encounter problems with people not paying for product, as long as their credit numbers are good on the platform and they have future cash flow, Ali Small Loans provides them with supplemental assistance. By means of operating measures on its e-commerce platform, it provides support to enable the enterprise to recover its ability to pay back its borrowed money.

Alibaba's microfinance services group has used big data and cloud-computing platforms to prove that the data amassed on the Internet has value and can be used to provide evidence of the credit situation of its enterprises. Through a combination of Internet technology and unique innovations in finance, Alibaba's small loan model is truly achieving the motto, "Turn trust into wealth and make it easy to borrow money." It is bringing benefits to ever-more microenterprises engaged in e-commerce. The small loan system of Ali Small Loans is providing China with a feasible path toward funding microenterprises in the Alibaba ecosystem. It has provided the life blood for more than 300,000 grassroots entrepreneurs by providing the indispensable financial support for releasing their entrepreneurship.

YuEbao: Internet Ways to Manage Personal Wealth

YuEbao is a value-added service that was created by Alipay. Users shift funds from their Alipay accounts into YuEbao in order to invest in a wealth-management fund called the Tianhong Zenglibao Money Market Fund. In shifting funds into YuEbao, they can gain relatively high returns from current deposits while still being able to use funds in their YuEbao accounts. At any time, they can purchase goods on the Internet, use Alipay for payment functions, and so on. The advantage of YuEbao lies in the fact that funds shifted into its account not only earn higher returns but also can be used to pay for consumption in ways that are flexible, quick, and easy.

Collision Between the Internet Business
and the Financial Industry

After YuEbao saw the light of day on June 13, 2013, it was broadly regarded by the public as yet another historic episode that changed the use of the Internet for finances following on the innovations of Alipay. By January 31, 2014, this fund had already reached a scale of 350 billion RMB. More than 58.95 million people had YuEbao accounts. It had become the largest fund in the Chinese domestic market. It would have been impossible to realize such a magnitude by using offline sales methods.

By June 30, 2014, YuEbao had amassed 100 million users and had taken in some 574.2 billion RMB into its accounts. YuEbao had created a publicly funded Chinese money-market fund with the greatest number of users of any fund in China. It also counted as the fourth largest money-market fund in the world (Figure 5.2).

FIGURE 5.2 *Customer number and investment value of the Tianhong Fund shown on YuEbao website as of January 15, 2014*

This initial "round of cannonballs" shot off by YuEbao quickly attracted the attention of Baidu, Tencent, and other large Internet companies, as well as commercial banks. They all rushed into the competition and began to innovate with a number of wealth-management products as well. On November 2, 2013, seventeen fund companies registered on the Taobao site and opened their own "stores." They were quite proactive in promotional activities surrounding the upcoming 11.11 Shopping Festival. In the 11.11 Shopping Festival of 2013, the business volume of transactions relating to wealth-management products came to 908 million

RMB. The official flagship store of Guohua Insurance did 531 million RMB in business, the official flagship store of the Yifangda Fund did 211 million RMB in business, and the official flagship store of Sino Life Insurance did 101 million RMB in business. The competition between the Internet and the world of finance was underway.

The direct-sales method employed by money-market funds, other types of funds, and customer account services on e-commerce platforms is actually not new. Instead, the major breakthrough of YuEbao lies in the way it merges a form of direct-sales method organically into its system. This takes full account of the experience of its Internet users. Part of the key thinking behind the Internet model of finance is that the user is the center. It attacks key demand directly and focuses strongly on the customer experience.

Most users belong to grassroots classes of people. YuEbao guides this portion of users in learning to use new wealth-management products to make reasonable plans for their modest sums of money. In actuality, this is a powerful impetus to releasing entrepreneurship among the public at large. The enormous attention that YuEbao is getting from the public and the debates going on about it naturally have attracted the attention of many others. Consumers who have never done any online purchasing now want to try it. In the end, this has had a very positive effect on increasing the number of transactions going through Taobao. "Pull on one hair, and the whole body is affected," as the saying goes. Every time Alibaba pulls another "hair," the entire chain of e-commerce is affected. If this very vital emerging industry, this sunrise industry, did not get refreshed by the morning dew all the time, it would not be as sparkling and lively as it is today. It can be said that innovation is its fundamental driving force for constant development, as well as the most effective route to growth.

At the current time in China, quite a few issues have become apparent in the way banks and securities firms market financial products. For example, they aim for short-term profits. They promote high-risk products to a clientele that can only handle low risk. They engage in churning, make inappropriate recommendations, and so on. In contrast, Internet sales platforms have the advantage of being able to tap latent customer demand among targeted customer groups and with targeted product designs. They can be more precise in marketing to appropriate customers. The powerful interactive nature of Internet technology and its precision can effectively lower the costs of service.

From the perspective of financial institutions, therefore, fund companies have for many years wanted to break out of their excessive reliance on banking channels. They want to move away from being forced into a passive position. It is no exaggeration to say that Alibaba's cooperation with the Tianhong Fund stirred up a "channel revolution" in the fund world. No longer do fund companies have to line up to go through bank channels to achieve distribution. They can go through innovative forms of cooperation with Internet companies. With much less trouble, they can achieve an increase in customers and ramp up the scale of their business.

Naturally, the partnership between the traditional banking industry and Internet companies has been achieved by grinding down the edges. It has not all been smooth sailing. In the early period of cooperation, one of the differences of opinion on the part of both sides was the starting point at which YuEbao would sell the fund. Normally, funds solicit a minimum of between 100 and 1,000 RMB. Ali Small Loans felt that this should be reduced, and it proposed that the threshold for wealth management should be just 1 RMB. The fund felt that there wasn't too much problem in handling a 1 RMB starting sales point but that customers would not directly see any tangible results, which would influence customer confidence. After repeated discussions, both sides agreed that the target customer for YuEbao was someone with no professional experience in how to handle money management and that therefore 1 RMB would be easier to accept psychologically. Alibaba's approach to always putting the customer first is what persuaded its partner in the end. The 1 RMB starting point was a precedent in the fund world, and it is clearly stated on the Taobao page. After this, 100 funds saw notable results. From this single example of the initial sales quantity, we can see that collisions with the Internet financial industry have helped to change the old concepts of traditional companies. Internet business has changed their customary ways of doing things. In the information age, they have had to change their own strategies and pick up their pace to keep up with the times.

The collisions between Internet finance and traditional finance are a long way from being over. Some traditional financial institutions have already begun to be aware that cooperation may be the best choice if they do not want total confrontation. The fusing of traditional finance and Internet finance and the mutual interpenetration of the various links of the financial industry will necessarily lead to more innovations in distribution channels but also in the industry overall. It will have an enormous impact on the reform of China's financial structure.

A More Dispersed Approach to Personal Wealth Management and Money-Market Funds

YuEbao is essentially a money-market fund. It mainly invests in short-term bonds, repurchase agreements (repos), central bank notes, bank deposits, and other money-market products. As of 2013, money-market funds were returning an annualized yield of between 3 and 4 percent, which is roughly 10 times the return on current deposits. Because money-market funds and current deposits fall in different categories with different kinds of risk, it is not right to try to compare their yields directly on the basis of just two years of returns. Nevertheless, for investors who cannot accommodate much risk, money-market funds may be regarded as a fairly good investment choice.

In addition to this aspect of being a money-market fund, YuEbao is tailor made for grassroots classes of people. The average investment amount put into YuEbao by a customer is 1,912.67 RMB. This is definitely a grassroots kind of figure, but it also manifests the force of common people in creating a great potential "long tail" made up of many small, fragmented financial transactions. It is also an important signal that the age of Internet finance is on us. What traditional forms of financial management focus on is the wealthy investor. This conforms to the 80-20 rule in traditional business. The profits of banks and other traditional financial institutions rely predominantly on their 20 percent of high-value customers. Focusing on high-net-worth customers is rational because the rate of return is highest. Meanwhile, the 20 percent of high-value customers enjoy extremely good financial service from banks and financial institutions, whereas the common person, from whom banks make very little, does not.

According to data from the American Bureau of Labor Statistics, in 2008, there were 208,000 people professionally engaged in financial consulting services in the United States. This means that around 1,500 people, on average, could share the services of one financial consultant. Nevertheless, Robert Shiller believes that there are still too few people engaged in the financial consulting industry.

We lack comparable statistics for China, but there is certainly reason to assume that in a country with such an undeveloped financial industry the number of professionals in finance is not large enough to satisfy the demand for financial services. This is particularly true of people who are at the middle and lower levels, what we are calling the *grassroots classes*. Excluded from the financial industry or unable to get relevant information, it is possible that these people are subjected to unfair treatment given that they do not themselves participate in financial decisions or cannot themselves make effective decisions. To reduce the possibility of this happening, we should do all we can to ensure that financial services are more universally available. We should lower their costs and enable finance to truly benefit the public at large.

YuEbao and other similar Internet funds have lowered the barriers to entry for financial services. They have enabled young people with small change and grassroots people with middle to low incomes to participate in managing their own money and have a chance at making it increase in value. An investment of 10,000 RMB may only earn a net income of around 1 RMB per day on average. This kind of return is not going to satisfy high-net-worth people. What YuEbao has recognized, however, is that by means of software that is designed to be user friendly, this 1 RMB return is also enabling the whole subject of personal finance to reach grassroots people.

A shop owner who lives outside the fifth-ring road in Beijing is the typical YuEbao user. The shop owner, Xiaolong, has never invested in any kind of personal money-management product before. All his savings reside in the bank. His little brother has recently introduced him to YuEbao. His shop already uses Alipay Wallet for payments when customers buy things. Those receipts can be transferred directly into YuEbao—it is extremely quick and easy—so Xiaolong begins to put his money there.

These mornings as you are walking along the street, you can hear the customers in front of breakfast stalls talking about how the cash for their morning roll came from yesterday's earnings on YuEbao. YuEbao has already become one of the most active applications of Alipay Wallet. More and more of Alipay's customers wake up in the morning and immediately check their earnings on YuEbao on their cell phones. YuEbao is now trying to make the service more interactive and participatory, so through a new app called "Little Happiness Broadcasting," users can share the news about their own net worth on YuEbao with their friends.

Having more Internet companies and financial companies participate in the business of Internet-based money-market funds is also helpful in cultivating a more knowledgeable public when it comes to investing and money management. It is particularly helpful in educating younger people. The 21–25 age group makes up 30 percent of Alipay's current customers, while the 25–30 age group constitutes another 28 percent. This means that over half of Alipay's customers are young and may be constrained by their budgets and lack of experience in investing and money management.

Analyzing the subject according to levels of income, China's low wage earners tend to put their money in banks to earn interest. Over time, however, currency holding is not a good strategy in the face of inflation in the long run, so the more these people put money in banks, the less they have in actual wealth. This means that low wage earners in the country, the people with the least financial security, are actually taking a smaller and smaller share of the society's wealth. For this one reason alone, their income disparity with others is getting greater and greater.

How to enable the public to spend without too much worry while also being able to put funds into investment is a multilayered issue. One of its aspects involves cultivating an awareness of and knowledge about how to handle personal finances. YuEbao does not restrict the amount of money one can invest or the time horizon. The funds are available and can be pulled out any time the customer wants them. This unique feature makes it possible for an awareness of personal finance to begin to enter people's lives while also benefiting the further nurturing and growth of China's entire personal-finance market.

The *Survey Report of 2013* on China's e-banking indicated that 87 percent of "netizens" had already heard of YuEbao. Among these, some had used YuEbao as the starting point for their path toward handling their own personal finances. It can be said that YuEbao has provided China's public with quite a broad form of universal education about money management and finance.

By August 2013, the amount of money in China's personal savings accounts in banks surpassed 43 trillion RMB for three months in a row. Bank deposits now stand at their highest point in history. In per-capita terms, deposits are over 30,000 RMB for every single Chinese citizen. China has more personal savings deposits than any other country on Earth. The savings rate of its citizens exceeds 50 percent, which is one of the highest in the world. In addition to helping dispel worries about having enough money for security, this high figure also reflects the ignorance of the Chinese public when it comes to consuming and investing.

During the same period, the savings rate of citizens in the United States was 4.6 percent (Figure 5.3). The contrast between the two is extreme. There is a saying in the United States, "Money doesn't grow on trees, but if people not only save up money but invest it wisely, money can indeed be treelike, always putting out new green leaves." Investment concepts are more universally understood in the United States than in China. By handling investment products wisely, people can earn a return off their own savings.

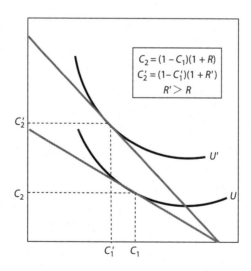

FIGURE 5.3 *Intertemporal utility changes with respect to a change in saving rate*

A short vignette reflects this contrast in financial experience between the two countries. An older American woman and an older Chinese woman have the following exchange. The Chinese woman says, "Now that I'm getting older, I guess I've saved up enough money to go buy myself a home." The American woman says, "A few days ago I paid off the 30-year mortgage on my home, so I now own it." In contrast to the United States and other Western countries, the Chinese public is less familiar with net present value and the time value of money. The degree to which borrowing and loaning money and investment decisions are understood is still at a preliminary stage, which means that the industry still has plenty of room to grow.

The primary customer group of Alipay is 20- to 30-year-olds, a market segment that still has limited savings. These people are less able to muster financial power and so are neglected by traditional financial institutions and fail to get adequate financial services. In the equal and open environment of online platforms, however, not only can they receive more information and better services, but they also can earn a return by using money-management services that are provided on a micro or dispersed basis. From a macro perspective, this is also useful in raising the financial awareness of the generation that came after the 1980s and the 1990s. As understanding of money management improves in China, and as people upgrade their capabilities, they will not be so severely reliant on their children to take care of them when they are older. Through financial planning and thinking ahead, they should be able to provide some security for themselves.

In addition to providing people with an alternative to bank savings deposits as a way to manage money, money-market funds are also highly useful in pushing forward the development of China's interest-rate markets. The goal of liberalizing interest rates involves relaxing controls over rates. It involves allowing capital to flow toward higher rates of return via market-determined methods and thereby breaking the monopoly that banks have over capital markets.

The experience of the United States in "marketizing" its interest rates is instructive. The result of these rates was that participants in the market, including depositors and lenders, derived higher returns from banks. The main impetus for this kind of marketization of interest rates came from the fast development of money markets at the time. During the 1970s in the United States, because of a nonmarketized environment for interest rates and the constant innovations among many different financial institutions, America's money markets developed very rapidly. Meanwhile, as commercial banks constantly put out new products and raised levels of services, the gap between the return on money-market funds and the return on bank deposits shrank. After the start of the twenty-first century, the size of America's money-market funds compared with current deposits in banks had already greatly declined. It can be seen from this that money-market funds do not, in themselves, "shake the foundations" of bank deposits. On the contrary, the growth of money-market funds can stimulate better banking services and in the end bring benefits to all users.

Statistics from China's Securities and Investment Funds Industry Association indicate that by September 30, 2013, the net value of the money-market type of China's open-type funds came to 575.448 billion RMB. In contrast, the net value of such funds in the United States came to US$2.6797 trillion. Clearly, the scale of China's money-market funds is far behind that of developed countries such as the United States, which means that there is a great deal of room to grow into this area in China.

As demand is being generated among the public for investment and money-management products, to a certain degree the growth of money-market funds will also open up new channels for the flow of capital among different markets. This, in turn, will push forward China's process of reforming its interest-rate markets. The overall goal is to upgrade the efficiency with which resources are allocated in the country. From a macroeconomic perspective, this benefits the common person and the entire society.

In this current great wave of Internet-based finance, what each major enterprise is trying to figure out is how to gain greater market share in the course of competition. In addition to dividing up the pie, however, a more significant task will be figuring out how everyone can cooperate to make a bigger pie. This will be far more beneficial to society. Whether through Alipay, Ali Wallet, or YuEbao, all at Alibaba are trying to use the Internet and big data to open up financial channels to increase the size of the financial pie.

Alibaba is using lower-cost and higher-efficiency means to do this and making sure that common people can participate in the process. If people engaged in the financial industry and Internet companies can work together to integrate the spirit of the Internet with financial innovations, that is, use openness, equality, cooperation, and sharing to build a sound financial ecosystem, finance will then truly create wealth for society.

CHAPTER 6

E-COMMERCE LEGISLATION AND INNOVATIONS IN REGULATORY SUPERVISION BY THE PUBLIC

HUANG LINGLING

We are all beginning to be aware of a new kind of commercial civilization given the rapid development of three aspects of the Internet, namely, e-commerce, e-goods, and e-rules. To grow this new kind of commerce in a sound and sustainable way, it is becoming especially important to have standardized regulation of the industry. China's existing laws and regulations have not kept up with the Internet's fast-paced change. This means that we need a new structure, which can be called *Internet rules*, to serve as a support.

China's existing laws and regulations originated in the era of large-scale industry and in China's unique planned-economy period as dominated by state-owned enterprises. There is quite an obvious generation gap between the laws of that age and the modern laws required by an age that is based on IC, the Internet, and big data.

Meanwhile, the language of existing laws is based on the advanced economies of the United States and Europe. Again, there is obviously a major chasm between such laws and the economics, society, culture, and history of a country such as China, which has the advantage of being later-to-develop but that still lacks a certain degree of development.

The regulatory system of the platform of the Alibaba Group is constantly undergoing innovative improvements. In this regard, it may provide useful lessons for the regulatory aspects of the new age.

A Smart Regulatory System

The Internet has already been going for more than 40 years now. At the outset, it was manifested mainly through tools. Sina was, for example, a tool for disseminating information, whereas Tencent was a tool for communicating among people. 360 was a tool for ensuring security, Baidu was a search-engine tool, and so on. As the Internet developed, however, the network itself began to take on social attributes. It became a space in which people live and grow.

The formation of a *social* condition has to satisfy two conditions. One is that people exist within a certain environmental space. The second is that people do not exist in isolation within this environmental space. Instead, the mutual interaction between them forms a fairly stable interconnection and relationship.

In the Alibaba Group, the social attributes of the Internet have two particular characteristics. The first relates to the material level of things in the virtual society of Ali, namely, commercial activity and money transfers, as well as the mental level, namely, people communicating with one another. The second relates to the way Ali has taken on the functions of social management or, one could say, governance in this virtual society. For example, Ali is responsible for account security, for providing tools, and for formulating rules and regulations.

Based on the preceding two characteristics, Alibaba's difficulties have been greatest with respect to carrying out regulation of security. Given the need to standardize rules and regulations, in innovative fashion, Alibaba set up an Information Security Department. This department is responsible for tying together all the security aspects of the Taobao trading platform, which include ensuring the security of information, ensuring that online merchants and online products are authentic and reliable, and ensuring the security of consumers. The Information Security Department has endured years of pulling together the efforts of many different departments with respect to the systems governing transactions on the Internet. It is different from the Information Technology Department and also different from the Internet Rules Formulation Department. It involves an extremely broad range of topics, including virtual products and real products—and then there are considerations of information, logistics, credit, and transactions, and there are enterprises, and there are individual people. Figure 6.1 illustrates the framework of the functions of the Ali Information Security Department.

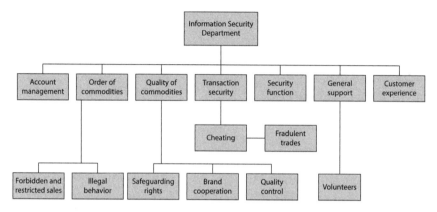

FIGURE 6.1 *Framework of the various functions of Alibaba's Information Security Department*

To achieve harmony among the platforms over which it has jurisdiction, the Information Security Department has used innovative approaches to turn certain real-world management methods into "Internet-ized" methods. It has applied offline methods to online procedures to form a set of unique management models. Ali has put them into three main categories, which it calls the three main lines of defense of the Ali security framework.

First Line of Defense: Protecting the Security of Accounts
The Information Security Department uses three primary measures to ensure the security of accounts. First, when vendors open a "store," they must certify their identity. This identity certification system is linked directly to the Chinese government's Public Security Bureau and its population information system. The two systems are synchronized and check whether or not the data that the vendor has supplied are valid. Second, vendors must use their registered identity certificate to open a credit-card account with a bank. By remitting money to that account,

Ali confirms whether or not the account does indeed belong to the said vendor. Third, the vendor has to have his or her photograph taken as he or she holds his or her identification card so that the information can be checked and confirmed. These measures are used to confirm the account information of the vendor and the actual name and integrity of the vendor.

Alipay's Identity Certification System

Identity certification in a virtual environment is a challenge to the intelligence-based capabilities of the management system. If you don't carry out identity certification, it becomes hard to control the risk of the platform. In carrying out identity certification, however, you come up against all kinds of resistance. For example, in 2010, the Ministry of Industry and Information Technology of the People's Republic of China made it clear that any individual wanting to start a website had to go in person to go through procedures and have his or her photograph taken. This provoked considerable unwillingness on the part of people responsible for websites to divulge their personal information.

Faced with this dilemma, Alipay came up with a creative solution. It set up a test of the identity of the person being certified by sending money to his or her account. This ingenious solution resolved the problem and at the same time reduced the burden on the person being certified as much as possible. Alipay's handling of the matter in this way also displayed an open and creative mind-set; that is, it resolved the problem through the support of already existing channels (in this case, the enormous network of banks). It turned virtual into real and turned "what the other has" (namely, a bank's confirmation) into "what I have."

Second Line of Defense: Protecting the Security of Products

Taobao currently encompasses more than 800 million online products. Among these there is no dearth of illegal, prohibited, restricted, and counterfeited items. Another dilemma confronting the Information Security Department therefore soon became how to ensure effective regulatory supervision over all these products.

With respect to illegal and prohibited items and restricted items, the Information Security Department first divided them into categories by consulting both Chinese law and the provisions of international conventions. It calculated that more than 40,000 items currently on its platform are illegal, prohibited, or restricted. What's more, it estimated that the figure would go up over time, not down. To deal with this problem, the Information Security Department cooperated with the public security system in China, including such parts of the system as the Internet Security Department, the Food Safety Department, the Anti-Illegal-Publications Department, and so on. It synchronized the online and offline categories of behavior that were defined by all as contravening laws and regulations.

With respect to counterfeited goods, the Information Security Department's main strategy could be summarized as protection + maintaining legitimate rights and interests + supporting and helping. The category of supporting and helping could be seen in such things as educating vendors, providing official sources to buyers for the original makers of the goods, cooperating with the Ministry of Commerce and Industry to open up channels for registering copyrights on a preferential basis, and so on. With respect to fake trades and counterfeit goods, it is sometimes hard to distinguish which are authentic and which are not. To do so, on the one hand, Ali used its massive database system and applied its research and development (R&D) system to develop an intelligence-based (or smart) discriminating system. Some 99 percent of goods can be put through this system and recognized accurately. If the machine has any question and the system cannot confirm authenticity, then it transfers the order to a human labor order, and a person carries out the final differentiation. On the other hand, Ali cooperates with the makers of authentic goods who inform Ali of the array of their authentic products. Ali enters this information into the intelligence-based or smart discriminating system. Naturally, attacking counterfeit products is a constant battle for Ali. Not only must Ali undertake this effort, however, but the government and the public also must cooperate in the effort as well.

Louis Vuitton and Coach Team Up with Taobao to Attack Counterfeiting Behavior

On October 11, 2013, the Taobao platform and Louis Vuitton announced the signing of a memorandum of agreement in Paris. Under this agreement, the two sides set up proactive cooperative mechanisms to jointly protect intellectual property and to jointly attack counterfeiting behavior on the Taobao sales platform. In fact, starting in 2010, Taobao had already instituted regular periodic meetings with Louis Vuitton to carry out a series of cooperative measures to protect property rights and attack piracy. In 2013, it went further in cooperating with the Public Security Department on the issue, starting a series of actions on this single issue to punish the makers of a group of counterfeited goods.

Around the same time, Coach, a designer brand for luxury accessories, signed a memorandum of agreement with Taobao in New York that renewed an agreement signed earlier in 2011. The purpose was to deepen anticounterfeiting cooperation and work together with Taobao in suppressing counterfeit sales on Taobao and infringement of Coach's intellectual property. Both sides also committed to protecting the rights and interests of consumers.

Protecting Intellectual Property Rights

Intellectual property rights are an important target of regulatory concern. The subject involves a wide range of things from commodities (products) to store names to illustrations, movies, and so on. Often it is unclear whether or not infringement has occurred because there is a certain degree of difficulty in distinguishing real from fake. Because of this, the Alibaba Group has set up a synthesis of rules and regulations. It incorporates all parts of intellectual property rights that have to do with material things. It includes things about which the Internet still has no legal determination, and it includes a full set of mechanisms for bringing legal action. Figure 6.2 shows Alibaba's rules for punishment of fraudulent sales practices.

FIGURE 6.2 *Illustration of an event: Taobao small vendors surround and attack Tmall*

Third Line of Defense: Protecting the Security of Transactions
As in the real world, such illegal phenomena as swindling, extortion, and stealing cannot be wholly avoided in the Ali virtual society. To keep such behaviors from getting worse, however, the Information Security Department first divided all kinds of such behavior into categories and analyzed the features that characterize each behavior. It set up models using big data. Through intelligence-capable systems, it set up uninterrupted real-time "lining up and examining."

Another form of criminal behavior that is unique to the Internet happens when someone suspected of committing a crime issues an invitation from an outside network that is then transmitted to Taobao to carry out the crime. This kind of activity is generally concentrated in virtual (nonmaterial) products, on game programs, and so on. In order to attack this kind of criminal behavior, the Information Security Department intends to set up long-term cooperative relationships with external networks to synthesize and organize information from all networks and thereby use all lines of attack.

The System of Security Deposits
The "Taobao Rules and Regulations" stipulate that merchants who operate on the Taobao marketplace must possess a Tao Gold Certificate. This gold certificate is mainly a security deposit used

to ensure that the merchant operates in line with Taobao's rules and regulations. When a merchant violates the rules, according to the service agreement he or she has signed with Taobao, as well as relevant other rules and regulations, that merchant must pay a violation fee as per agreement to Taobao and to the consumer. This is done to diligently protect the rights and interests of consumers and to preserve the confidence of the public in e-commerce (Figure 6.3).

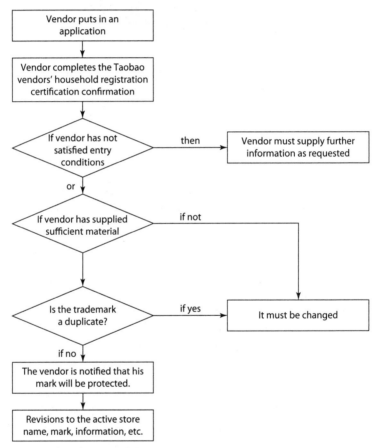

FIGURE 6.3 *Flowchart describing the protection process for getting a Tao-mark*

The Information Security Department is the core of the Alibaba Group's regulatory control over its platforms. Its mission is to guard and protect Alibaba's "treasure," namely, its prosperity and success, in a stable and orderly way. It does this through intelligence-based or *smart regulatory measures, namely, the three lines of defense of the Alibaba security framework.*

Taobao's Evaluation and Indexing System

Taobao's evaluation system is based on rating a number of indicators about the subject in question that are mutually interconnected and form an internally consistent organic whole. To ensure that this indexing system is scientific and standardized, the system was created in compliance with a number of major principles. Specifically, the indicators must be systematic, representative, concise, scientific, comparable, manageable, quantifiable, and comprehensive.

Taobao's Indexing System for Evaluation

Taobao's indexing or grading system for evaluation is a method by which both sides of a transaction can evaluate each other after the transaction has taken place, that is, after buyer and seller on the Taobao platform conduct business with each other. These evaluations then are used as a reference by other buyers and sellers, given that the evaluations of both sides are made available in ways that are fair, open, transparent, and accountable.

In contrast to traditional ways of rating companies that are derived from official sources or third-party professional institutions, this type of evaluation is bottom-up as opposed to top-down. It involves a broadly based group of people, and it is dynamic. Taobao's evaluation and grading system is built on three main cornerstones, namely, Alipay, AliWangwang,[1] and real-name certification.

The Online Payment Tool Alipay

The online payment tool called Alipay is one of the cornerstones of Alibaba's evaluation system in that it serves to defend the security of online

---

[1]Translator's note: From the official website of Alibaba: "AliWangwang is a personal computer–based instant-messaging tool that facilitates text, audio, and video communication between buyers and sellers. It operates on Taobao Marketplace."

payments on the platform. As a third-party payment platform, Alipay serves as guarantor of the goods being sold by the seller and of the payment being paid by the purchaser. Taobao stipulates that only once the purchaser has received the goods and confirmed receipt on Alipay can both sides appraise each other through the evaluation system. At the same time, irrespective of whether the buyer chooses to pay through Alipay, an online bank, quick-and-easy pay, or a credit card, confirmation of payment must be done through Alipay. Because of this condition, in addition to serving as escrow agent or guarantor, Alipay can effectively prevent any fake transactions from occurring.

The Online Chat Tool AliWangwang

The online communications tool called AliWangwang is a free online business communications form of software that was tailor-made for merchants on Taobao and Alibaba. It enables buyers to get in touch with sellers at any time to discuss details about products and negotiate a transaction. At the same time, it allows for eyewitness confirmation in the evaluation system. Taobao's regulations stipulate that if any dispute arises from a transaction, the record of conversations on AliWangwang may be used as evidence in resolving the case.

Certification of Real Name

Taobao's regulations give buyers the option of registering their real names or not, and generally buyers are only required to fill in basic information. Registration and activation can be done using the Taobao platform. In terms of sellers, however, real-name certification is required to ensure account security. As mentioned earlier, sellers must fill in their real names, addresses, telephone numbers, identity registration numbers, photographs of themselves as on their identification cards, and bank account numbers. The system confirms the bank account numbers. These measures are taken to guarantee authenticity of the certification and to guarantee the security and authenticity of the account.

In abiding by the main principles according to which the evaluation system was formulated (systematic, representative, concise, scientific, comparable, manageable, quantifiable, and comprehensive), the Taobao evaluation system includes two main parts. Those are *credit evaluation* and *rating of the store.*

Credit Evaluation System

The Chinese term for credit that is used by Alibaba can refer to both credit and integrity. In the context of someone's financial strength, it is used in the sense of credit. In the context of trustworthiness, it refers to a quantified measure of integrity. In the United States and other Western countries, the use of credit cards is pervasive and is based on a reasonably well-established credit evaluation system. China does not have such a system, and this has been a bottleneck choking the development of Internet businesses. Alipay has been helpful in serving as a credit evaluation system via evaluation of the transaction records of Alipay users, but this still has not been sufficient. As a result, Alibaba's Ant Financial Group recently organized a company called Sesame Credit Management Co., Ltd. This is an independent credit assessment and credit management organization. Sesame Credit assesses the personal credit situations of individuals based on objective measures by connecting a variety of services and applying big-data and cloud-computing technology.

The Ant Financial Services Group was itself spun off as a financial branch of the Alibaba Group in October 2014. The launch of this financial arm was an expression of Alibaba's ambition to develop financial services based on its innovative online payment platform Alipay. Such services now include payment (Alipay), credit evaluation (Sesame Credit), microlending (Ant Micro Loans), cloud computing (Ant Financial Cloud), and such financial management services as YuEbao and ZhaocaiBao.[2]

In terms of quantified measures of integrity, the following procedures apply on the Taobao platform. Based on a real transaction, both buyer and seller "members" on the Taobao platform are asked to complete

---

[2]Websites relating to these are as follows: Ant Financial: http://www.antgroup.vn/; Sesame Credit: http://zmxy.antgroup.com/index.htm; Ant Micro Loans: http://www.antgroup.com/page/xiaodai.htm; Ant Financial Cloud: http://www.antgroup.com/page/jinrongyun.htm; YuEbao: bao.alipay.com; and ZhaocaiBao: zhaocaibao.alipay.com.

mutual evaluations within 15 days of the successful completion of a piece of business. Buyer may rate their purchased goods according to a three-level rating of good, medium, or poor, and sellers may rate certain criteria on the same three-level rating. Overall, these ratings are known as *integrity evaluations.*

Rating of the Store

The store-rating system is conducted after Taobao members complete a successful transaction. It is limited to a one-time evaluation, with the purchaser rating the seller using the seller's Taobao membership identity. It includes four items: whether or not the description of the goods tallies with the actual goods, the service attitude of the seller, the speed with which the seller dispatched the goods, and the speed of actual delivery. The store ratings are dynamic indicators, so the average rating of a store incorporates all ratings of the past six months.

Reference Standards for Grading Sellers

Degree to Which the Purchased Goods Tally with Their Description

5 points: Extremely high quality, completely tallies with the description of the seller, extremely satisfied

4 points: Not bad, basically the same as what the seller described, still quite satisfied

3 points: Only so-so, not as good as what was described by the seller

2 points: Included some damaged goods, not in line with what the seller described, dissatisfied

1 point: Inferior and unacceptable, not in accord with what was described by the seller, extremely dissatisfied

Seller's Service Attitude

5 points: Wonderful service on the part of the seller, all things taken into consideration, exceeded expectations

4 points: Quite good service, communications smooth and easy, generally satisfied

3 points: Responses from seller slow in coming, attitude just so-so, not able to say we had smooth communications

2 points: Seller rather impatient, service did not come up to what was promised

1 point: Very poor attitude on the part of the seller, used foul language and shouted, did not treat the customer with any kind of respect

Speed with Which Seller Dispatched Goods
5 points: Extremely fast, packaging was well done and sturdy
4 points: Fairly on time, shipping costs quite reasonable
3 points: Timing just so-so, only shipped after being reminded
2 points: Slow in dispatching goods, had to chase the seller several times
1 point: Finally shipped after I insisted, made me waste time, and packaging just so-so

This system quantifies objective impressions on the part of consumers. They form a specific rating system that enables merchants to see at a glance how customers feel about their product quality, attitude toward service, speed of dispatching goods, and degree of integrity. Integrity thereby becomes a standard that can be measured across different merchants, that can be anticipated and made use of by buyers, and that also tells merchants where they can change things and improve.

A Comparison Between Taobao's Integrity Evaluation System and Its Store Rating System
Taobao's two different evaluation systems coexist on the overall Taobao evaluation indexing system. The information displayed by each is different, but they share the same purpose, namely, to provide buyers with multidimensional information with which to make decisions and to provide sellers with multidimensional incentive mechanisms.

As Asia's largest Internet retail sales platform, Taobao is responsible not only for creating a secure purchasing environment that inspires consumer confidence but also for building standardized regulations for the Internet and instituting a spirit of integrity on the Internet. The three cornerstones and the two main systems, as just described, combine to form the Taobao evaluation indexing system. This is the basis for constructing an e-commerce platform Internet integrity system that is characterized by the qualities of fairness, equality, and transparency. The fact that this system actually does play a role in promoting e-commerce integrity and accountability is something that can be seen daily on the Taobao platform.

Efficiency of Systemic Innovations and an Evaluation

In this context, the term *systemic innovations* refers to how Alibaba creates new systems on top of its existing ecosystem to incentivize certain behaviors by the entities that carry out transactions. The purpose is to allow Alibaba to ensure the ongoing sound growth of its platform.

All such innovative activities rely on the long-term effect of incentives that are sustained and consistent over time. Over an extended period, these incentives become cohesive enough to serve as institutionalized methods that play an ongoing role in healthy functioning. With respect to the overall evaluations process, the key to creating new innovative systems that are truly effective lies in analyzing the costs of each new system. Such costs are characterized by six specific dimensions, including design costs, opportunity costs, timing factors, risk involved, friction with established systems, and implementation. Each of these is described next.

Design Costs

A new regulatory system cannot be built out of thin air. It has to be designed in meticulous fashion by planning personnel who first conduct detailed surveys. The design process of such a new regulatory system includes training the planning personnel, broadly based surveys, plan for design components, plan for comparative analysis, decision making, refinement of the plan, and so on. In this process, all the costs involved are incorporated under the term *design costs*.

Opportunity Costs

When a new regulatory system is generated, it necessarily accompanies the elimination or revision of a previous system. That long-standing system had its own rationale for having come into being as a way to provide regulatory supervision. Because of this, the opportunity costs referred to here are the benefits that the previous system was able to maximize, benefits that now will be eliminated and that lose their former function.

Costs of Time Lag

It is not hard to understand that there is always a time lapse between the complete elimination of a previous system and the launch of a new system. During this period, entities initiating systemic change have a continuous stream of inputs that they have to cover, and in monetary terms, these affect such things as profits. These then become the costs of time lag.

Costs of Taking Certain Risks

Like investment risk, with which we are all familiar, building a new system also entails a certain risk. The returns on systemic innovations are necessarily uncertain. In the period between now and a given time in the future, many variables can intervene to affect anticipated returns. As time goes on, the impact of ever-changing risk factors becomes greater. This, then, is what we refer to as *risk costs*.

Costs of Conflicting Interests

In theory, systemic innovation should abide by the principle of the Pareto optimum. In reality, however, any innovation in a system cannot accomplish this totally for the reason that change will affect the interests of those who were vested in the former system. Their resistance will generate a certain amount of conflict and friction. Damage to anticipated profits will be the result, as measured by the *costs of conflicting interests*.

Costs of Implementation

After a new system has been launched and put into operation, its implementation and handling or the running of the system will have an impact on income. For the moment, we divide this kind of cost into *implementation costs* and *handling costs*, but both are influenced by four main factors: the degree to which the new system is scientific, its comprehensiveness, its manageability, and the people who execute it, that is, the caliber of those who run the system.

In the process of carrying out institutional innovations, Alibaba tries to minimize the preceding six costs by focusing on the following. First, it attempts to make the process of formulating the new system as democratic as possible. That is, it solicits the opinions of buyers and sellers as broadly as possible. Second, it attempts to weigh the value of old and new systems in a comprehensive way so as to avoid issuing orders in the morning that have to be retracted in the evening. Third, it tries to limit its "battlefront" to precise objectives in order to have a "short war that is quickly resolved." Fourth, it adopts an incremental method of systemic innovation as opposed to a revolutionary mode.

The process of improving systems must necessarily confront pressures and opposition from vested interests both inside and outside the system. Since 2008, when Taobao came up with the concept of Internet rules, it has encountered three major incidents of large-scale group opposition as it reformed its own system of rules and regulations.

These three incidents are the incident when Taobao changed its search-engine rules and regulations, the Tmall incident, and the Taobao attack wrecks reputations incident. In dealing with these and similar kinds of efforts that sought to block systemic innovations, Taobao came up with its own unique set of countermeasures. In these countermeasures, the relationships between Taobao and small and microvendors, between Taobao and the government, and between Internet rules and legal-system rules are worth our close attention. They involve the relationship between Alibaba's regulatory supervision of itself and its external environment.

The Three Large-Scale Taobao Vendors Protest Incidents

First Protest: Taobao Changes Its Search-Engine Rules and Regulations
On July 8, 2010, Taobao revised its search-engine rules and regulations. This was done to craft a platform environment that allowed for fair competition among vendors, to provide a purchasing experience for consumers that was quick and easy by a guided purchasing service, and to push forward the sound development of e-commerce markets. Taobao formally announced seven major kinds of behaviors that constituted fraud: manipulating integrity, duplicating stores and goods, commodities that are actually advertisements, misrepresentation of categories and product attributes, arbitrary use of key terms, postage fees that are out of line with product prices, and product descriptions that do not match up with illustrations.

Taobao's search engine could automatically recognize whether or not any of these fraudulent practices was occurring, and Taobao could adjust its search engine accordingly by making it delete duplications and put the search results at a lower, less desirable level. In the most egregious cases, the search could result in having a protective screen put over a store so that it could not be accessed at all.

To take the category of duplication of goods as an example, some vendors change the attributes of a product very slightly to make the search engine find it in multiple ways. They change its measurements, its color, or even its name. After Taobao's change in search-engine rules and regulations, if the search engine determined that this was redundant, then it would not list even the original product among the first few pages of search results. In doing this, Taobao intended to provide a better purchasing experience for consumers while also providing incentives to vendors to supply a greater real diversity of products.

However, this move by Taobao stirred up considerable discontent among some vendors. They felt that this new regulation was intended only to win more business for Taobao, while it dramatically lowered the traffic to small and microvendors. It therefore reduced their orders. They complained that the Taobao rules and regulations were changed "once every three days in small ways and once every five days in a major way," with each change bringing them unnecessary trouble. Between early July and early September 2010, Internet vendors held demonstrations outside Taobao's offices. This attracted widespread public attention.

This was the first time that Alibaba had encountered such questioning from vendors. Faced with increasingly shrill queries, Jack Ma composed an internal letter for all Alibaba staff that he called "Living for your ideals." In this letter, Ma confirmed the correctness of the change in search-engine rules. He said that he believes that the action "gives up immediate benefits on our part in favor of long-term sustainable growth on the part of users by setting up more fair and equitable business practices." He warned those who were attempting to use the incident as a way to gain personal benefit out of it, "Your actions not only are damaging the ideals of more than 20,000 outstanding young people, but you are also attacking and hurting the interests of tens of millions of small businesses who rely on the Internet and several hundred million consumers as well." He encouraged Ali-people to carry on doing upright and proper business and to hold to their ideals. He called on them to "choose the path that holds to principles, that holds to ideals, and that holds to our mission."

Second Protest Incident: The Tmall Incident

To have the merchants on Tmall operate in a more engaged and serious manner, on October 10, 2011, Taobao Commerce City (Tmall) announced new platform regulations: "Announcement Regarding the Renewal of Merchant Agreements for 2012 and Regulatory Changes" (the "Announcement").

Third Protest Incident: The Taobao Anticounterfeiting Incident

On July 22, 2013, Taobao announced to the world its latest regulations on selling counterfeit goods. This was done to ensure that the ongoing growth of the Taobao ecosystem would proceed in a sound and prosperous way and to ensure that consumers have a positive experience when they purchase things on the Taobao platform. The new rules and regulations included the following main modifications:

1. They increased the overall severity of measures taken against counterfeiting behavior and extended the period during which offenders lost certain rights and privileges.
2. They intensified the punishments for behaviors that were particularly egregious, including multiple instances of violations, particularly serious violations.
3. They set up a system to calculate and add up the number of violations. Excessive violations then triggered a red flag, and repeat offenders were prevented from using the Taobao platform for business.

Starting in October 2013, Taobao began to increase its regulatory controls over and punishment of the community of copiers on the basis of these new rules. These two severe anticounterfeiting actions then became a "guided missile" in the history of Taobao. They elicited tremendous dissatisfaction from small-scale vendors, who intensified their virtual attacks on the Taobao platform. On December 3, 2013, yet another e-commerce mass incident occurred, following on the previous Tmall incident. Some Taobao stores declared that Taobao had, in attacking transactions for counterfeit goods, mistakenly deleted their own goods from the platform. As Double Twelves[3] approached, so-called hot-selling items were deleted, which was equivalent to cutting off their path to sales. (Hot-selling items are products with high flow, high exposure, and high order volume.) A number of small vendors gathered together through QQ groups and maliciously attacked some of the famous large vendors on the Tmall website. On December 8, small vendors put forward to Taobao eight explicit conditions for a ceasefire of this war:

1. Restore all items and stores that were misconstrued to have offered falsely sold items and stores that violated the rules.

---

[3]Double Twelves is a second online sales promotion launched by Alibaba that occurs on December 12.

2. Conduct a thorough investigation of counterfeit trade on the Taobao and Tmall sites, and realize greater fairness between the two sites.

3. Separate out Tmall (B) and Taobao (C) stores and put an end to enabling the Tmall stores to absorb the Internet data volume from C stores.

4. Provide evidence of any violations on the part of a store before taking any disciplinary action.

5. Adopt modified rules only after the Taobao Vendors Association has voted on them.

6. Restore Tmall's middle and inferior rating/grading mechanism or abolish the similar mechanism on Taobao so as to realize fair treatment on both and a spirit of free competition.

7. All official activity on the part of the Alibaba Group must treat Tmall and Taobao stores on an equal basis.

8. The Alibaba Group must provide a public apology about this incident.

Three days after the incident began, Taobao made a formal reply via WeBlog (China's blog site). On the one hand, Taobao improved the procedures for initiating appeals or legal suits. Moreover, starting on November 14, 2013, the deadline for appeals being made by vendors who were implicated in counterfeit trade was postponed until January 20, 2014. (This provision made an exception for the 48 cases of severe violations.)

On the other hand, Taobao emphasized in its message, which was entitled "Dispersing the Pollution Caused by Integrity Manipulation and Enabling the Market Once Again to See the Clear Light of Day," that it was determined to eradicate behavior that damaged integrity in the Internet marketplace. It indicated that some merchants had swindled consumers by selling counterfeit products and that this was beginning to endanger the entire trustworthiness of the platform. It declared that it would not give an inch in the battle against untrustworthy behavior.

At the same time, Jack Ma maintained a clear-cut position on the subject when he declared that he knew this incident would cause trouble for some people but that playing with integrity, dealing in counterfeit goods, and infringing intellectual property lines would not be tolerated. Any complaints would be useless. If any vendor was unwilling to accept the process of being tested for integrity, Ma invited them to go to any other platform that would support them. "Do not wait for Taobao to come to terms with you," he stated. He made it clear that he would take the attack on counterfeiting to the bitter end.

These three large-scale mass protests brought tremendous losses to Taobao, to vendors, and to the government. They hurt the enthusiasm with which the Alibaba Group's platform enforced its regulatory management. They hurt the normal operating order of the great majority of vendors, and they increased the difficulty of the government as it maintains stability in its own work. Because of this, the three protests occasioned considerable reflection within the Alibaba Group about how its own internal platform regulatory systems were related to the environment of the outer world. These reflections included the following.

Several Thoughts on Taobao's Relationships

Since established in 2003, Taobao.com as e-commerce retail platform went through tremendous challenge. Despite Amazon and eBay.com being leaders in the field, Taobao platform has grown into a very different business model that no one had done before. The major challenge was from how to deal with several important relationships.

The relationship between Taobao and Small Microvendors

Standardizing regulatory management of the platform is done to meet the needs of growing the new commercial civilization and of growing a modern market economy. It is in line with the needs of an information society and certainly even more in line with the needs of economic globalization. Meanwhile, systemic innovations must occur because they are a vital part of the ongoing process of regulatory management of the platform. In the context of the "tides of our times," the fact that the Alibaba Group has firmly held to its social responsibilities in the face of enormous obstructive forces and has maintained a way of handling systemic reform innovations that come straight from the heart and cannot be altered is something that deserves our confirmation.

Taobao has by now come up against a number of mass incidents. This makes one wonder if there are not certain "black hands" pulling strings behind the scenes, malicious attacking companies that target a company by giving false evaluations and blackmailing innocent vendors, or false trading companies that deliberately undertake fictional trades to stir things up for monetary gain.

Taobao cannot indulge or appease this kind of bad behavior. Instead, it must focus on it as a serious opponent and deal it a hard-hitting blow. We can imagine that as Taobao does this, however, it will unavoidably make mistakes that affect a certain number of vendors who are blameless. From Taobao's perspective, it must correct such mistakes in timely fashion and apologize. From the perspective of small and microvendors, however, they, too, should extend a certain amount of understanding for Taobao's situation.

As in the ancient saying about the solidarity of brothers, only if the Alibaba Group and the great number of small and microvendors stand united behind the sustainable and sound growth of the Alibaba ecosystem can they prevent third-party evil forces from opportunistically stirring up trouble to gain illicit profits.

Relationship Between Taobao and the Government

As we enter the new commercial civilization, the lines between individuals and enterprises become less distinct, as well as the lines between enterprises and government. This is a major new characteristic of the new era.

The preceding sections give examples of incidents that play with Taobao's reputation. With respect to sham trades behavior, in legal terms, this can be described as unfair competition and disrupting market order. When it comes to details, however, there are no relevant legal provisions on which to base a case. Prior to having any legislation that clearly defines the rules, and prior to having the government set its foot in the process, the Taobao platform itself must carry the appropriate social responsibility and must carry out corrective actions against behavior that violates the rules.

Part of the problem is that Taobao's platform is not in itself government. It does not have the authority to compel compliance. This is why it must launch counterincidents undertaken to maintain stability as its only way to respond.

In the realm of e-commerce platform governance, the government should come forth with major support for Taobao's platform by directing its actions in the correct direction. What are the criteria for judging the correct orientation? In answering this, we must return to the main topic of this book—whether or not actions serve to unleash the innovative forces of grassroots people and entities. If Taobao's governance benefits things that incentivize and protect the creativity of the grassroots, then the government should support it. If not, then the government should stop it.

E-commerce is highly dynamic and highly grassroots-driven, and it fuses various industries as it develops. These characteristics mean that it has to be managed by a governing model that allows for low barriers to entry and is highly dynamic. China's traditional government model employs the permitting system (licensing system) to allow market entry. It divides industries into categories in order to manage them. This model has long since become inappropriate to the needs of developing the new commercial civilization. In the sphere of e-commerce platform governance, therefore, the government should rely more on the relevant useful experience of platform enterprises such as Alibaba.

Relationship Between Internet Rules and the Chinese Legal System

Ever since the Internet came into being, it has spawned the creation of numerous new technologies and new industries. Search engines, Internet games, household websites, and e-commerce—each of these changes daily with a speed that no traditional industry can begin to match. By nature, the legal system is intended to be fair and upright, rigorous, prudent, and thorough—all of which means that it cannot keep up with the pace of an ever-changing Internet. One constant source of discussion, as we think of how to standardize the Web, is therefore the blank areas in Internet legislation and the lack of authority in many areas.

If we try to trace back to the source of Taobao's three large-scale mass incidents described earlier, in one way or another, they all relate to the lack of or inadequacy of legislation. If there were clearly defined legal language to serve as the criterion for behavior, small and microvendors would not have to express their appeals in such unreasonable ways. Taobao would not have to walk such a difficult path in the course of taking on social responsibility, and there would be no way for nefarious manipulation to occur.

In this regard, the deputy chair of the Policy and Law Committee of China's E-commerce Association, who is concurrently the chair of the Internet Regulations Research Center, A. Lamusi has proposed the following several considerations:

1. *Internet rules are supplementary to the national legal system.* As we move into the information age, markets constantly become more complex, whereas the traditional procedures by which laws are enacted are constraining. Regulation often falls behind as a result. The governance procedures by which Internet rules function are often able to avoid the shortcomings of traditional controls. They should be adopted as useful supplements to the government's methods of managing the Internet.

2. *The relationship between Internet rules and the national legal system is also substitutive.* What this means is that Taobao's "platformized" governance allows society to use fewer judicial resources. It lowers the costs of the judiciary and the burdens on China's judiciary. The Taobao platform's protection system of intellectual property rights is a good example. In 2011, Taobao determined that the personnel responsible for intellectual property rights infringement on the network should be divided into three teams, one for safeguarding rights, one for intellectual property rights cooperation, and one for quality control of products. It created a team made up of over 2,000 professionally trained staff engaged in an intellectual property rights system with diversified functions. To a very large degree, this reduced the government's burden of protecting intellectual property rights.

3. *The relationship is compensative.*

Conclusion

The Alibaba Group has made a tremendous number of innovations in the regulatory systems that govern its platforms. The areas in which such innovations are most concentrated include the real-name system, the integrity system, guarantees of secure transactions, prevention of fraud, and the areas relating to dispute resolution, protecting consumers, and core links surrounding the protection of consumers.

These efforts pulled together the intelligence, vision, and hard work of a great number of people working on platform regulatory supervision. Although changes in how platforms are regulated cannot help but stir up opposition, the Alibaba Group has never hesitated to move forward in the midst of tricky issues. This has led the group to undertake a great deal of interesting thought and consideration of the issues. Such consideration may be worth using as a reference when enterprises are determining the rules and regulations of the industry overall and assuming social responsibility for their actions. It also may be worth using as a reference when the nation is formulating relevant laws and regulations and breaking through the traditional methods of managing these things.

Naturally, what can and should be used for reference are not simply the innovations themselves but rather the thinking that went into how to realize innovations and improve governance. That thinking is of key importance and is precisely what we like to call the *Alibaba spirit*.

CHAPTER 7

THE "ROUTINIZATION" OF ALIBABA'S CORPORATE CULTURE INNOVATION

QUAN TAO

As an Internet company, Alibaba has made many crucial innovations in operating procedures, products, technologies, and business models. In so doing, it has been able to unleash the innovative forces of tens of millions of grassroots entrepreneurs. The question naturally comes to mind: How did Alibaba do this? Was innovation something that happened by chance, or was it a habitual state of mind within the company?

Established in 1999, Alibaba is quite young, but youth does not necessarily guarantee the quality of being innovative. Many newly founded companies fail by trying to emulate others or by not being able to turn ideas into innovative products. In contrast, many famous built-to-last companies that keep renewing themselves rely on constant innovation to stay in business, and some have stayed in business for over 100 years. The business results of Alibaba in the course of just 16 years are astonishing— the company is already one of the largest and most influential Internet companies in China. While there is evidence to show that innovation and business results are related, actual success relates to other factors as well. This was particularly true when the Internet was just getting started because competition was not nearly as fierce as it is now. At that time, reading the market accurately, focusing on execution, controlling costs, and being opportunistic all may have been just as important as innovation.

Before 2011, in terms of strategy, Alibaba did not emphasize innovation in any particular way. Innovation was more of a by-product. It was akin to spontaneous behavior. As the Internet community gradually matured, however, and as Alibaba became weightier within that community, and also as unforeseen technological problems became more frequent, Alibaba realized that innovation had to become a conscious policy choice if it wanted to enjoy ongoing sustainable growth.

Alibaba's corporate culture has been encapsulated in six values, what it calls its six "Pulse Excaliburs" or "Six Sacred Swords": customer first, teamwork, embrace change, integrity, passion, and commitment. Except for the part about embracing change, which has a certain Internet feel to it, the others represent straightforward business values. They are useful in any situation and constitute a basic approach to how to conduct oneself and how to conduct affairs. They do not "aim the sword" directly at innovation. When one pursues the question of why it is that Alibaba has in fact done so many innovative things, however, one finds that these straightforward values have indeed played a fundamental role.

Culture is something intangible, but it has to come about by means of things that are real. Organizing a structure, creating mechanisms, and managing human resources are very matter-of-fact things. As Alibaba grew and its strategy shifted, the company began quite consciously to put effort into using what is real to stimulate creativity. For example, it carried out organizational restructuring, it promoted innovative mechanisms, it consciously hired innovative people, and it rewarded the results of innovation. As a result, the innovative nature of its culture became ever more evident—an intrinsic part of the company.

A great deal of research has been done on creating innovative structures. Some of the main elements of an innovative organization include a common outlook, the desire to be a leader in innovation, the appropriate organizational structure, a focus on individuals, effective team cooperation, all members participating in innovation, an innovative atmosphere, and a focus on key externalities. In analyzing factors that apply to innovative-type organizations under noncontinuous conditions,[1] the following three considerations are also key: individual development that continues beyond immediate goals, a great deal of communication, and having a learning-oriented organization.

---

[1] By *noncontinuous conditions*, we mean unstable states, when a company must do different things that are not in line with what it was doing before.

These elements can be grouped into four main categories. First, encourage an innovative corporate culture (e.g., a common outlook, a desire to be a leader in innovation, and all members participating in innovation). Second, create organizational structures that are conducive to innovation (e.g., effective team cooperation and the appropriate organizational structure). Third, make sure that the platform supports innovation (e.g., an innovative atmosphere, a great deal of communication, and a focus on key externalities). Fourth, nurture a type of human resources management that rewards innovation (e.g., a focus on individuals, individual development that is sustained and extends beyond the immediate goals, and a learning-oriented organization).

In what follows, each of these categories is used to evaluate which methods allowed Alibaba to become an innovative organization.

Promoting Innovation as the Corporate Culture

During an interview with *Fortune* magazine in 1981, Steve Jobs made the comment that innovation is not related to how much money you have for research and development (R&D). It isn't a question of money. It's a question of people—what kinds employees and how you lead them. Innovation involves tremendous uncertainties. It requires having actual people—the workers who do the innovating, or call them entrepreneurs— looking for opportunities, making choices, implementing decisions, and taking on risk. In addition, its complexities require a high degree of team solidarity; that is, a number of individuals must form an organic group. Even with these things, plus meticulously created plans, well-executed systems, established processes, efficient machinery, and even one or two geniuses—you cannot necessarily ensure ongoing innovation. (I don't rule out the "hitting it lucky" accidental kind of innovation.)

The difference between an innovative-type organization and one that is not innovative lies in the difference between people who have an innovative mind-set and those who do not. When I talk about an innovative-type organization, therefore, I absolutely am not describing some kind of structure that is simply a static environment. Instead, I am implying that the people themselves have a certain set of values and feel the atmosphere, support, individual growth potential, and mutual stimulation of others who feel the same way. It is with respect to these things that corporate culture plays a key role.

Vision, Mission, and Set of Values

An innovative corporate culture must, first and foremost, explicitly set forth a vision, mission, and set of values.

> *Alibaba's vision:* "Being the number one data-sharing platform, being at the top of the well-being index as an enterprise, living 102 years."
>
> *Alibaba's mission:* "To make it easy to do business anywhere[2] (or "To make it no longer difficult to do business around the world").
>
> *Alibaba's values:* "Customer first, teamwork, embrace change, integrity, passion, commitment."

Vision, mission, and values are important for innovation for two main reasons. First, they have a direct impact on stimulating innovation. Alibaba's culture itself incorporates innovative behavior—from the moment it was founded, the company had an "innovative gene." In 2001, after Guan Mingsheng joined Alibaba, together with some of the founders, he tried to summarize the "interesting things" about the organization, its general atmosphere, and came up with nine items that could be called a set of values, a kind of "Dugu Nine Swords of Solitude." These were passion, innovation, teaching that benefits the teacher as well as the learner, openness, simplicity, team effort, focus, quality of service, and respect each other.

Later these were combed through and simplified into three categories. The first was the *driving force of innovation*, which included four items: innovation itself, passion, openness, and teaching that benefits the teacher as well as the learner. When the "Nine Swords" were further simplified into the "Six Swords," the term *innovation* was no longer mentioned explicitly, but all the values incorporated the concept itself. Some played

---

[2]Translator's note: The English-language Alibaba website uses the first sentence for its official mission statement in English. The original Chinese is a little less concise. It is "To make it no longer difficult to do business around the world."

a direct role in supporting innovation, such as customer first, embrace change, and passion. Later, I discuss the influence these key qualities play in promoting innovation.

Second, vision, mission, and a set of values stimulate innovative behavior among people in indirect ways. Matt Kingdon has suggested that behind the paradigm of successful innovation lies "innovative energy." This is the fusion of three different forces, including personal attitude, team behavior, and the organization itself. Regarding attitude, he notes that the great majority of people one sees who make a difference in a company have an inner desire to do something significant. They want to make an impact, and they want the approval of the team. They like pursuing the objectives of the corporate entity—it feels good to them, and they are happy to be a part of it. This is why vision and objectives are the key to innovation. They set the pulse of innovative energy.

All people are creative. The difference lies in the degree to which this is sparked and the direction in which it is applied. An inspirational vision and mission can serve to galvanize the creativity of people and their enthusiasm for work. At the same time, these things can guide the creativity of different people in the direction of a common goal. The combined force of innovation is that much stronger as a result. This is why one of the founders of Alibaba, Peng Lei, has said that "the essence of innovation is idealism."

Major innovations can face all kinds of internal obstructions if they cannot break through the core rigidities that were the original sources of the organization's strength. At such times, clearly defining the company's new vision can lead to consensus among all workers and allow for repositioning and smooth change. Alibaba's major transformations have all begun with a redefinition of the corporate vision. When the company was established in 1999, its vision was "to become one of the world's top 10 websites." By 2008, as the company's strategic plans changed, this was changed to "becoming the largest e-commerce services provider on the globe." In 2013, this changed again to "being the number one data-sharing platform."

Changes in the company's vision reflected the changing times. They also reflected the way in which Alibaba defined its objectives and its group strategy in a more targeted and specific way. For example, Alibaba has now come to define its positioning in the market as an *ecosystem*. At the same time, recognizing that the core operations and management of the company will be existing in a digital age, it sees that its current organizational structure, management methods, mode of thinking, technological demands, and so on need major adjustment. The new vision, "being the number one data-sharing platform," serves as a foundation for future changes and innovations as well as those currently underway.

Customer First

Where does innovation come from? In its most classic form, innovation is *pushed by knowledge* and *pulled by demand* as the two primary forces that bring it into being. Later models that address this subject have added all kinds of new factors and improvements, but these two, push and pull, still occupy a fundamental position. Alibaba's innovation has benefited enormously from the pull of demand. It set its sights on helping tens of millions of enterprises grow, providing job opportunities to 100 million people, and providing services to a billion consumers. The very first value of the company states this ideal in succinct terms: "Put the customer first."

For a long time, Alibaba was positioned as a services company and not a tech company. It was not even regarded as an Internet company. During the period in which its business-to-business (B2B) enterprise was being established, salespeople ran the show, not technical people, and as a result, this was not a productive period in terms of technical innovations. Instead, salespeople crisscrossed the country making sales calls on customers. When the Internet bubble burst and tech companies went into a dormant period, senior management formulated correct strategies that enabled Alibaba to weather the hard times. They increased customer services and investment in staff and employees and stopped "burning" investors' money, which is where the idea first arose of customer first, employees second, and investors third.

The reason Taobao was able to beat out eBay was almost totally due to eBay's blind spot when it came to understanding Chinese business. By using the not-very-original motto of "Customer first," Alibaba honed its consumer-to-consumer (C2C) business into what became a fine skill.

First, it was free. At the time, per-capita income in China was one-thirtieth that in the United States, and a market economy had only been going for 25 years. The Internet was a new kind of thing for communicating, and people were not very sure how reliable it was. Asking people to pay a fee to sell on the Internet was psychologically unacceptable. It was outside the bounds of Chinese people's tolerance at the time. As Jack Ma later said, "We did not adopt this free policy in order to compete with the opposition. We adopted it because the market demanded it. We did it completely in order to serve the customer."

Second, it dealt with the issue of payment. At the time, Chinese people rarely used credit cards, and there was no system in the country as yet to certify individual credit. In the United States, eBay fundamentally did not have to take creditworthiness into account, whereas in China, this was a monumental problem. In essence, Alipay was nothing more than an intermediary guarantor of payment, a new form of a very ancient kind of service. By creating this innovative product called Alipay, Alibaba found a solution to the problem.

Finally, it improved communications. The no-compensation model that Alibaba adopted meant that varying qualities of products were all commingled on the platform. Excellent communications between buyer and seller were the sole route to actually achieving sales because they reduced the asymmetry of information. In addition, of course, what Chinese buyer does not like to haggle over price at a market? AliWangwang arose to meet the need. In contrast, eBay heartlessly blocked any communication between buyers and sellers. This action on the part of eBay allowed Taobao to satisfy customer needs all the more easily.

The story of Alibaba's product "Zhao Cai Jin Bao," which means "bring in wealth and treasure," lends another perspective on how customer first influences innovation. In June 2003, a product that Taobao had spent three months of concentrated R&D effort on was summarily taken offline after just one month, voted down by the public. This astonished everyone. At the time, this had been a secret innovative project given preferential treatment by Taobao. A superteam had been selected to work on it, with all the resources the company could offer. In its initial period, it went through a week of detailed testing, analysis, and modeling. The software-engineering phase was carried out on Ali's "blessed venue"—the

Lakeside Garden. The CEO of Taobao.com, Sun Tongyu, personally took on the major responsibility for the project. During the R&D process, the entire team, top to bottom, coordinated secretly and worked flat out. The trial run passed, marketing was successful, but the formal launch of the product then aroused totally unexpected controversy and opposition. In the end, Sun Tongyu decided to allow public opinion to determine whether to keep or to toss the product. He decided to ask users themselves to vote on it. After 20 days, the votes of those opposing were greater than those supporting it. In the end, the product was taken offline.

Innovation is a business process that incorporates four main links: search, selection, implementation, and the harvesting of results. Search involves looking for innovative ideas, though in fact the mechanisms that spark innovation are omnipresent. Even the best-funded organization is not able to undertake everything, however, so selection of projects becomes critical—formulating the right proposals and allocating the appropriate resources. At this point, customer first becomes an important selection criterion. No matter how good the idea or how much money is spent on it, without customers' approval, it will not generate value. It then becomes unfeasible as an innovation. The code of putting the customer first at Alibaba is what led the team to cut loose from an idea that, from every other perspective, had seemed the perfect innovative project.

As an aside, this story has a good sequel. The hard work that the R&D team put into the project was not in vain. All the ideas behind the product eventually flowed into a different channel and were realized in other products. Taobao's pay-for-peformance (P4P) product and its Tao-customer product are the concrete expressions of the original ideas.

Embrace Change

When you choose to be in the Internet business, you are opting for change. The Internet is a place where companies "can emerge in a second and go out just as fast." The years between 1995 and 2000 were the springtime of the industry, when companies blossomed everywhere, and just the idea of a dot-com was enough to make investors compete against one another to pour in money. The larger web portals piled into listing on the market. In 2001, the bubble burst. Internet companies entered a frozen period in which many died and those that survived went through hard times. Taking just the one aspect of e-commerce, after a preparatory period that lasted several years, the industry entered an explosive stage of growth in 2010. Already-existing e-commerce companies went for round after round of massive amounts of financing. New vertically integrated e-commerce entities emerged in droves, and *platform transformation* became the new buzzword. Merchants who dealt in the real world also began transforming their business models, and price wars began to heat up. Mergers and acquisitions threw off sparks in all directions. By the time the situation had calmed down a little, the age of big data and mobile Internet then arose like a mighty wave, creating innumerable new variables to deal with in the future.

In the bigger picture, things are changing constantly, but they are at the micro level of individuals as well. Personal demand changes daily, and the essence of the Internet is that it is personalized. Even the biggest and mightiest of contenders have to consider the "long tail" and ply their wares there. They also have to recognize that tastes change. "It is not enough to say [that] you understand someone since that person is different tomorrow. Today she may want a pineapple, but tomorrow she may want something else."[3]

In an industry that is growing so rapidly, in which nothing is nailed down for sure, innovative opportunities are all over the place. The prerequisite for success, however, is having an attitude that embraces change. When it comes to the elements that make for an innovative organization, it is more fundamental to embrace change in innovative activities than it is to have an innovative atmosphere. Embracing change is to innovation what water is to fish. When Alibaba changed the value of innovation in the Dugu Nine Swords into "Embrace change" in the Six Swords, it was in fact inserting an even more fundamental requirement into its code of values.

One interesting example of this idea of embracing change can be seen in Alibaba's practice of making people stand on their heads. Alibaba would like for its staff and employees to look on the world from a new

---

[3]The quotation comes from the Hong Kong movie, *Chongking Express*.

perspective, upside down, in order to learn to change. So the company has every new employee, old or young, fat or thin, learn to stand on his or her head against a wall within three months. Men must hold that position for at least 30 seconds. Women have to hold it for 10 seconds. Otherwise, the new recruits are told to roll up their mats and go home.

Many people inside and outside the company have explained this in various ways, saying, for example, that it is done for health or that it makes people realize that the impossible can actually be possible. The most significant thing about it in terms of culture, however, is that it forces people to think from a different perspective. Jack Ma has said, "Everyone has to learn to stand on his head because when you're upside down, the blood rushes into your brain, and you see things differently than you normally would. You also can think over issues in ways that you would have found unimaginable before."

Rotating positions is another of the ways that Alibaba's systems express the company's spirit of constant change. Alibaba has always had a strict program of rotating positions. Every year, management-level positions are reassigned. If managers have any desire to be promoted, they must have fulfilled two considerations. First, they must have a good plan in mind for who is going to succeed them in their current position. Second, they must have experienced the process of rotating positions. Many of the more outstanding staff at Alibaba have done every single job in the company. Alibaba's highly qualified Deputy CEO Deng Kangming explains it this way: "As you change positions, you eliminate the barriers between one position and the next. Only if you do that can people really understand things from a different perspective, use different ways of thinking about things. Only by analyzing things from different perspectives can you truly cultivate the capacity to think systematically, that is, in terms of the total system."

Sometimes the difference between jobs is considerable. Someone in charge of human resources will be sent to run sales channels and major customers, or personnel from sales will be sent to do human resources. Someone with no background in technology, who is involved in editing content on the website, may be sent to manage technology. A chief financial officer may be transferred to management of business in general. In early 2013, Alibaba spun off 25 different business units (BUs), which represented "the hardest reform of all in the past 13 years." In considering all the horizontal and vertical business interactions, cooperation among business units had become extremely important. The frequent rotation of positions for many years was a good preparation for this organizational change. It also helped business continue to function properly after it had taken place.

Another unusual feature of Alibaba's system of rotating positions is that it sometimes does not happen according to predetermined processes, which is extremely important in testing people's ability to embrace change. The need for employees to participate in new projects may have no forewarning at all—people may find out from one day to the next that they have been transferred to a different department.

If one wants to be successful in embracing change, the necessary attitude is said to be, "Forget about success; start over again." A previous situation may have been one that felt successful and that therefore was hard to relinquish. After the fact, we always think that a given innovation is a great success. Before it comes about, however, the people who have to do it must be brave enough to forget about success and actually embrace change.

Alibaba's earliest website was built by one of the founders of the company, Zhou Yuehong, using a language called Perl. As inquiries to the website increased in number, the system quickly became overloaded, and it also became hard to increase the number of its functions. Despite the extremely high hurdles that the program now presented, it was something Zhou was extremely proud of, a kind of asset that he owned. Nevertheless, it was making it hard for the website to continue working. An American engineer was asked to come in and look at the situation, and he decided to use Java, new at the time, to completely rewrite the system. This made Zhou Yuehong, who knew everything there was to know about the old program, feel terrible. His opposition to this proposal was strong enough that this founder of the company eventually had to be let go. After a great deal of persuasion, he came back into the company on a trial basis of three months as a completely new employee with a salary that had been cut in half. The change worked; he applied himself to learning the new technology, and he soon became a master of Java.

Not only can individuals become infatuated with their own past successes, but companies too can sometimes find it hard to move forward from a basis of existing success. Taking such a step often can be an important form of innovation, however. The independence of Taobao Mall is one such example (in January 2012, Taobao Mall was renamed Tmall). Between 2008 and 2010, Taobao held 80 percent of the market share for C2C business in China. Because of this, the idea of making the business-to-consumer (B2C) business part of Taobao independent was not given much serious attention, and anyway, the feeling was that this would affect the size of and the traffic on the Taobao Marketplace. Because of this, that segment of the market went through various twists and turns. The first "independence" was in 2008, when senior management decided that the B2C model had no future, so the people responsible for it, who were both capable and trustworthy, were notified that they would have to leave. The board of directors then used an operating procedure that gave Taobao Mall the least degree of independence because they were unwilling to upset their C-store vendors. Half a year later, Taobao Mall Department was disbanded, and the mall was again merged with Taobao. In August 2009 came another attempt to operate it independently, but again, little progress was made. On November 1, 2010, six days after the B2C company Mecox Lane Limited was listed on the Nasdaq, Taobao Mall finally declared real independence. Only then did its managers hold a news conference and announce an independent domain name, and only then did they begin to do major brand publicity. Before that, other companies had been allowed to grab the stronghold of B2C opportunities first. Only in final recognition of the need to do so did Taobao agree to cut out a chunk of its own livelihood and release Tmall. This then formally enabled Taobao itself to put its energies toward developing its B2C model. One of the founders of the Taobao Marketplace, Huang Ruo, summarized this by saying, "What Taobao Mall did was to deny itself on an already successful platform, thinking in a 'headstand' way. It was trying to cast off its existing procedures and to find new operating models according to how the market functioned. Meanwhile, it also had to make the operating rules and design the architecture of a B2C platform."

Fortunately, Alibaba finally allowed Taobao Mall to become independent. A number of innovative ways of thinking in the Taobao Marketplace that could not previously be realized then found good use in the Taobao Mall. Furthermore, Taobao.com finally found a winning model. Thanks to all of this, Tmall now holds over 50 percent of the B2C market share in China, and the 11.11 Shopping Festival has been a miracle of sales for three consecutive years.

Passion

The passion of Ali-people is expressed in many different ways. When sales champions lost bets to Jack Ma, they had to jump in Hangzhou's West Lake in the wintertime. When Taobao's ranking exceeded eBay's, Taobao staff beat thunderously on garbage cans out of sheer exuberance. When Alipay's sales figures exceeded 7 million RMB, the technical staff who had worked night and day on perfecting the product ran naked in a special kind of celebration. After this, the "naked-run tradition" in the company has continued. These things are how Alibaba staff members express their emotion at peak moments, but they also express it in other ways in everyday work. You only have to see how many people are still in their offices after working hours and how there is real fire in their eyes when they talk shop with one another. You can see it in the way it is hard to grab a conference room. Passion permeates every aspect of this company's circulatory system.

Innovation requires this. It is an activity that involves massive amounts of energy and enthusiasm. Not only do people need to create and organize new things, but they also need to break through the constraints of old things. Just as energy is needed in physics to break through inertia, innovation implies the breaking out of routine ways of thinking and doing things. This puts demands on mental forces, physical forces, and the force of a person's ambition or desire. The expression of this kind of force is *passion*, whether it stems from enthusiasm or from responsibility. In general, an organization that is well endowed with passion finds it easier to generate innovations.

The place in which Alibaba was founded, namely, Jack Ma's old apartment complex, the Lakeside Garden, has become a cultural symbol within the company. In 1999, eighteen founders gathered there to set up Alibaba. After this, the company moved constantly and each time to a more favorable location, but whenever the company encounters an occasion of which it is particularly proud (especially when secret new projects come to completion), the team working on the project gathers at the Lakeside Garden to reexperience the feeling of being founders themselves, "very foolish and very innocent, very vigorous and very long-lasting."

If you ever mention these Nine Swords to Ali-people, they immediately think of several crucial moments when the founding team abandoned excellent prospects and conditions in Beijing and followed Jack Ma back to Hangzhou to set up the company. Everyone scrounged together 500,000 RMB, but nobody was allowed to borrow from his or her own family. Furniture was brought in from the founders' own homes or dredged up from secondhand stores. A few newer pieces were the self-assembly kind that everyone helped to screw together. People used a dozen computers on a rotating basis. Everyone worked 10 or more hours a day, and when they got tired, they would just lie down for awhile. On especially cold days, they even used a bath heater for heating. Despite these conditions, everyone believed that they were engaged in creating something truly great. Shoulders together, they worked day in and day out—no hardship or simple fare was going to disturb their peace of mind.

This founding team worked at the Lakeside Garden for just one year, but during that year, the Alibaba website was completed and put online and then revised, as the number of staff in the company started a continuous ascent (Figure 7.1). When it broke through 100,000 people, the company registered itself in Hong Kong as Alibaba China, Ltd. The Alibaba Research and Development Center was then registered in Hangzhou, and the company went through two rounds of funding, taking in a total of US$25 million.

In 2003, during the SARS crisis, Sun Tongyu and over a dozen people signed a secret agreement before moving back into the Lakeside Garden. There they worked day and night on a particular project. Within a month, Taobao.com went online. Three and one-half years later, eBay retreated from China.

FIGURE 7.1 *Photograph of a staff meeting with Jack Ma, held at the Lakeside Garden, Hangzhou, during the early period of the company.*

Inside the company, Ali-people use a great deal of what is called "Alibaba slang." The term that most galvanizes people is *da zhang*, which means "fighting a war." In the Alibaba sense, it refers to crossing swords head-on with an opponent, particularly one that is bigger than you are. Despite this, Jack Ma often says, "Only if you feel internally that you have no enemies will you really have no enemies in the actual world." By this he means that competition is a by-product of what you should be doing anyway—the key point is to provide incomparable service to customers. It seems a nice thing to say, but it also seems to sum things up after the fact. The reason is simple: in some spheres and at certain stages, Alibaba has truly been a company without any contenders on the horizon, "even if you look for them with a telescope." Alibaba has no competitors for various reasons: its model is unique (it was the earliest B2B company), and its forces are already too strong (today's C2C business). Given such things, there naturally is no need to pick a fight with anyone.

However, when competitors do appear, nobody is going to ignore them either. You may put the customer first, but so does the competition, so why should the customer choose you? When strong competitors appear in important areas, therefore, even Alibaba does not disregard them and go its own way. Instead, it makes its moves depending on the specific qualities of its opponent. What enables it to beat that competition is not only customer first but also a kind of invincible passion. Meanwhile, the pressure of competition makes it easier to force innovations out of the company, whereas passion ensures that these innovations get implemented. This reinforcing process continues until the battle is won.

The classic example of a winning campaign was when Taobao went up against eBay. In terms of marketing and promotion methods, Taobao's innovations were absolutely forced into being by its situation. In July 2003, eBay set up exclusive advertising agreements with other Chinese sites, including Sina, Sohu, Netease, and TOM. If any of these major sites cooperated in any way with Taobao, Yabao, or other online auction houses, in promotion or otherwise, eBay was allowed to levy high fines on its site as punishment. Faced with this kind of "tyrannical" blockade, all Taobao could do was stage a kind of guerrilla war and "encircle the cities by taking the countryside."[4] At fairly low prices, it put advertisements on thousands of smaller websites. Taobao's sales staff swept through the ranks of China's "website alliance" and got all these small and medium-sized sites to post Taobao advertisements from one night to the next. At the same time, its salespeople covered the offline advertising territory—subway stations, train stations, lampposts along the streets, any possible venue. In the end, Taobao was also advertising on television. Back at the Lakeside Garden, Sun Tongyu, one of the original founders, led the exhausting but dedicated charge of all the company's various departments. The up-to-date rankings of the two companies hung beside each employee, motivating everyone each moment of the day. Many people waited every night until 11 p.m. or even later to go home to sleep—they would not leave until Alexa[5] changed its rating for the day.

---

[4]Translator's note: A reference to the way the Chinese Revolution was won in 1949.

[5]Translator's note: A company that provides information on website traffic for free.

Loose on the Outside, Tight on the Inside

Is a tense work atmosphere more conducive to innovation, or is it better to have a relaxed environment? Peng Lei, vice president and head of the Human Resources Department, encapsulates the answer to this question within Alibaba by noting that the company is "externally loose [or relaxed] while internally tight [strict or intense]." A loose approach to interacting with the external world allows the company to maintain an open attitude and be more receptive to new things. It also gives people the freedom to unleash their own imaginative forces. A strict internal environment keeps the work results oriented and focused on execution, which allows innovative ideas to come to fruition more quickly.

Alibaba's "loose" culture is expressed in a number of ways, but three specific aspects are most apparent. The first is the physical environment of Alibaba. A company's physical surroundings are very important for innovative energies. As soon as you walk into Alibaba, you sense that the company is young, vital, and encourages unconstrained thinking. Any sense of hierarchy is quite muted. Work areas are open style, with more senior people stuck in among a crowd of young people. Walls are adorned with amusing caricatures and photographs of Alibaba recreational events. Meeting rooms are named for places that hark back to Alibaba's *Outlaws of the Marsh* type of culture.[6] All kinds of excellent facilities are available for exercise, recreation, eating and drinking, and studying.

The second aspect of looseness is a management style that gives full rein to individual expression of employees. Taobao acts as an incubator that fosters a list of Alibaba's innovations, including Alipay, Tmall, eTao, Juhuasuan, and Taobao Wireless, among other businesses. Taobao represents the beginning of Alibaba's innovation culture. It is the most innovative platform within the Alibaba Group. This is related to the way in which senior management "looks after the bigger picture and doesn't concern itself too much with small things," as expressed by former Taobao CEO Lu Zhaoxi.[7] Operating innovations are more likely to be generated from the bottom and move upward as a result of this unconstrained atmosphere. People can be more experimental. The downside is that

---

[6]Translator's note: A reference to the influence that the sixteenth-century classic *Outlaws of the Marsh* has had on Jack Ma and the company (also known as *The Water Margin*).

[7]Jonathan Lu Zhaoxi, former CEO of Taobao, appointed CEO of Alibaba.com in 2011.

efforts may be duplicated as too many people focus on a given product or business. The advantage is that people are free to do something new without worrying too much about making mistakes, which increases the probability of successful innovations.

Finally, Alibaba has a kind of "gene" that inclines it to enjoy having fun. This is not to say that people who enjoy having fun are necessarily more innovative, but there is something about refusing to be mediocre that links the two things together. Most people who know Alibaba well would agree to this characterization. A small anecdote reveals one way in which this works. Within the Alibaba Technology Association campus, a person in the technical department ran into a problem when he could not get a certain program to complete its response in less than 600 seconds. He therefore put out a notice offering a reward—a case of Coke—to the person who could reduce the time to less than 200 seconds. Someone was intrigued by the problem, spent a couple of days looking into it, and was able to reduce the response time to less than 50 seconds.

Alibaba's more stringent environment is demonstrated first and foremost in the company's very results-oriented performance standards. A person can have as much fun as he or she likes, but ultimately he or she must come up with results. What's more, that person must ensure that the results are reproducible through a defined process. As the saying goes, results without a process are no more useful than garbage, while a process without results is like a fart. Second, Alibaba enforces strict discipline. Economist William Baumol has noted that entrepreneurship within an entity can be productive but also nonproductive and potentially also destructive. People's energies are finite. If entrepreneurial efforts are poured into nonproductive or even destructive endeavors, this necessarily reduces the amount of energy going into productive endeavors. An organization's entrepreneurial capacities will suffer as a result, which is why the right kind of disciplined approach plays such an important role.

Integrity is one of the cardinal rules in Alibaba when it comes to relations with the outside world. It is one of the Six Sacred Swords. In December 2009, the Alibaba Group set forth regulations on business conduct. These established a "high-voltage line" with respect to the company's code of values—they went further in explicitly defining the standards of ethical conduct. If any employee "touched" this line, he or she would be asked to leave the company. Alibaba has in the past asked a number of superlative salespeople to leave the company despite their excellent performance record. In 2010, Jack Ma went so far as to "kill" Wei Zhe as a result of the way certain B2B staff had colluded with merchants to defraud customers.[8]

With respect to internal relations, Alibaba espouses simple and straightforward human relations and rules out any kind of office politics. The company advises employees that the Alibaba Group is still in the midst of rapid growth, which means that there will be abundant opportunities for all, with new job positions and new benefits coming along every year. People do not have to fight over limited resources and interests. If each person does his or her own job well, the prospects for personal development are huge.

An Organizational Structure That Is Conducive to Innovation

Take a look at what Alibaba has done in recent years to restructure itself:

In 2008, Koubei.com merged with China Yahoo! to set up Koubei Yahoo, Alimama merged with Taobao, and the Alibaba Group's Research Institute was established.

In 2009, AliSoft merged with the R&D Institute of the Alibaba Group, the Business Management Software Department of Alisoft was injected into Alibaba's B2B company, and Koubei.com was inserted into Taobao.

In 2011, the Alibaba Group spun off Taobao into three separate independent companies: taobao.com, tmall.com, and etao.com.

In 2012, the Alibaba Group announced that it was upgrading its existing subsidiaries to become seven business groups, including

---

[8]David Wei Zhe, former CEO of Alibaba.com. In 2010, some employees of the direct-sales group of the B2B company were found to be colluding with China Gold Suppliers, resulting in an increase in fraudulent transactions. This was investigated and confirmed, with the result that Wei Zhe took responsibility for the problem and resigned in February 2011. Jack Ma later issued an e-mail to all staff reconfirming Alibaba's code of ethics.

Ali International, Ali Small Business, Taobao, Tmall, Juhuasuan, eTao, and Alibaba Cloud Computing.

In 2013, Ali Cloud Computing and net.cn merged to form a new Ali Cloud Computing Company, and the Alibaba Group reorganized into 25 business units.

The reorganizations within business groups and subsidiaries were even more frequent. In 2013, starting at the beginning of the year, all available conference rooms within Alibaba were crammed to capacity. Because there was still not enough space, it is said that all neighboring coffee shops and restaurants were pressed into service. Business was booming, and the reason was easy to see. Both internal and external changes were happening too fast and too often—nobody seemed to have a clue about where the next step might take them, and nobody knew what the more distant future would bring.

In 2009, when Ali Cloud Computing was being reorganized, an employee wrote: "Suddenly, this earthquake. The wind changed directions, and I, without the slightest internal preparation, realized I had lost my way. Comrades at arms were being spun off to other departments and subsidiaries. Everyone felt the same, lost, each person now trying to find his [or her] own path."

Every single year, the organizational framework of Alibaba is adjusted in one way or another. New employees are confused and troubled by changing bosses every six months. Older employees joke among themselves: "When we say hi to one another, we ask 'which department are you in now?' The answer is different every time since departments change over every few months." In 2012 alone, Alibaba had a total of 30,000 employee job adjustments, including changing departments and switching bosses, yet Alibaba only had a total of 24,000 employees that year. This means that each and every person had an average of more than one adjustment to make.

As organizational change occurs, it absolutely is not the case that employees take it in stride, all smooth and easy. Generally speaking, however, Ali employees have become familiar with and accustomed to the group's changes. In 2013, one story that illustrates this made the rounds in the Beijing subsidiary of the company. The group was setting up a wireless department. At the outset, transferring people to the new department met up with resistance and even outright refusal. At the kick-off of the wireless OE, once Lu Zhaoxi explained the rationale for all this, many people felt that it was an honor to be included and sprang to recommend themselves. Because the department was based in Hangzhou, the person in charge in Beijing sent an e-mail to the employees being transferred so that they could get ready to go to Hangzhou. He mistakenly sent it to one person who was not connected to the wireless department at all. The next day, this person responded conscientiously with an e-mail: "I have my things ready. Where and when are we supposed to meet?"

Organizational Change and Innovation

The overall environment of an organization has a major influence on the creation of new products and on innovative processes. Within a rigidly hierarchical organization, it is rare for functions to cross lines and then be reassembled in creative ways. Communication generally goes from top to bottom. Being unidirectional, it cannot support the free flow of information and the kind of cooperation that transcends functional lines despite the fact that these things are precisely the things most critical to the success of innovations. Scholars believe that the higher the degree of nonprocedural decision making in an organization, the more it needs loose and flexible structures. Research indicates that the more uncertain the environment and the more complex, the more the entity needs to employ a flexible structure and nimble processes.

At the end of the 1950s, Tom Burns and George Stalker divided organizations into two types—*mechanistic* and *organic*—depending on how the organization is designed to deal with its external environment. A mechanistic organization is characterized by tasks that are divided into independent professions, functions, and responsibilities that are meticulously defined and restricted and authority that is ordered in a hierarchical system with many procedural rules and regulations. Knowledge relating to the work and supervisory control over tasks are concentrated in the upper levels of the organization. This reinforces the tendency to have a strictly hierarchical and vertical form of communication, coordination, and control between upper and lower levels.

In contrast, an organic organization is characterized by employees who are structured around a common task. Functions and responsibilities are constantly being revised as roles shift. Levels of authority are fluid, and there are fewer rules and regulations regarding procedures. Knowledge about the work at hand and control over tasks are dispersed throughout the organization. Communications that are horizontal as well as diagonal are encouraged. Coordination and control frequently depend on mutual readjustments and organizational systems that are fairly flexible. (This describes a matrix-type organization.)

Both mechanistic and organic organizations represent two poles of a continuous spectrum. In between are an infinite number of transitional variations. Alibaba as a whole is positioned in the middle but tending toward the organic end of the spectrum. In terms of innovative processes, however, it has carried out far more exploratory attempts at organic structure than most organizations.

Within Alibaba is a special type of structure called a *virtual organization*. This refers to a department and a whole business that grows out of the organization itself. Like many companies, Alibaba may pluck individuals from various functional departments to carry out specific projects. They then become the team for that project. In Alibaba, these people still belong to their original departments, although they have been selected to be part of a small team—in overall terms, they still have to do their original work, hence the name *virtual* for the ad hoc team. As it goes along, however, and the project becomes routine, and the virtual becomes more real. Members may well gradually become members of a whole new organization. Alipay is an example of such an entity that grew out of Taobao. In this way, a small group of people who were originally in the Taobao Finance Department gradually transitioned into the largest third-party payment company in China.

As a fast-growing company within the fast-growing Internet industry, Alibaba has never stopped its exploratory approach to organizational structure. In recent years, Alibaba has become a larger entity with over 20,000 employees, and the tendency to seek stability as per larger companies is already in evidence. Reorganizations in any company face greater coordination problems the larger the entity gets. The reason is that any change involves the interests of a greater number of people. However, the age of big data and the great wave of mobile Internet that is upon us require that companies have fast responses. They must follow quickly on the heels of any change.

The very business that the Ali system is in means that previous structures inevitably become restraints. Given this situation, Alibaba opts for change. Moreover, it wields a real knife and a real gun as it achieves that change. The ultimate purpose is not simply to move from a mechanistic organization to an organic organization. The intent is rather to move in the direction of being a higher level of ecosystem or one could say an "ecologized" organization. Behind organizational change lie changes in strategy. The future strategic orientation of the Alibaba Group incorporates what are being called the "four-izations," namely "marketization," "platform-ization," "ecologization" (which refers to a greater diversity of species), and "data-ization." Another way to put it would be to have Alibaba become more market oriented, more platform oriented, more diverse in terms of constituent parts, and more data driven. Innovation has been raised to an unprecedented level of strategy. Any completed structure will always serve as an obstacle to innovation—given this recognition, Alibaba's method of dealing with it is to relinquish control.

The first step in such relinquishing of control is to go from centralized to decentralization control. Before 2012, Alibaba was "a one-man Ali," that is, a one-man show. All strategies, policy decisions, personnel matters, organizational structure, and even issues of implementation came from one man, Jack Ma. Starting in 2012, this centralized management style began to change. For example, the new management system is now composed of two core units: a *strategic policy committee* and a *strategic management and execution committee*. Jack Ma is in charge of the former.

The second step is to decentralize and restructure. In May 2013, the seven business groups that had been created just six months earlier were now spun off into 25 different business departments that were managed correspondingly by the group's strategic management and execution committee. Three months after that, four more business departments were created under the auspices of the Ali Finance Group.

In wanting to expand the outer boundaries of its ecosystem, it has been logical and necessary for Alibaba to reform internally as a means of "ecologizing," or creating a greater diversity of species. Not only do these internal adjustments more fully interweave the horizontal and vertical aspects of business, but also they gave more weight to the horizontal ways in which all parts of the company take advantage of the platform. As vertical lines of business generate features that can be used in common, the system precipitates those out onto a platform that is shared by all.

For example, if a given line of business has a certain set of marketing processes, other business units can take advantage of them as well. The shared platform becomes an internal system that allows for broadening the whole. It enables the advantages of one to be shared by all through the application of common standards. The new organization is managed through the use of data and supported by a shared platform. In general terms, the hope and intent are to rest easy about relinquishing control by turning the organization into a networked structure.

Previously, the group relaxed its hold over the "Seven Swords"[9] in order for them to operate with more freedom, but at a certain point, they still needed to be linked to headquarters. The comparison could be made to a small sapling that can grow at will to a certain size but then begins to come into contact with the trees around it and needs to share space with them. The business of all departments is mutually interwoven so that nobody can avoid becoming involved in the growth of the neighboring community.

New organizational change becomes opportunistic in the positive sense—by having a finer structure of individual units, each can more quickly line itself up within new combinations, and the growth of the entity as a whole more resembles wild growth. As long as the growth of any individual business is oriented in a correct direction and the business is "planted" into the platform at a basic level, it will grow. In this kind of dynamic networked structure, the generation and transmission of information, the interactions of personnel, and the coordination of businesses all reach a new and higher level. At this level, innovation becomes routine.

---

[9]The original reference is to a martial arts novel by Liang Yusheng.

A Platform and Mechanisms That Support Innovation

Alibaba's platform has always contained mechanisms that allow for the free flow of communications, bottom up, that enable innovation. As the phrase goes, "If you dare to be crazy, I dare to invest."

Free and Unhindered Communications
Equality and openness are said to embody the spirit of the Internet. If this is so, an Internet company should quite naturally implement this free spirit in how it conducts itself. Jack Ma has said, "The hope of the Internet lies in innovation." However, such innovation must be born out of a climate that allows all voices to be heard equally and that allows different ideas to contend freely with one another. Alibaba works hard to create an atmosphere in which this can happen. Not only can people debate issues, but the debates can be heard.

Alibaba espouses communication methods that are simple and direct. The embryonic form of Ali's code of values is "believable, intimate, simple"—this was the corporate culture with respect to communications when the enterprise was still in its early period. Jack Ma believes that "[i]f I have something to say to you, I should go knock on your door and talk to you for a couple of hours. Either we have a fight, or we get the thing resolved. If you have something to say to me, you should come find me as well. If you have to go to some third party, then you should get out of this team." In Alibaba, if personnel have any problems, they take notebook in hand and clump together to talk it through. One can see small groups of people discussing things all the time in the company. Teams may be located in different cities, but there still is a sense of close communication.

In terms of the actual content of this communication, internally, what people talk about relates to business, customers, and products but also to corporate culture and the work environment. In terms of the forms that communication takes, there are annual meetings, "Open Day," and other large-format occasions, and then there are "Open" post boxes, microrecommendations, T-lines, a "woods bar," and other smaller formats for informal communications. Every month, the Communications

Department of the company monitors and analyzes data with respect to each format of communication. It then prepares an evaluation on the effectiveness of communications for the group and all subsidiaries. From these data, it analyzes and summarizes any hot issues, any discoveries, and it looks for the wellsprings of any innovations.

The internal communication network of Ali is called "Ali Flavor." The name of its forum is "Say What You Want." On this network are such bulletin boards as business chats, news on customers, and other such subjects, but then there are also bulletin boards relating to hobbies, interests, and sundry other enjoyments. On these things, items that receive an unusual number of hits are called "Magic."

As an example, in early 2013, the company was thinking of outsourcing its security, something that had been handled internally in the past. Staff uploaded the departure statement of one of the security officers of the company, which then turned into a sensation on the internal communications system. His statement complained that the company had no sense of humanity whatsoever—the incident almost turned into a cultural crisis. The result was that senior management overturned the decision and maintained security internally.

Alibaba's position is that anything should be allowed on the internal network—"poisonous weeds" included. They should see the light of day. Anything should be open for discussion and should not be the occasion for censorship or shutting down the internal network. Senior management takes the attitude that it is willing to be criticized and does not control what people say. No individual point of view is censored. Upper levels cannot force lower levels to hold back a very lively way of thinking, which creates an atmosphere that is conducive to innovation. Alibaba in its earliest days was a simpler organization—as soon as new products were put online, the internal bulletin board service (BBS) would start criticizing them. This part was faulty, that part had problems—and products were gradually improved in the midst of the clamor. This tradition continues.

Yet another unusual format for communications within Alibaba is called WCBBS (which stands for Water Closet Bulletin Board Service). The Human Resources Department puts a pad of paper on the back of the door of every toilet in Alibaba, with A4 paper on which people can write their opinions and ideas. The pad has topics that can be addressed and that are changed from time to time. Whenever employees feel the urge, so to speak, they can jot down their thoughts. Subjects vary from light topics to the more serious and provocative. One, for example, said, "If Edison were alive today, what would he do?" This kind of thing often provokes spirited responses: "He would open an Edison light bulb flagship store on Tmall." Some of the notices are essentially advertisements for new products, and responses give opinions on how to improve them. Every month, the Human Resources Department collects the WCBBSs and conducts a statistical analysis of opinions—from that, one can see the lengths to which Alibaba goes to encourage a grassroots spirit.

Innovative Mechanisms That Go from Bottom Up

In its early days, Alibaba's innovations generally took the form of top down and were called "CEO projects." Once senior management had proposed an idea and it had been approved for preferential handling on a top-tier basis, its implementation was guaranteed by having the company invest money, staff, and materials. Results were often not all that impressive, however. Vice President of Human Resources Lu Yang says that the reason was that people were not able to internalize a project that they had been ordered to do. They did not "take it into their own bones."

One of Taobao's innovations was to change the direction of idea generation and make it go from bottom up. It adopted all kinds of methods to enable the voices of ordinary staff members to be heard by senior management. This process unearthed new ideas via competitions, ways of encouraging staff to innovate, and so on. The general approach was to enable ordinary people to do extraordinary things. This concept ran through all the innovative activities of the company.

One classic example from Alibaba's early period was called "My Growth." In 2005, at the time of the "second founding" of the company, each person was asked to keep a diary every day called "So-and-So's Growth." Each was then uploaded onto the internal Taobao network in diary form. One of the tasks of the Human Resources Department back then was to check to see if each employee had written in his or her diary or not. Many innovations came out of discoveries from these diaries.

A second example is the annual competition for innovation held by Alibaba. Starting in around 2007, when the Taobao platform was fairly large and had quite a few products on it, the "innovation points" came in so fast that staff started compiling them into a weekly report. A competition began among the different departments that resulted in a prize at the end. At the time, people would say to one another, "Have you written your weekly report yet? What new innovations have you got?"

One of the more influential innovative mechanisms was the annual "horse race." Lu Zhaoxi was CEO of Taobao at the time it started, in 2010, and it was his idea to have a contest to determine what companies would be started up from within Taobao itself. The project took two different forms. One was purely among the people in that any staff member could come up with an idea, organize his or her own team, and run with the idea if it was voted in and approved. The second used ideas generated by the company. People could still form their own teams, vote, and run the idea if it won. The idea was an instant hit. At the time, Taobao had around 4,500 employees, and close to 1,000 of these poured energy into their own ideas. Their teams would gather after work every day and on weekends, discussing and planning. Out of this, 350 project ideas were generated and passed through several rounds of evaluations. Ten were approved in the end. The company had high hopes for these 10 projects. It dedicated a specific working area to these efforts and gave the people the authority to pull together a team as they wished (naturally, this also led to some conflicts). It gave them half a year within which to hand over their completed proposals. Despite the fact that this was year one of the contest, a number of excellent products came out of it.

In the first season of the contest, the greatest virtue of the entire scheme was that it made every person realize that the company was serious about encouraging innovation. The process in 2011 basically continued what had been begun in 2010, and 85 projects came out of it. In 2012, after considerable reflection, the orientation shifted somewhat. The purpose was no longer founding companies internally but rather resolving the major issues that the company was encountering in the course of innovation. Under the influence of the key performance index (KPI), it had become easy for innovative thinking that went from bottom up to be stolen by someone else. This meant that the company had to work harder to keep open a path to protect creative thinking, and the "horse race" became that path. The positioning of the contest went from being internal founding of companies to microinnovations.

The third season of the race made two major changes. First, the race was extended from Taobao to the entire group and to innovations that went from the bottom up. One of the key issues was the number of "dots"—the group allowed these to increase suddenly in number to more than 20,000. Second, multiple racecourses began to appear in addition to the main racecourse. Given the complex structures of various subsidiaries, many companies or departments instituted their own races, and the best ideas were then fed into the main racecourse of the overall group.

In 2013, the main racecourse proposed 155 projects, while each company handled its own projects and selections in more flexible and well-developed ways, as seen in the following three examples.

"I want to send it by express": Several employees in the Customer Satisfaction Department suggested a project that stemmed from their understanding of the "pain points" of customers with respect to shipping. In the end, this was adopted by the Logistics Department, and the winning team quickly changed positions and began to do things in which they took a stronger interest.

Juwuba:[10] A staff member involved in technology suggested a tool designed to automate certain internal processes, which resulted in saving the cost of several hundred jobs. In the end, the KPI of this person was successfully adjusted so that he could spend his entire time working on this tool.

A History of Taobao Products: A product manager suggested that Taobao should have a book describing the history of its products. The company agreed and allowed him to spend 20 percent of his time working on it.

When the contest (horse race) entered its fourth season in 2013, it was upgraded in several ways. First, it became the vehicle for explorations into a new form of organization. Alibaba's original intent was to have people doing what they themselves wanted to do because this would motivate

---

[10]In Chinese, this sounds like "exceptionally huge."

them more than having the company tell them what to do. However this works out, in the future, the corporate structure will definitely not be as it is today, namely, a bureaucratic system that operates in hierarchical layers. It may be supplemented by the kind of task-oriented system, as practiced in the United States. A group working on a given task can assemble in a bottom-up mode and then disband once the task is completed.

Second, the horse race became a channel for communicating a culture of innovation. As with other forms of organizational culture, it turned intangible things into real things. For example, starting in 2013, the evaluation group communicated much more thoroughly with projects that had been selected. Innovation is necessarily something with a high failure rate, and in the early period of any project, the company cannot invest too much. Alibaba, like Google,[11] talks about 20 percent, but Google's 20 percent is 20 percent of 100 percent, whereas Alibaba's is 20 percent of 120 percent. An Alibaba employee must first complete his or her own work, and well, before he or she does any extra innovating. Because of this, employees must choose things that they themselves are truly interested in doing—the kinds of things where it doesn't matter how things end up as long as they can have a try at them because the learning and growing are what make them happy.

In the fourth season, the horse race also had some very practical break-throughs. First, it combined the two ends—individual microinnovations that go from the bottom up and the organizational need for innovation that goes from the top down. For individual microinnovations to work, they must pass through a kind of innovation funnel that includes guidance from periodic infusions of resources. The main stages of the funnel are the idea, registering its name, online screening, gestation period, offline evaluation, and realization. Resources that can be applied at the various stages include such things as service tools, testing environments, horse race vacations, training drills, legal and financial consulting, horse race trainer, bonus money, testing of formats, and so on.

Meanwhile, the organizational need for innovation is now divided into three stages as well. One is the official call for projects, similar to

---

[11]Before 2013, Google staff could spend 20 percent of their time doing things not relevant to work, which was intended to encourage innovation.

the way the first season called for subjects. The second is an activity that draws ideas together. In this process, a small team can have access to more minds than just those within his or her own department. The third is individual horse races in different companies and subsidiaries. These are managed by the department or team itself, with the group supporting the efforts. These individual horse races (or contests) take all forms. As long as they revolve around the subject of innovation, they are fine. For example, they could be an engineer's night that is aimed at technical personnel or the Ali Cloud Computing horse race put on by Ali Cloud Computing.

Finally, the horse race changed directions somewhat in the fourth season. It was made more of a habit and less of a one-off event. It became a path that allowed for the year-round gestation of new ideas within the group. To ensure that this happened, the company set up what it called an "Innovation Farm" on its online platform. This was open all year. The interesting thing is that this site was one of the ideas proposed by a group of employees in the course of participating in the horse race.

In addition to being made an ongoing event, the horse race became market oriented. Instead of having a few high-level committee members decide on which projects would live and which would die, the company now thought that the market should decide the issue. In 2014, it therefore added an online filtering link to the process that enabled all 20,000+ employees of the company to judge each concept. This too was something a former winner had proposed. In the future, the company hopes to broaden the market-oriented nature of the process even further by asking Ali's customers at large to evaluate projects. They will determine who is up and who is shot down.

A third shift in orientation was that the contests gave more rein to particularly outstanding projects. Everybody felt the same about these contests, namely, that their creators should be allowed to run with an idea more fully. The people winning the races should be true winners. Although for many contestants, ideas being recognized by existing business was an acceptable path, learning and growing from the course itself was fulfilling, and for the race, its goal had already gone beyond just founding a business within the company. Alibaba dreamed bigger, envisioning a future in which altogether new subsidiaries and companies would result from these competitions. What this required was the latter part of the innovation funnel. It involved many follow-on decisions that were summarized by the term *special zone of results*. For example, an employee might gradually stop receiving a salary and, in incremental stages, start receiving actual investment from the company.

Human Resources Management That Nurtures Innovative People

Alibaba is a company with extremely high regard for its employees. As Jack Ma says, "Customers first, employees second, shareholders third." Innovation is fundamentally about people, while human resources management can guide employee behavior to a very large extent. It can help fashion the corporate culture, and it plays a key role in determining whether or not innovation increases within that culture.

Forging Innovative Ali-People

Human resources at Alibaba are divided into *functional human resources* and *operational human resources*. The first is responsible for formulating human resources policies and researching and developing related tools. The second is the so-called political commissar or human resources generalist (HRG).[12] It is composed of specialists in the field of human resources who are partners in the businesses carried on by managers of the business departments. These people coordinate with departments in devising strategy and handle the corresponding human resources tasks. Most of the time, they sit together with employees in units responsible for business. They constantly change positions so as to make it easier to "smell" what is in the wind, to sense any changes in the atmosphere of teams in a timely fashion, and understand any abnormal perturbations in employee emotions. They scope out any hidden management problems. HRG is something that Jack Ma was inspired to set up as actual positions in the company after seeing a film entitled, *The Sky of History*. It is a unique characteristic of human resources management in the Alibaba Group.

---

[12]Author's note: This term originated in the People's Liberation Army. It was a role or position established by the Communist Party of China to strengthen political leadership over the army.

The human resources people of many companies cannot push forward innovation because they are not positioned as a top-line department. In Alibaba, HRGs assume precisely this function. They constitute a 500-person human resources specialist system situated throughout the company. Depending on the number of people in each department, one such person covers one or several departments and handles between 50 and 100 employees. However, these people serve as a communications channel. Any needs or new ideas that employees have can go through HRGs and be transmitted to senior levels of management or directly to the Human Resources Department to be addressed. As a result, innovative ideas have a chance of being realized more quickly. In addition, these people serve as the vehicle for transmitting corporate culture. Alibaba figures that the company was set up by people who were born in the 1950s and 1960s but is mainly staffed by people who were born in the 1980s and 1990s. Ensuring that culture is actually brought home to these younger people requires a transmission channel. The HRGs serve as disseminators of a culture that moves forward with the times.

Three primary aspects comprise the actual processes by which human resources management takes place: hiring people; training, research, and development; and evaluating qualifications and deciding on compensation.

Hiring People

Alibaba has continued to hire more people every year as it has grown. In recent years, this hiring has been characterized by the need for more technical personnel, which has led people outside the company to feel that Alibaba is shifting from being business led to being technology led. As Alibaba's Chief Technical Officer Wang Jian says, however, the way the business has developed has brought with it a host of unanticipated technical problems, which have led to the need for technical talent.

It is certainly true that Alibaba has confronted problems nobody else ever handled, so the company has had to devise its own ways to handle them. Innovative solutions have been applied with tremendous frequency as a result, and coming up with solutions is a capability that the group as a whole has emphasized. To give one example, many companies use Hadoop (a distributed form of basic framework system), but this cannot cope with the superfast speed at which Alibaba's data are growing. Alibaba therefore uses its own multifunctional Flying Apsaras for its cloud-computing platform, which has already surpassed Hadoop. The previously used Oracle is already useless within Alibaba, and the company has instead substituted OceanBase for it, a system that the company developed itself, as supplemented by a reconfigured MySQL. IBM's small-scale computers were always the mark of high functionality, but they too have already been replaced by hardware that Alibaba has made for itself. Alibaba has an internal team that focuses exclusively on optimizing and revising the Linux system for internal use. It has had a custom-made Linux system built for its own purposes. Alipay processes tens of millions of transactions every day, with total transaction amounts in the tens of billions. The company's business requires a dedicated security solution. Given this level of activity, Alibaba requires not just technical personnel but highly creative thinking.

The launch of a plan called "A-Star" (for "Alibaba Star") was the ultimate expression of Alibaba's desire to attract innovative technical personnel. In 2013, Ali selected 10 trainees from among college graduates entering the company to participate in a training exercise. It sent them to the most challenging of its various projects, where the head of the technology team was directly responsible for them and focused on training. The compensation package for these people: 600,000 RMB in annual salary with no cap on increases, a certain number of stock options, and obtaining a Beijing *Hukou*[13] for the person. This generous compensation package went beyond what other companies offered, but the things required to get it also were quite stringent. Candidates had to undergo a face-to-face interview with Alibaba's chief technical officer to test a number of considerations. In terms of competitive nature, did the person aim for the ultimate in technical excellence, and was he or she qualified to be an expert in his or her field as well as competent to write about it? In terms of technology, was the person passionate and immersed in his or her subject and wanting to find technical solutions wherever possible? In terms of empirical experience, was the person the kind who talked about soldiers on paper as opposed to getting things

---

[13]Author's note: Registered permanent residence.

done, and was he or she a core member of any project because of being adept at solving problems? In terms of logical thinking, was the person able to define the key issue in a complex situation, did he or she think through to the underlying issues, and was he or she then able to arrive at his or her goals in a structured and logical way? In terms of approach to learning, was the person strongly curious about new things, and could he or she absorb them quickly into his or her own way of structuring a conceptual approach?

Innovative qualifications are emphasized more and more in job postings and review procedures for other kinds of positions as well. In the personal interview, the "Official Smeller" (an experienced Ali employee who investigates whether or not the applicant has the "Ali Smell") focuses particularly on whether or not a person is curious, and has a natural passion for understanding things and a strong desire to know what is not yet known in the world. This is in addition to finding out the normal things about a person—ambitions, interests, sense of mission, ability to cooperate with a team, and so on.

Training, Research, and Development

Alibaba puts considerable effort into training its human resources. During the Internet freeze of 2003 and during the global economic crisis of 2008, when Internet companies and indeed most companies were in dire straits, Alibaba chose those worst of times to invest in humans themselves. The company began to practice what is called *Nei Gong*[14] and to improve training of personnel.

By now, Alibaba has created a powerful and systematic process of training. It is becoming a learning-type organization, which is a key requirement if today's innovations are to be successful. Following are two cases that illustrate Alibaba's unique form of training.

Technology Carnival: The importance of technical advances to Alibaba was described earlier. The Technology Carnival is a platform that enables people to get together, interact, and learn from one another. It was started

---

[14]Author's note: Inner power.

by some engineers in the Alibaba Group who are passionate about technology. Held in Hangzhou in July of every year, this forum had been going for three consecutive years. By 2013, participants had increased from an initial 1,600 people to 3,400 people—the event has become wildly successful. Software engineers from many companies gather to discuss what is happening in the industry and what the future will hold. They discuss framework design, HTML5, and other such subjects. Since participants are all top-tier R&D people, the sense of "actual combat" is fairly intense, and the event has become known for sharing truly useful content and getting real work done.

Alibaba also has maintained the ability to do self-study within the organization by designing a variety of systems or institutions. First, it has set up training halls within the Park campus. Each can accommodate between 80 and 100 people, and each holds a full set of learning facilities. Second, each business department holds learning sessions at regular intervals, with specialists who are invited in to discuss specific subjects. Third, Alibaba's internal network has a learning platform that contains materials on courses taught by experts from within as well as outside the company. The employees are informed of specific sessions via mass e-mail or internal notice, and attendance is limited to a certain number of people. Sessions are almost always fully booked. Course subjects range from big data to wireless Internet and from insurance to individual tourism. Fourth, people on the internal network can both upload and download learning materials, so this has become a resource that the 20,000+ Ali-people are building together. By June 2014, this resource already had 15,000 items on it. Fifth, once major projects are completed, the team will review the process to learn lessons from it.

Performance Evaluations and Compensation

Alibaba may be the only company in China to put the evaluation of an employee's code of values on a par with an evaluation of his or her business performance. Most companies are guided solely by business results. Alibaba instead uses two coordinates. The vertical coordinate measures business results, whereas the horizontal coordinate measures the person's values. The "Six Swords" are further subdivided into 30 smaller items, each with a potential grading. If one's business performance is excellent but one's values are not up to what is required, this is called being a "wild dog." And wild dogs must be "killed." If one's values are excellent but business results are not, this is called being a "little white rabbit." Little white rabbits also must be "killed." In the company's grading system, 50 points go to business results and 50 points go to values. If values are poor, the person will definitely be asked to leave. If business results are poor, however, the person may be given another chance. Twenty percent of people in Alibaba are allowed to get higher increases in salary, bonuses, or promotions. Seventy percent of people get average salary increases and bonuses. Ten percent are given no bonuses, whereas some may well be asked to change positions, may be demoted, or may be asked to leave the company. This is "Rule 271[15]." Because of these strong incentives, the company has achieved an extraordinary sense of cohesion.

In 2013, Alibaba launched a reform in its performance evaluation system. This had many specific details to it, but it also included two main points that had to do with innovation. First, Rule 271 became Rule 361. Behind this change was the desire to elicit a greater number of outstanding employees and a greater diversity of voices to provide support for innovative strategies.

Another more important part of the reform was to moderate the effect of KPI on how people were graded. This was in line with the strategic adjustments and organizational changes in 2013. At the group level, the gross merchandise volume (GMV) within a period and the KPI of each business department were uncoupled to the degree that each department could decide for itself whether or not the teams under it should be judged at a similar level. In traditional enterprises that are operating on a stable basis, the pursuit of the KPI ensures that operations continue to be highly efficient. In a highly volatile environment, however, the KPI can become an obstacle to generating completely new things. In volatile situations, nobody knows what KPI is reasonable. Alibaba deeply understood the reasoning behind this and therefore took the risk of experimenting with

---

[15]This was the Alibaba's human resources department management principle. The employees are reviewed annually: 20% of all employees are evaluated as outstanding, 70% meeting the expectation, 10% at the brink of elimination. The proportion later changed into 30%, 60% and 10%, respectively.

employee evaluations. For example, innovation itself had already become an important item by which people are evaluated, but the method of doing evaluations proceeds by a kind of case-example system. If a business department can justify high marks by saying that a certain innovation has opened new markets and is being adopted by customers, that consideration is enough to merit points.

Conclusion: Releasing the Grassroots Entrepreneurship of the Company

In managing for innovation, what are known as the *4P laws* are being used to create business opportunities: *p*roduct innovation, *p*rocess innovation, *p*osition innovation, and *p*aradigm innovation. In its 14 years of existence, Alibaba has had considerable success in applying all four of these laws.

YuEbao, Alipay's online money and finance product, is an example of *product* innovation. Alipay itself is an example of *process* innovation. The way Alibaba transitioned from an emphasis on e-commerce to one on being an ecosystem and a data-sharing platform is an example of *position* innovation. B2B is an example of a *paradigm* innovation of the transactions of small and medium-sized enterprises, as well as of the overall business model of the Internet.

All these innovations, large and small, have added to the company's vitality and competitiveness while at the same time creating massive value for China's microenterprises and for consumers. Behind these results lies an enterprise that supports innovation and a group of people who believe they themselves can develop their own creative abilities in a relatively unconstrained way.

When we turn to look back at the main elements of an innovative-type organization mentioned earlier in this chapter, we see that Alibaba has done quite well in some respects. It has employed a common vision, leadership, intent to innovate, ongoing and sustained personal development, and effective group cooperation. Meanwhile, it is putting more and more effort into other aspects, such as an appropriate organizational structure, all members participating in innovation, and having a learning-type organization. The company is intentionally raising its own innovative capacities as appropriate to its growth and strategic repositioning. It is trying to make itself into an innovative-type organization that directly supports innovation through systems and corporate culture. The most noteworthy change is that it has moved to a greater emphasis on bottom-up innovation and is consciously attempting to stimulate grassroots entrepreneurship.

In the company's earlier period, what we saw in Alibaba was a tendency to focus on the key senior individual as playing the decisive role in the innovative process. By now, participation in innovation by all employees is becoming the trend. For example, the creation of Juhuasuan in 2009 is something that burst forth from the lower levels of the company. Meanwhile, the competition has expanded to the point that the "ecologizing" reform of the entire group and its organizations is providing more fertile soil for innovations that go from bottom up.

In addition, Alibaba is focusing on using more external networks to generate innovation. That is, it is opening up innovation to vendors and consumers as well. In 2013, the new operating concept of Taobao was to "give vendors their own stage and let them dance their own dance." Zhang Yu, vice president of the group and the person formerly responsible for Taobao, cites one example of this. Taobao.com always puts on a swimsuit activity in the summertime. In the past, the company developed the categories of products itself. Later, it handed this kind of classification over to vendors on the theory that they themselves are most familiar with consumers. The results have been extremely interesting—vendors have come up with successful categories that people inside the company would never have thought of. Taobao.com is now in the process of experimenting with delegating more authority to vendors. In the future, it will just provide basic marketing and data tools. How they are used will be up to the vendors themselves.

Edmund Phelps believes that unleashing grassroots entrepreneurship is the greatest source of prosperity for a country. Alibaba is in the process of using its own actions to prove that unleashing grassroots entrepreneurship can be a source of major prosperity for a company as well.

CHAPTER 8

GRASSROOTS STARTUPS ARE THE WAY TO EXPAND EMPLOYMENT

SUN XIAOYU, XIANG SONGLIN, AND YING LOWREY

Ever since Thomas More (1478–1535) described a peach-blossom paradise in *Utopia*,[1] people have never stopped aspiring to and also criticizing such a utopia. In Chinese, the term is synonymous with a kind of fantasy land.[2] If there is a utopia in the labor market, what kind of work would people do there?

Since the time Alibaba was founded, it has consistently maintained a low barrier to entry for people who create startups on its platform. It does not charge fees for listing a storefront. It conducts routine training of store owners, public self-policing, convenient supply-chain services, and grassroots financing that is based on integrity capital. These things have

---

Note: Unless otherwise noted, the material and data quoted in this chapter come from research conducted by Tsinghua University and the Alibaba Research Institute and a report entitled, "Joint Research on Internet-Related Job Creation." This is the first formal attempt to apply big data from Alibaba's platform to economic research.

[1]For the Chinese reader, the reference also ties in to the fabled land of the "Peach Blossom," as described by Chinese author Tao Yuanming in AD 421. This describes an ideal place where the land is level, open, and fertile; houses are neatly arranged by beautiful ponds and mulberry trees; young people all have jobs; and old and young can relax and everyone is kind and friendly.

[2]Translator's note: The term *utopian socialism* had something to do with this—in the term in Chinese, the characters for "empty thinking" or "fantasizing" are used instead of the characters *u-tuo-bang*, which is a direct transliteration. This paragraph plays on the contrast between ways to define utopian in Chinese and therefore speaks to a Chinese reader.

enormously lowered the risks of starting up a business. They have made it possible for a large group of people who have little experience and no capital and who otherwise would not have been able to start their own businesses. Star companies have been founded by an extraordinary range of people, from students, to handicapped people, to formerly unemployed people, to rural migrant workers. The stories of these successful startups have encouraged even more people to start their own businesses, which is pulling up employment figures of society at large.

Alibaba therefore has created jobs of a whole new kind in the new economy. These are different from old forms of employment in quite distinct ways—Internet employment has provided jobs in particular to more vulnerable segments of the population. It has served as a force in generating more equal employment opportunities and improving social equality in general. The Taobao net e-commerce platform could indeed be called a utopia of the real world's employment markets.

Rapidly Growing Scale of E-commerce

In the years 2008–2009, economic conditions deteriorated dramatically around the world as the tsunami of the global financial crisis hit, and e-commerce, too, was unable to stand firm. Online business-to-business (B2B) foreign-trade business was affected first, given the turbulence in industrial supply chains. Some export-oriented e-commerce services companies either experienced slower growth, reorganized and laid off workers, or closed down altogether. At the same time, however, online B2B domestic business within China started a new round of fast growth, as well as the vertically differentiated business-to-consumer (B2C) business.

A new kind of economic pattern began to develop, characterized by modern methods of circulating goods. It came about under the multifaceted impact of technological innovation, changes in market demand, and the increasingly socialized[3] nature of investment. The size of e-commerce

[3]Translator's note: That is, investment from the public as opposed to investment by the state.

markets continued to expand as enterprises used e-commerce more intensively. Both purchasing and then related services via the Internet grew swiftly as the process began to galvanize primary industries, upgrade secondary industries, and refashion tertiary industries.

In 2011, e-commerce entered a new stage of fast-paced and scaled-up growth that could be seen most notably in three specific respects. First, website businesses grew exponentially in the areas of B2C and consumer-to-consumer (C2C) e-commerce. Second, small and microenterprise use of e-commerce expanded rapidly. Third, a large group of enterprises engaged in traditional forms of goods circulation now began a powerful entry into the realm of e-commerce. In 2013, China's e-commerce transaction volume reached 10.2 trillion RMB, which was approximately 12.5 percent of gross domestic product (GDP) in that year. Within three to five years, we anticipate that e-commerce in China will maintain stable growth and increase at a rate of 35 percent per year on average. By the end of 2015, it will have reached 26.5 trillion RMB.

According to materials provided by China's E-commerce Research Center, the market shares of companies engaged in retail sales in the Internet-based B2C market were as follows: by December 2013, the number one company in China's Internet-based purchasing market was Tmall, which held 50.1 percent; Jingdongming was number two, with 22.4 percent of the market; whereas Suning Yigou was number three, with 4.9 percent of the market. The next seven in line were Tencent (3.1 percent), Amazon China (2.7 percent), #1 (2.6 percent), Weipinhui (2.3 percent), Dangdang (1.4 percent), AOL (0.4 percent), and Fanke Chengpin (0.2 percent). The market share of online retail markets in the C2C arena was as follows: Taobao was firmly entrenched, holding 96.5 percent of the market by December 2013; Bobo held 3.4 percent; whereas Yiqu held 0.1 percent.

The Boston Consulting Group recently released a report that indicated that the scale of China's e-commerce is currently ranked second in the world but is positioned to experience explosive growth. By the end of 2015, the number of Internet consumers in China is expected to reach 329 million people. This will include 44 percent of all urban residents. By that time, China will have become the largest e-commerce market in the world. IDC

Consulting estimates that by the end of 2015, sales volume via China's e-commerce platforms will be 5 to 10 times what it is now, given the current trajectory of growth in sales. As the most representative example, Taobao's retail sales platform will provide coverage to 500 million consumers, and transaction volume is expected to exceed 2 trillion RMB.

This increase in e-commerce will drive the creation of direct and indirect employment of 30 million people. The penetration rate of e-commerce is expected to surpass 60 percent in China.[4] The rating company Neilsen says that China's Internet purchasers will go from 34 percent in 2010 to 48 percent in 2015 to 60 percent in 2020. This means that in the future there may be 700 million people buying things on the Internet, roughly 10 times the current figure. According to a recent report by the Chinese E-commerce Research Center, online shopping transactions in China in 2014 came to 2.8 trillion RMB. This was an increase of 47.4 percent over the previous year's total retail sales of social consumer goods, and it was the first time the annual penetration rate exceeded 10 percent.[5]

Business Creation Is Job Creation

In trying to encourage job creation, those who formulate policy should be aware that enterprises who are in the business of doing business are also creating employment. They are creating employment for others, but particularly for themselves.

Alibaba's e-commerce platform directly creates job positions, but it also indirectly creates employment. Direct employment includes all the founders of companies on Taobao's and Tmall's retail platforms, that is, the business owners of storefronts (including partnerships) as well as the people hired to manage the platforms and the people hired by

---

[4]The penetration rate in this context is turnover value from e-commerce as a percentage of total turnover value.

[5]See http://www.100ec.cn/detail--6262173.html.

the entrepreneurs. Indirect employment includes people who are closely connected to online stores as well as the increased employment of people in other industries that is generated by the whole chain of e-commerce operations. Employment generated in areas that serve online sales is a good example of indirect employment, including such things as transportation, warehousing, and delivery. The reason Alibaba's e-commerce platforms have been able to create such huge numbers of jobs is twofold. On the one hand, the financial crisis stimulated a new round of high-speed growth in e-commerce. On the other, small businesses became the primary entities involved in e-commerce platforms, injecting new vitality into labor markets.

In 2009, faced with the impact that the financial crisis was having on small and microenterprises, the State Council of China issued a statement entitled, "Various Opinions on Taking Further Steps to Stimulate the Growth of Small and Microenterprises." This was in recognition of how the growth of such enterprises affects people's livelihood and well-being and therefore how it affects social stability.

According to the way in which the State Statistical Bureau categorizes enterprises, called, "Methods of Accounting for and Differentiating among Large, Medium, and Small-Sized Enterprises," virtually all the stores on Taobao belong to the small and microenterprises category. Ying Lowrey has estimated (2011) that over 70 percent of newly created jobs in the United States every year come from the vast number of small and microenterprises as well as self-employed people in that country. This percentage went to 80 percent after the financial crisis, with the number of people being hired by others constantly declining.

In China, the primary entities active on e-commerce platforms are the huge numbers of small and microenterprises and entities operated by individuals. The ability of the Internet economy to generate jobs is substantial. According to a report issued by *People's Daily* on November 3, 2013, by June 2013, China's e-commerce service companies were directly employing more than 2.2 million people, while indirect employment generated by such business came to more than 16 million people (Table 8.1).

TABLE 8.1 *Transaction volume of e-commerce in China and the number of jobs that the business has mobilized*

YEAR	TRANSACTION VOLUME (100 BILLION RMB)	EMPLOYMENT (10,000s OF PEOPLE)	
		DIRECT	INDIRECT
2008	3.2	45	570
2009	3.8	100	800
2010	4.6	160	1,200
2011	5.9	180	1,350
2012	8.5	—	—
2013	10.2	220[a]	1,600[a]

[a]*Source: People's Daily*, November 3, 2013.

Source: 2011 and 2013 Annual Reports, *China E-commerce Market Data Monitor*, published by the China E-commerce Research Center.

Patterns of Employment Generated by Alibaba's Innovative Economy

The jobs created by Alibaba could be described as *new-economy employment*. For a very long time, people have generally thought that the only proper form of employment was that done by official enterprises and institutions, including all types of work performed within such entities. Such employment was highly traditional, based as it was on an industrialized modern factory system. Most aspects were predetermined by labor contracts that included provisions to do with working hours, work site, compensation, insurance and benefits, labor relations, and so on.

In the past 20 years, more flexible forms of employment have sprung up in developed market economies that have had a very positive impact on local labor markets. The Internet and cloud computing, as the basic infrastructure for the new information age, are generating massive amounts of data and pooling resources that gradually incubate new forms of production factors. Using these new production factors (or inputs), a new division of labor that is socialized, that permeates throughout society, is now emerging on a large scale. The people generating Internet-based employment are also the beneficiaries of this new basic infrastructure. They are pioneers in taking advantage of the new production inputs. They are both the creators of the new division of labor in Internet industries and also the operators whose cooperative innovations propel the e-commerce ecosystem toward greater prosperity.

The Alibaba Research Institute sums up four main features of e-commerce retail employment as follows: it is self-employed, dispersed, simultaneous (i.e., carried out concurrently), and cooperative. These four characteristics depict a work pattern that is flexibly driven by innovative approaches and that gives prominence to the individualized nature of employment demand.

The self-employed nature of new employment patterns means that the employed person is neither hiring others nor being hired by others but instead is working for himself or herself. Supported by the Internet and the mobile Internet, the sole condition of his or her work is that it be online. The time and place of work are now dispersed as opposed to being concentrated, which breaks out of the conventional mold of person-hour labor.

The appearance of simultaneous work allows for one person to engage in multiple tasks and for a diversification of income sources. The Internet "employee" works cooperatively with e-commerce services providers to carry out long-distance cooperative efforts; pay depends on the tasks that are performed; and new forms of organization come forth to meet whatever needs present themselves. Survey data from research conducted by Alibaba regarding retail Internet employment indicates that the average number of self-employed people who operate self-run independent stores on Taobao and Tmall comes to 1.2 per store, figuring in both individual store owners and partnerships that jointly operate a store. From this statistic, the research calculates that a total number of 4.76 million people are self-employed on the Taobao and Tmall platform. Some 80 percent of these self-employed people are between the ages of 23 and 35.

In this new employment pattern, the quality of being dispersed refers to both time and place. Without any time restrictions, work time and nonwork time are intermixed. Without spatial restrictions, it becomes possible to work at home. While working online, one also can attend to daily life so that living and working become fused, and work becomes more an integral part of daily existence. This can enormously improve a person's sense of well-being. Alibaba's Internet retail employment surveys indicate that among those who consider their online store to be either their sole or their primary source of income, people work for 46.9 hours per week on average on the Taobao platform. Of the 42.9 percent of people who work fewer than 10 hours per week doing e-store business, 71 percent have other sources of income; that is, they are part-timers (Figures 8.1 and 8.2).

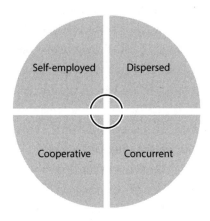

FIGURE 8.1 *Four major characteristics of employment in the new economy*

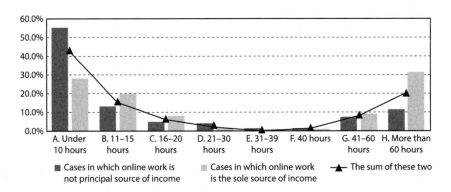

FIGURE 8.2 *The number of hours worked per week by two types of e-commerce vendors on the Taobao and Tmall platforms: vendors' e-commerce retail income is the sole or major source of income versus not the major income*

The time of day that people who conduct Internet store business work tends to revolve around the peak time for purchasing. The Internet is open for business around the clock, which has created a unique feature of e-commerce, namely, the peak hours at which people buy things. The peak purchasing time on the Internet is between 8 and 10 in the evening. During this period, most stores that conduct regular business are hard at work. "Melting time" generally comes after 10 p.m. Where do these people work? The preference of the great majority of people who operate stores on a platform is to work at home and to have their home serve the combined functions of office, warehouse, and living quarters. In October 2013, the number of people who used a mobile seller's app called Qianniu Workbench exceeded 1 million users per day. Online store owners have already gone from living in an age of e-commerce as operated by personal computers to an age of e-commerce as operated by hand-held devices. As the joke goes among those who operate stores, "I can do business even when I'm lying down, which means that I have much more time for romance."

The 2013 online research on living conditions of Taobao vendors indicates that over one-half (54.7 percent) of Taobao vendors operate their Taobao stores at their own homes, and another 29.7 percent rent other space as an independent office, generally in housing districts or residential areas. The percentage that has offices in regular office buildings or industrial districts is 13.5 percent. Of vendors who have turnover between 100,000 and 1 million RMB, nearly 32.6 percent have offices in office buildings or industrial districts, whereas nearly one-half (46.4 percent) of those with more than 1 million RMB in turnover have offices in such places.

The simultaneous nature of new-employment work patterns means that one person does more than one job and has diversified sources of income. The hours one has to work at doing Internet business can be flexible. While online, the vendor can log onto his or her store at any time, so this sort of work quite naturally accommodates the person's day job. His or her part-time job is compatible with work that can be done concurrently. E-commerce store income is supplementary income and even primary income for people who work at it on a part-time basis. Statistics from Alibaba's retail e-commerce employment research show that 65 percent of those who are employed in e-commerce stores also have other jobs, whereas 44.3 percent of those who are employed in e-commerce stores regard this as their primary source of income. In addition to operating e-commerce stores, owners of such stores work in a wide range of other occupations. Close to 30 percent are hired by other occupations or are part-time workers for individual businesses, and some 3.5 percent are students. The research even discovered that 6 percent of online store owners are government workers or staff employed by government institutions (Figure 8.3).

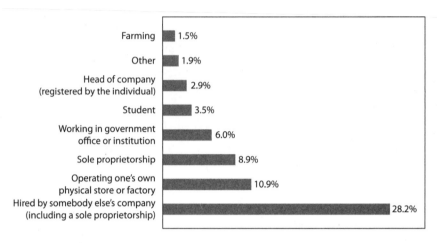

FIGURE 8.3 *Other occupations in which e-commerce vendors engage outside their work in e-commerce*

The new employment patterns require long-distance cooperative work among e-commerce services providers. Within the e-commerce ecosystem, more and more e-commerce is being handed over to services companies to handle. The densely interwoven nature of stores and services providers requires closely cooperative networked connections. Vendors pay for specific needs. This lowers their cost of transactions and improves efficiency. In addition, task-oriented organizations have emerged to meet demand. They gather depending on the particular job at hand, and they disperse once the job is finished.

A prosperous e-commerce ecosystem also has fostered a highly developed e-commerce services industry. In 2012, Taobao had 490,000 third-party service providers assembled on its open platform. These provided services to more than 9 million nonpaying users and 1 million paying users. Taobao's vendors use all kinds of e-commerce services, including software tools, trusteeship of e-commerce stores, information systems, data research, quality control, marketing, photography and modeling, consulting and training, supply-chain accounting, legal services, human resources services, and so on. Alibaba's e-commerce retail employment surveys indicate that the usage rate of third-party software tools is highest, followed by customer service, video making, guided purchasing, designing, warehousing, modeling, quality inspections, subcontracting, and training.

To give an example, Wu Guifen has a store on Taobao that only sells down-padded pants, which is a seasonal business. When she needs more labor, she hires local women. She hires women from the village who are over age 50, who are generally also responsible for sending off and picking up children from school, as well as older seamstresses who are over age 60. When sales are slow, she works on the e-store by herself. This kind of task-oriented organization is flexible—it comes together depending on the particular job at hand and disperses once the job is finished.[6] When times are busy, this model absorbs surplus labor from elsewhere, and when times are more relaxed, it at least allows for ongoing self-employment. It thereby embodies the unique features and advantages of being self-employed.

Alibaba's Platforms Encourage Equal Employment Opportunities

Not only has Alibaba created a tremendous number of new job positions in the new-economy type of employment, but it has done a great deal to stimulate equal opportunity and social equality by unleashing grassroots entrepreneurship.

Distribution of Online Stores Reflects Employment Equality

By looking at sample surveys of Internet merchants on Taobao, we can evaluate their distribution in terms of physical location within the country, industries, and types of professions. Such distribution turns out to be very helpful in equalizing job opportunities.

1. *Regional distribution of online retail employment.* E-commerce startups are generally concentrated in the eastern and central parts of China. From Taobao's platform statistics, eastern China accounts

---

[6]Translator's note: This takes off on a famous saying the way life itself comes together and is and then disperses and is no more: "One coming, one dispersing, that's it."

for 57.4 percent (within which figure Guangdong holds 23.5 percent, Shanghai 17.7 percent, and Zhejiang 16.2 percent). Although merchants in the East hold a dominant position, the growth rate of new startups in specific parts of central and western provinces is beginning to exceed that along the coast. From this trend, we can see that e-commerce is breaking through the traditional spatial patterns of commerce in China, which means that there is considerable room for growth in the western and central parts of the country that are less favorably situated in geographic terms (Figure 8.4).

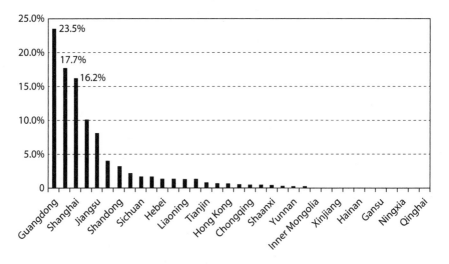

FIGURE 8.4 *Regional distributions of employment of people involved in e-commerce on the Alibaba platform as of December 2011*

With respect to the locations of e-commerce startups, 85 percent of all startups are in cities. Among these, 27.3 percent are town centers, 29.3 percent are capitals of provinces, and 18.7 percent are the largest municipalities. Large cities currently represent the mainstream location of e-commerce operations. For one thing, merchants can handle logistics more conveniently, and for another, cities allow for the hiring and retention of staff more easily. At the same time, the pace at which merchants are setting up in rural areas and the outskirts of county seats is picking up. The growth of the Internet economy offers a golden opportunity for lesser developed rural parts of China.

2. *Industrial distribution of online retail employment.* E-commerce startups are mainly concentrated in service industries relating to production and to daily life. Taobao's platform statistics indicate that clothing, accessories, and shoes accounted for 35.1 percent of the direct employment created by the Taobao platform in 2011, 3C-digital accounted for 14.4 percent,[7] and services accounted for 7.9 percent. Jobs attributable to household goods, automobile spare parts, furniture, and other production-type services are all increasing. Barriers to entry are low for such things as clothing, accessories, shoes, and bags, which is why so many grassroots entrepreneurs without capital or technology start in this arena.

3. *Occupational distribution of online retail employment.* In terms of the professions that provide jobs for people in e-commerce startups, the distribution includes knowledge-intensive, labor-intensive, and technology-intensive enterprises. According to Taobao's statistics, in 2011, 89 percent of direct employment positions attributable to the Taobao platform were in customer services in general. Some 73 percent related to packaging, 53 percent to website design or fine arts, 47 percent to Internet store management and operations, 33 percent to marketing, 30 percent to finance, and 15 percent to production processing. Newly created job positions that are knowledge and technology intensive include people from rural areas who have left to seek jobs in cities and college students in rural areas. The industry is giving them the chance for upward mobility and a way to make a living (Figures 8.5 through 8.7).

Weakening Discriminatory Behavior in Employment Markets

The fair employment practices followed by Alibaba are reflected in the demographics of store owners. They demonstrate store ownership by women, people with rural household registrations,[8] and people with physical disabilities. Most of these categories have been subjected not only to social discrimination but also to government discrimination. None of these owners' characteristics should have any effect on the productivity or the operations of online stores at all!

---

[7]*3C-digital* refers to computers, communications, and consumer electronics.

[8]The Chinese government's household registration status is the way to distinguish between people who are urban citizens and those who are rural peasants. Members of the latter group have typically been discriminated against by Chinese culture and society.

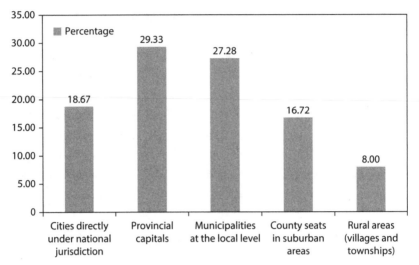

FIGURE 8.5 *Urban versus rural distribution of people engaged in e-commerce on the Alibaba platform*

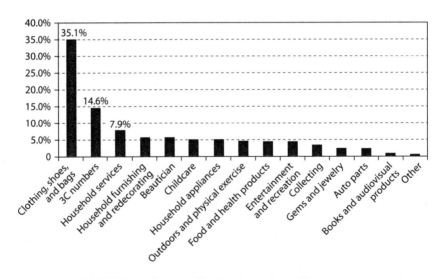

FIGURE 8.6 *Sector distribution of employment on the Alibaba platform as of December 2011*

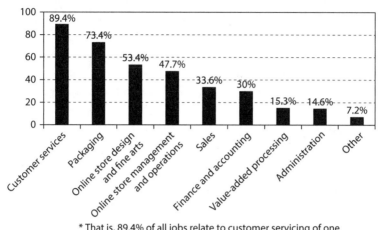

* That is, 89.4% of all jobs relate to customer servicing of one
from or another. Similarly for other status.

FIGURE 8.7 *Main categories of jobs on the Alibaba platform*

In More's *Utopia*, useless industries do not exist. All people in Utopia, male or female, are engaged in agriculture while at the same time being involved in wool spinning, hemp weaving, metallurgy, woodworking, and so on. Anyone may learn what he or she wants and choose the profession he or she likes. In today's reality, however, labor markets are not so perfect. Those hiring others do not rely exclusively on the requirements of a given profession or job in selecting workers. Instead, they evaluate and categorize prospective employees according to gender, apparent physical disability, household registration status, and various other forms of discriminatory behavior. They seek to differentiate among different types of people, some of whom may then get into high-paying professions with welfare benefits and good prospects for the future, whereas others are excluded and can only work at low-paying menial tasks that have no benefits whatsoever.

With respect to gender discrimination in China, according to a survey conducted by Nankai University, over one-half of all employers who were interviewed reported that one of their requirements was that the person being hired had to be male. With respect to the household registration system, generally speaking, rural migrant workers can only work at low-paying jobs. In addition to this, the work is unsteady and the unemployment rate is high. Such facts may well dispel anyone's rosy impression about the employment situation or any optimistic hopes for the future, but this may well not be the entire situation. As [9]Shu Ting's poem says, "All of the present holds the future within its embrace, and all of the future is born out of its yesterdays. Not all consequences are marked by tears; the countenance of the future does indeed allow for hope." The information economy, with Taobao's e-commerce platform as a representative example, may well be our future hope.

By analysis of sampling data on the Taobao platform, we discover that the transaction volume of Taobao online stores does not depend on the gender or household registration status of the owner. This is in distinct contrast to the way labor has to be put through a kind of grading process in order to qualify for different kinds of occupations in the real world.

Empirical research comes up with a similar conclusion. Since 2009, a large group of startup stars emerged from rural areas and among people with disabilities. Their experience in successfully starting businesses has encouraged many others to do the same. According to the Alibaba retail employment survey statistics, nearly one-half (49 percent) of job positions in stores on the Taobao and Tmall platforms are held by people with rural household registrations, and 90 percent of these people work in cities or surrounding suburban areas (Figure 8.8).

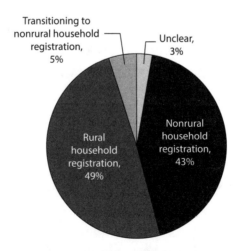

FIGURE 8.8 *Permanent household registration status of people engaged in retail sales on the Taobao platform from sample surveys*

---

[9]Shu Ting was born in 1952 in Fujian, a contemporary women poet, a representative of Hazy Poetry in China.

China's e-commerce maintained rapid growth in 2014, with total transaction volume breaking through 13.4 trillion RMB (8.1 trillion in 2012, a 65.4 percent increase in two years). Within this overall figure, e-commerce retail sales came to more than 2.8 trillion RMB (1.3 trillion in 2012, a 115.4 percent increase over two years). E-commerce services for e-commerce retail business emerged as a new industry sector, creating new online businesses and jobs in the process. Within total e-commerce turnover, e-commerce services for e-commerce retail business came to 0.77 trillion RMB in 2012 and then increased to 1.35 trillion RMB in 2014, a 75.3 percent increase in two years.

TABLE 8.2
E-Commerce in China: 2012 and 2014.

YEAR	TURNOVER OF TOTAL E-COMMERCE (TRILLION RMB) [1]	TURNOVER OF E-COMMERCE RETAIL (TRILLION RMB) [1]	TURNOVER OF E-COMMERCE SERVICES FOR E-COMMERCE RETAIL (TRILLION RMB) [2]
2012	8.1	1.3	0.77
2014	13.4	2.8	1.35
Two-year growth rate	65.4 percent	115.4 percent	75.3 percent

Sources: [1] 2014 Report on E-Commerce in China, by Chinese Ministry of Commerce; [2] estimated by Alibaba Research Institute.

Accompanying this fast growth in the Internet economy and e-commerce is an ongoing extension of the industrial chain, that is, the range of goods linked to the process. This has resulted in a surge of new occupations and created a tremendous number of new job positions. In cumulative terms, it has pulled employment figures up by 10 million people. It has given work to many grassroots level people who are disabled in one way or another in particular, allowing them to start their own companies and creating room for them to grow. It has forcefully propelled China's economy and society in the direction of sustainable and sound growth.

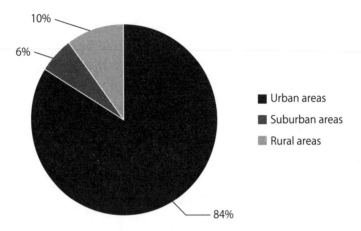

FIGURE 8.9 *Physical locations of people engaged in retail sales on the Taobao platform*

Because people are running their own businesses, such self-created employment on the Alibaba platforms has broken out of traditional constraints in terms of the age, gender, level of education, and physical condition of the people. Self-generated employment is providing a much fairer job platform for grassroots personnel who otherwise face problems and will provide greater equal opportunity for people in the future. Traditional channels for employment make it hard for disabled people, single mothers, students graduating from university after the 1980s, and rural migrant workers with minimal education to get work. Through e-commerce business creation, not only are people able to create their own jobs, but they often also create a large number of hired positions as well, generating considerable wealth for society at large. In what follows, we have selected a few case studies from the large number of representative examples that the Alibaba Group's Research Institute has collected. Each has its own story to tell. Collectively, the stories are the message of the new age: getting a job in the traditional sense is no longer a restriction for people who want to work. E-commerce platforms provide access to jobs for those who really want to work and know what to work on.

Case 1: The Handicapped Advisor of Shaoxing[10] Starts a Business

Luo Runfa, 50 years old, handicapped from childhood, uses two small wooden stools as he propels himself along. Luo previously operated a small stand and then a shop that provided typing for people. Starting in 1995, he opened a computer repair center that proceeded to train more than 90,000 people from around the country. As a result, he was awarded national honors and was widely recognized for his service. Starting in 2008, Luo started a second business together with some other handicapped friends—he set up a nationwide training base for "handicapped heroes." By cooperative arrangements with enterprises, this base enabled handicapped people to have access to high-quality goods at the best ex-factory prices in order to help the manufacturers of those goods sell on the Internet. Luo's base cooperated with Taobao in setting up a Taobao marketplace. Sales transactions are handled by student staff, profits are distributed among all participants, and the base itself handles promotion. It introduces the most outstanding students to production enterprises, where they then begin to serve as e-commerce staff. They sell products of the enterprise on the Internet. In the short time of three to four years, revenues from this online sales activity have begun to exceed 5 million RMB per year.

Case 2: A Single Mother and Her Strong and Tenacious White Poplars Company

Zhou Liqun became a single mother in 2006 owing to a family misfortune and then worked for 12 years in the foreign-trade department of Hebei Province. When the government department underwent reform and cut back on staff, she was let go and became unemployed. She was "resting" at home when an old classmate looked her up and asked her to work in the export department of his electronics factory. Zhou Liqun gladly took up the challenges of

---

[10]The term *advisor* here (*shiye*) refers to a person attending to legal, fiscal, or secretarial duties in a local *yamen*. A *yamen* was the local government office in the olden days in China. This term therefore intentionally places a handicapped person in a senior and responsible position in the local community.

the new job, given her years of experience in foreign trade. In the short space of a little over one year, she had exported more than 50 million items for her friend. After helping her friend get on the right track, in 2008, Zhou Liqun returned to Shijiazhuang and set up her own White Poplars Trading Company, Ltd. Her main line of business involved selling various kinds of equipment. She registered for an account on Alibaba and put all her efforts into selling on the famous export platform. Heaven rewards those who work hard. Despite the severe problems caused by the international financial crisis, White Poplars realized a respectable sales income of 2 million RMB in 2009. From that point onward, Zhou Liqun was able to grow quite quickly and to realize the dream of setting up her own company as a single mother.

Case 3: A Member of the Eighties Generation Starts a Company That Serves as a Model for Young People

Liu Pengfei, graduated from college in 2007 and then made his way to Yiwu with only 5 RMB in his pocket. Given his poor academic record, Liu Pengfei first had to work as a manual laborer with payment in room and board. The work was for a foreign-trade company, with packing and shipping jobs on the side, but Liu did not miss any chance to keep studying. After a few months, he became proficient at his task and was well regarded by his superiors. As other classmates gradually drifted southward to work as well, Liu Pengfei discovered that many of them were finding it hard to find suitable work. This, together with his own tough situation, led him to the idea of starting an online business. A chance opportunity came up when Liu Pengfei discovered that there were still not many people selling Kongming lamps on the Internet. He began selling them on the Taobao site. After a year, much to his own surprise, he had created a business of considerable size, and after three years, he had created a kind of business miracle—he had successfully provided jobs for more than 1,000 people. In order to help even more college classmates, Liu Pengfei then set up a specific Feitian Startups Foundation. This provides startup funding for people who have just graduated from college so that they can start their own businesses. While realizing his own personal goals and helping his classmates get jobs and become successful, Liu Pengfei has also addressed the unemployment problems of society at large. His story has become one of the legends among e-commerce startups, particularly because it relates to the many unemployed college students born after 1980.

Case 4: The Taobao Dream of a Young School Dropout

Zhou Liheng, 29 years old, is from Tianjin City, Wuqing District, Cuihuangkou Town. In 2003, when he was just 18, Zhou Liheng quit school and made his way to Shanghai to work as a laborer. When that did not go well in terms of making enough money to live on, he had the bright idea of starting his own business. Hand-woven carpets were made in small workshops around his home town, giving the place a reputation for good products, but production and sales remained limited. Given the lack of marketing channels, Zhou decided to try to sell the carpets on the Internet. After six months of careful preparation and then the launch of operations, his Hengyasi Carpets quickly entered the ranks of the top five carpet sellers in sales volume. In 2007 alone, he sold roughly 1.5 million RMB worth of carpets. However, even as his C-store was growing like wildfire, redundant (duplicate) Hengyasi Carpets were discovered by Taobao's relevant authorities, and he was shut down in August of 2009. In order to start up again, Zhou Liheng put his efforts into management of the marketplace and took to heart the lessons learned from the closing down of his C-store. He focused on the design of his storefront and made sure to indicate the quality and skilled workmanship of each product to the extent that, by 2010, his sales volume had reached 3.28 million RMB. After that, Zhou Liheng formally signed a KA (large-customer) vendor's agreement with Taobao. He invested over 1 million RMB in a new carpet factory. Not only had this young dropout from school used the Internet to realize his dream of starting a business, but he also created jobs for his local community. As a result, he became famous as a successful new kind of rural migrant worker of the Internet age.

These success stories will no doubt inspire people to realize that fair and equal employment opportunities are in fact possible.

Given the situation on Taobao, one wonders what it is about Taobao that operates against gender and status discrimination as practiced in the real world. Put another way, why do these forms of discrimination continue to play a role in categorizing people in the real world of job markets?

According to scholars who analyze this subject, discrimination in China mainly works by affecting a person's ability to get a job, whether that discrimination is with respect to gender or household registration status. That is, women and people holding rural household registrations are kept out of high-paying industries, and this leads directly to their relatively low incomes and lack of social security as a group. The phenomenon of "same work, different pay" is seen less in China in relative terms for the simple reason that rural residents and women fundamentally cannot even get "same work." Naturally, they do not have a chance at "same work, different pay." For women, the initial job interview can be highly intrusive. Interviewers first judge whether or not women have the same capabilities as men, but then they also ask about age, marital status, children, location of the husband, plans to have children if there are currently none, and so on. This is similar to the way in which Western countries also evaluate a woman's social background, the social status of her parents and husband, schools attended, and so on, all of which may be important in determining a job offer.

Opening a store on the Taobao platform is quite different. First, the threshold requirements for entry are extremely low, especially for shop owners of online stores, for which there are essentially no rigid requirements at all. Whatever your status, Taobao still provides you with free space on its network as well as an online storefront and technical support. This provides an equal-opportunity platform for entrepreneurs, particularly those with less education and rural household registrations—all enjoy "same work." If you want to enter, you are welcome to do so.

Second, once the online store is set up, the retailer can view supply and demand and sales figures in real time, which lowers inventory costs. Many Taobao vendors are able to detour around branch retailers and issue their orders directly to factories, which lowers channel costs.

Naturally, e-commerce is also able to avoid all the different levels of rather complex items in accounts that must be dealt with by conventional retailers, which lowers the financial burden.

It can be said that the Taobao platform provides everything necessary for Taobao online stores. All store owners have to do is focus on the selling links in the process, gaining the approval of consumers' "eyeballs" and trying their best to establish a loyal group of fans. Up to a certain amount of Internet volume, all online stores on Taobao can display their goods for free, so competition among stores is mainly based on the quality of goods and services. The personal characteristics of the individual person operating the store have very little to do with it. It can be seen from this that Taobao has eliminated the kind of concrete channel that discriminates on the basis of gender, human capital, and household registration status. It has limited considerations that prevent people from entering certain professions (e.g., a country woman might find it impossible to enter a given industry and yet might make a good income from online sales). Discriminatory considerations do not work on the Taobao platform.

Another point should be reinforced here, which is that the Taobao platform possesses an extremely powerful search engine and the capacity to sort through data, which shakes the very foundations of the causes of discrimination. Those causes include asymmetrical information, the costs involved in looking for a job, and the social bias that has built up over a long time as a result of these things.

The core of Alibaba's service is integrity, sharing, and responsibility, and among these, integrity is particularly important. The Taobao platform must have reliable information on online stores in order to make decisions about whether to support or penalize them for the purpose of ensuring the soundness and security of the entire trading environment. To provide a secure trading environment, Taobao launched Alipay, which provides not only third-party payment solutions but also third-party escrow services. By means of this service, Alipay serves as the guarantor of transactions. By means of the Alipay trading mechanisms, after a buyer and a seller come to agreement on a transaction, the buyer advances payment to Alipay, which temporarily holds it in escrow. Once Alipay receives confirmation of receipt of goods by the buyer, it releases payment to the seller to complete the transaction. Not only does this resolve the issue of trust in two different links of the process, the buyer being willing to pay money and the seller being willing to release goods, but it expands the market size of online purchasing and in the process amasses an absolute ocean of data on Internet store transactions. This allows Taobao to have a very good handle on the degree of integrity of each store.

In addition, a host of Taobao personnel work behind the scenes, monitoring any plagiarizing being done by online stores of other people's product information and photographs. Punishment for such behavior is stringent enough that the great majority of online stores voluntarily follow the principle of integrity. Third, the Taobao platform has massive backup support. Relying on big data, it has collected sufficient information on online stores to enable it to resolve many management issues caused by asymmetrical information. Finally, Internet transactions rely primarily on the nature and efficiency of service, so many of the social prejudices that come, consciously or unconsciously, from face-to-face contact do not have an opportunity to arise. As long as the customer is satisfied and gives good feedback in return, more of them will recommend the given vendor.

Developing Systems That Promote the Employment Generated by E-commerce Startups

China's Human Resources and Social Security Department is working closely with Alibaba to find ways to resolve certain social employment issues. Specifically, both are considering targeted measures to allow the inclusion of Internet entrepreneurs into national statistics. They hope that people employed in e-commerce startups will begin to gain national policy support under the definition of this newest form of industry. Both particularly hope that people employed in e-commerce startups will begin to enjoy social security benefits. This will preserve and protect the basic social security rights and interests of people involved in e-commerce startups. It will also protect the overall employment situation in e-commerce startups. We are not policy specialists, but would like to provide a record of a few specific policy recommendations that the Ministry of Human Resources and Social Security has been discussing with Alibaba.

1. Setting Up a Better Statistical System That Covers E-commerce Startups and Employment

Being employed by e-commerce startups has already become the first choice for many college students and unemployed people. In order to enable e-commerce startups to play an even bigger role, we should establish an *e-commerce startups employment statistical system*. In doing this, we should encourage people already engaged in startups and whose business is going fairly well to come to their local administrative office of the Ministry of Commerce and Industry to register their business. They should follow current procedures so as to be incorporated into official employment registration and employment statistics.

The people operating e-commerce businesses who are not doing well should be handled as a separate category. If people employed in e-commerce startups have been working for three months or more, if their trustworthiness ratings are up to certain standards, and if their monthly net income is over a certain minimum level, they can be certified as a person who is employed in an e-commerce startup. If someone has been working for more than three months and has good trustworthiness ratings but not sufficient net income per month to meet requirements, then that person should be defined as unemployed. For the time being, that person should not be described as employed and should not be listed in employment registration figures and data.

What's more, the government should unify all parts of the country in issuing a national *registration of employment and unemployment certificate*. This should register the actual names of people employed by e-commerce startups. The government should set up a service platform for people employed by e-commerce startups and should provide policies that allow for making startups convenient on their behalf, as well as information and consultation services. It should provide applications for startups with a list of startup projects that can receive financial assistance, that connect funding to projects, together with startup guidance. The aim is to encourage e-commerce startups that grow in a sound and orderly way.

2. The Government Should Provide Supportive Policies for People Employed by E-commerce Startups

We should incorporate e-commerce startup personnel into the scope of the supportive policies that the country is providing for job creation in general. Those self-reliant startups with Internet-generated employment also should have access to financial services and opportunities for e-commerce training. The local government and relevant institutions should work out ways to assist self-employed vendors and their employees for social and medical insurance payments. For unemployed people who want to start an e-commerce business, they should enjoy such supportive job-creation policies as a one-time startup award and a one-time drawing from the unemployment insurance fund.

Disabled people who start an online store should be exempted from certain administrative fees, including management, registration, and identity-card fees. The line fees for the Internet and the costs of incubating startups should be subsidized, together with assistance in logistics, warehousing, and rent, in order to stimulate better growth of startups being undertaken by disabled people.

3. We Should Ensure That People Employed by E-commerce Startups Participate in Social Insurance Programs and Are Entitled to Enjoy Their Benefits

Depending on the situation of different kinds of people employed by e-commerce startups, those involved should be encouraged to participate in social security and health insurance systems. Depending on their contribution to the social security and the various insurance premiums, they will be financially covered when they are older and will allow them to draw on pooled funds for basic living major illnesses.

Meanwhile, for people whose businesses have poor operating results and have low and uncertain income prospects and therefore are unable to pay premiums, we should ensure that they join into the town-and-village (or township) residents' basic pension insurance program and basic medical insurance program. With lower premiums and with local community government special policies, they will still be sure of their basic rights to some security. As their situation improves, they can then be incorporated into regular employee insurance.

It is not as though people employed in e-commerce startups would not like to be insured. The main reason many are not is that they have been in business for such a short time that operations are still unsteady and income is low, and they cannot afford the premiums. By improving government policies on basic level premiums and rates, the government can lower the threshold for gaining access to the insurance system for e-commerce startup personnel. Not only will this reduce the burden on these people as they are getting their businesses going, but it will also enable them to continue lower-level payments and to have continuous insurance coverage. This will promote a better employment situation in e-commerce startups.

Another situation with respect to e-commerce startups relates to the tax bureaus at national and local levels and specifically to their often dubious attitude about e-commerce startups. In fact, too skeptical an attitude will hurt the development of e-commerce and therefore lead to problems in job creation in grassroots startups. The concept of a sole proprietorship in the United States serves as a good comparison because it is similar to the e-commerce startups on Alibaba. One telephone number or one e-mail address can be enough to cover the registration requirements for such sole proprietorships in a given area. After registering, if the sole proprietor has a certain level of operating income, he or she can pay the annual tax on that without having to pay the additional enterprise tax.[11]

There is no need for the tax bureaus to investigate the tax-paying compliance of the sole proprietor directly. If tax evasion has occurred, all a bureau needs to do is ascertain accurate information from third-party channels, for example, from banks and investment companies. With this in hand, it can calculate the actual amount of tax that should be paid and instruct the entity to pay. If the entity has sufficient evidence to refute this, it can present this to the tax bureau. If not, then the entity will be allowed to supplement its already paid taxes to the degree required within a certain period of time.

---

[11]Translator's note: The enterprise tax is unfamiliar to most Western readers but is something that is generally required in China. According to the author, "Enterprise taxes and fees are usually high and complicated, which has been why people go into business but do not like to register the business with the government. For example, an enterprise has to pay a Security Deposit if it does not hire employees with physical disabilities. This is well intentioned, since it is good to encourage enterprises to hire disabled people, but on the other hand, the burden of disability as a social issue should be managed by government and not borne by the business sector."

Why should sole proprietorships with sufficient income to warrant paying taxes actually want to go ahead and pay those taxes? The reason is that the costs of not doing so are very high. First, anyone who evades taxes is put on a special list of names by the tax system and will receive particular scrutiny every year thereafter. Second, anyone put on the list immediately damages his or her own reputation. When applying for such things as a mortgage, an automobile loan, a student loan, or a business loan, he or she may well be refused or may be subjected to a very high interest rate. Third, many business loans that are of a policy nature look at the last two years of income.[12] If income is not respectable, the possibility of getting a loan at a low rate is minimal.

In its attempts to promote e-commerce startups and employment, government departments should make full use of information technologies and big-data resources. They should attempt to minimize the costs of enforcement by government departments. They should try to maximize the effect of various incentive mechanisms to encourage the greatest employment effect of grassroots startups.

In this respect, putting incentive mechanisms in place not only will help startups to stay in business longer, but even more important, it will also reinforce the establishment of ethical business practices. It will help to nurture market systems for small businesses that are orderly, based on trustworthiness and reputation, and comply with rules and regulations. It will help a constant stream of grassroots entrepreneurs to emerge in the market that operate on their own in free competition and that are therefore highly creative and responsive to the challenges they are willing to take on.

---

[12]Translator's note: So-called policy loans are subsidized by the government because policy considerations dictate supporting the endeavor.

POSTSCRIPT

In the course of writing this book, my writing team and I were fortunate to receive enthusiastic help from many people within Alibaba as well as from Internet vendors, service providers, and government personnel in various departments. We would like to extend our warm appreciation to Alibaba staff for their assistance in so many respects, including Liang Chunxiao, Hu Xiaoming, Zhang Ting, Yu Siying, Song Fei, and Sheng Zhenzhong, among many others.

In July 2013, Hangzhou experienced an extended period of extremely hot weather, with temperatures hovering over 40°C. Our interviews of Alibaba staff were conducted during this period. Their unstinting support and enthusiasm made us realize that this was indeed a company with far-reaching ideals and a high sense of social responsibility. The mission of the enterprise was obvious in each person's approach to our questions and concerns.

I want to extend particular thanks to Chen Liang of the Alibaba Group's Research Institute. In addition to contributing Chapter 2 of this book, Chen Liang was careful to ensure that all the book's contents reflect reality and are legitimate. As a representative of the grassroots of Alibaba, Chen Liang has the kind of upright attitude that is rare in today's society, particularly with respect to making sure that e-commerce develops in China's rural areas. Without his contagious passion about that endeavor, we would not have appreciated the role that Ali-people and Alibaba are playing in unleashing the innovative forces of the grassroots in China.

In undertaking research for this book, my team and I have done field research in a number of places, including various cities and counties in the provinces of Jiangsu, Zhejiang, and Shandong. From close up, as well as from a distance, we have observed the living conditions and business models of small businesses engaged in e-commerce, which has deepened our understanding of the ideals and social values of people doing e-commerce. In these places, we were fortunate to receive the help of both government personnel and Internet vendors. We apologize for not being able to list here the names of all who were helpful to us. We simply express our gratitude to everyone we interviewed. Without your cooperation and hard work, we could not have fully understood innovation and recognized its astonishing spillover effect.

I personally would like to thank the School of Social Sciences at Tsinghua University for the enormous support it has provided for my research.

I am particularly grateful for the support of the coauthors of this book, students who have put substantial efforts into its making. These students are Fang Ruonai, Xiang Songlin, Dong Youying, Huang Lingling, Sun Xiaoyu, Quan Tao, and Kang Lili. Xiang Songlin and Fang Ruonai were highly professional and meticulous in both research and writing throughout the whole process. Like me, many of those who research economics in the academic recesses of Tsinghua University are not fully familiar with business operations and the range of activities involved. Nevertheless, all those involved in this project, including graduate and postgraduate students, have tackled this project on Alibaba and e-commerce with enormous interest and a great deal of hard work.

Despite the current environment, in which everything is aimed at making money, my students participated willingly in this project that did not have the slightest financial support for research and writing. They were the epitome of Tsinghua University's reputation for seeking the truth and its spirit of willing sacrifice. The study of economics began in ancient Greece and was more formally established on the eve of the industrial revolution. It then developed and effectively served the great industrial era of the twentieth century. Together with my students, I am fortunate to have had the opportunity to embrace change in the way economics is studied today. I am happy to dare to innovate, to observe, and to describe the economic laws of the new age.

I particularly want to thank two men for their profound insight, their friendship, and their teaching. These are 93-year-old William Baumol[1] and

---

[1] Translator's note: Baumol was born on February 26, 1922.

82-year-old Edmund Phelps.[2] As I was immersed in the study of how the dynamics of small businesses relate to the overall economy over a lonely and solitary 11 years, Professor Baumol gave me the strength to complete some pioneering research. He and I have worked together to organize sessions on the "Economics of Entrepreneurship" in annual meetings held by the American Association of Economics, and in 2008, he came to China to participate in academic symposiums on the same subject that we co-organized in Hangzhou and Wuhan. He tolerated my stubborn opinions and wrote and rewrote many drafts of research articles that we coauthored. He invited me to participate in many international conferences that he organized on innovation and entrepreneurship, where he introduced me to a number of Nobel laureates in economics, including Professor Phelps.

In 2013, Professor Phelps' book, *Mass Flourishing: How Grassroots Innovation Created Jobs, Challenge, and Change*, further confirmed my resolve to study grassroots innovation and entrepreneurship. This year (2014), Professor Phelps meticulously commented on and edited the paper I delivered at the Villa Mondragone International Economic Seminar in Rome. He stands as a tremendous role model for all of us in his tireless and diligent approach to scholarship in the field of economics.

I thank both my mentors for taking time in the midst of busy schedules to write Forewords for this book. I treasure the friendship I have enjoyed with them and their wives over many years. By writing this book, I hope that readers will come to a better understanding of concepts that these two men have explored in detail, including innovation, entrepreneurship, dynamism, and mass flourishing.

Finally, I extend heartfelt appreciation to my husband, Ernst Nilsson, for the sacrifices and contributions he has made in supporting my work. He is the source of my intelligence and my strength. I thank my son, Kendall Lowrey, for his understanding and support and for broadening my field of vision with respect to economic teaching and research in the new age. Precious little Preston grew up beside me as I worked, and it was on the eve of his fourth birthday that I left Washington to come to Tsinghua. He often asks his parents (my nephew and his wife), "When is Nana coming back?"

---

[2]Translator's note: Phelps was born on July 26, 1933.

As an innovative company, Alibaba is changing faster than anyone can write about it. More profound issues and phenomena remain to be unearthed as its story unfolds. Owing to time limitations, this book could not delve into all the details. Nevertheless, such things as small is beautiful, small is the new big, and a platform economy are becoming more and more familiar to the Chinese people, and the unleashing of grassroots entrepreneurship is becoming more significant to the country's strength and the prosperity of its people. The role these things must play in the future is becoming clearer to all. I hope that this book can be of some use in stimulating ideas and research on the subject.

Finally, being a native Chinese, I dare to have a certain hope for and pride in what may happen in the future—that Alibaba's innovations will lead the world's economy toward greater growth and that more Chinese startups will contribute to a more prosperous twenty-first century. Who can now say that China cannot produce entrepreneurs on the level of Bill Gates and Steve Jobs?!

The authors of this book are as follows: Chapter 1: Ying Lowrey; Chapter 2: Chen Liang; Chapter 3: Fang Ruonai; Chapter 4: Xiang Songlin; Chapter 5: Dong Youying; Chapter 6: Huang Lingling; Chapter 7: Quan Tao; and Chapter 8: Sun Xiaoyu, Xiang Songlin, and Ying Lowrey. Kang Lili also contributed to the writing of Chapter 3. Xiang Songlin and Fang Ruonai edited and unified the overall manuscript. I have been responsible for outlining, advising, and editing all chapters and therefore am responsible for any errors in the book.

INDEX

Note: Page numbers followed by f, t, and n denote figure, table, and note, respectively.

Dr. Ying Lowrey is an economics professor at the School of Social Sciences, Tsinghua University, and deputy director of the Tsinghua Research Center for Chinese Entrepreneurs, senior researcher of the Tsinghua Research Institute of Innovation Development, senior advisor for several privately owned Chinese enterprises and research or government institutions. Her teaching and research interests include economics of innovation and entrepreneurship in the Internet and platform economy, modern microfinance market, business demographics, characteristics of business owners, and the role of free enterprise in the macroeconomy. She received her economics Ph.D. from Duke University, economics MA from Yale University, and mathematics BS from Wuhan University. Before joining Tsinghua University in 2012, she served as senior economist at the Office of Advocacy, U.S. Small Business Administration. She taught many economic courses at George Washington University as assistant professor and at San Diego State University as an instructional professor. She was an assistant researcher at the Economic Institute, Chinese Academy of Social Science, and an assistant professor at Wuhan University.

Dr. Lowrey is an avid reader, rigorous thinker, and hands-on-data researcher. She plays a proactive role in partnership with academic scholars, government agencies, professional organizations, and foundations for fostering entrepreneurship as well as promoting economic research on the entrepreneur and entrepreneurship. She is an active member of the American Economic Association (AEA) and regularly organizes sessions and contributes papers at the AEA annual meetings. She was cofounder, vice president, and newsletter editor-in-chief of the United States–China Entrepreneurs' Association and vice president of the San Diego Chinese

Association. She was the recipient of many awards, including the Kauffman Foundation Fellowship, the Asian Foundation Fellowship, the Duke University Scholarship, and the Ford Foundation Fellowship.

Dr. Lowrey published numerous research papers in peer-reviewed journals, books, and working papers. She has become an important source in the United States, China, and abroad for research on entrepreneurship and macroeconomy, and on characteristics and dynamics of U.S. businesses, including those owned by women and minorities. She has often been interviewed and quoted by important media, such as the *Washington Post*, *Wall Street Journal*, and *USA Today in America* and *China Daily*, and renren.com in China. Her most recent publications include "E-Commerce Unleashes Rural Entrepreneurship," "Small Business Ecosystem and Job Creation," "Rapid Invention, Slow Industrialization, and the Absent Innovative Entrepreneur in Medieval China" (with William Baumol), "Business Creation Is Job Creation: Estimating Entrepreneurial Jobs," "Preference for Exerting Entrepreneurial Effort: A Neoclassical Model and Computational Simulation," "An Examination of the Entrepreneurial Effort," as well as "Business Density, Entrepreneurship, and Economic Well-Being," "Startup Business Characteristics and Dynamics: A Data Analysis of the Kauffman Firm Survey," "Minority Entrepreneurship in the USA," and "U.S. Sole Proprietorships: A Gender Comparison, 1985–2000."

About the Translator

Martha Avery began translating Chinese in the mid-1980s, when she managed the business of the publisher Wiley in China. She currently manages family farms in Indiana, while continuing to translate for a think-tank in China's State Council, among others. She is finishing the last of a series of 15 books by influential Chinese economists; a volume on Chinese agricultural policy and food security is being published in late 2015. Her home base is Boulder, Colorado.